World Order Discourses

World Order Discourses

Search for Alternatives

Sujit Lahiry

RAWAT PUBLICATIONS

Jaipur • New Delhi • Bangalore • Hyderabad • Guwahati

ISBN 81-316-0386-5

Published by
Prem Rawat for **Rawat Publications**
Satyam Apts, Sector 3, Jawahar Nagar, Jaipur 302 004 (India)
Phone: 0141 265 1748 / 7006 Fax: 0141 265 1748
E-mail: info@rawatbooks.com
Website: www.rawatbooks.com

New Delhi Office
4858/24, Ansari Road, Daryaganj, New Delhi 110 002
Phone: 011 2326 3290

Also at *Bangalore*, *Hyderabad* and *Guwahati*

Typeset by Rawat Computers, Jaipur
Printed at Chaman Enterprises, New Delhi

Dedicated to

My Parents

Contents

Preface

This book is based on my PhD thesis, which has been awarded by Panjab University, Chandigarh. This is a critique of scholarly interest in the studies on world order that took major shape in the late 1960s and early 1970s, when a group of eminent social theorists from various continents came together under what came to be known as the World Order Models Project (WOMP). I have critically analyzed WOMP and its normative values in retrospect.

The 'Introduction' looks at the origin of WOMP, while Chapter 2 looks into the foundation theories of WOMP and provides its philosophical context. Chapter 3 traces WOMP's genealogy of origin and delineates its history and evolution. Chapters 4, 5 and 6 deal with the ideas of prominent WOMP theorists such as Richard Falk, Rajni Kothari, Ali A. Mazrui, Saul H. Mendlovitz and Samuel S. Kim. I have tried to assess WOMP in Chapter 7 and provided a critique of it. In Chapter 8, I have examined the relevance of WOMP in the contemporary world. In an era of neo-liberal world economy and dominant positivist notions of world order, how can we rejuvenate WOMP? We have tried to move away from our current predicament to lay down the basis for an 'alternative' world order, which is more humane and just. *World Order Discourses: Search for Alternatives* is an endeavour in that direction – to lay down the basis of a humane world order.

This book is dedicated to my parents, who provided me constant encouragement and moral support in completing it. I express my deep gratitude to my father, mother and sisters. Special thanks are due to my sister, Dr Sharmistha, for teaching me the nitty-gritty of computers as well as her constant encouragement.

I express my deep gratitude to Professor Rajni Kothari of the Centre for the Study of Developing Societies (CSDS) for sparing the time for a lively discussion on WOMP. I also wish to thank Professor Yogendra Yadav for motivating me to complete this work. Thanks are also due to my PhD supervisor, Professor Bhupinder Brar.

Outside India, I would like to express my gratitude to Professor Richard Falk for answering my e-mail questionnaire. I would also like to thank Professor Saul H. Mendlovitz for encouraging me to complete this endeavour. Last, but not the least, I express my gratitude to Rawat Publications, Jaipur, especially Pranit Rawat.

I am also grateful to the staff in the libraries of Panjab University, Delhi University, Jawaharlal Nehru University, American Centre, Teen Murti and Institute for Defence Studies and Analyses for helping me in collating the necessary materials.

1 Introduction

History is replete with examples of both conflict and violence and socio-economic change and transformation, which may be either evolutionary or revolutionary. Little wonder, then, that thinkers and visionaries across times and cultures have contemplated how order can be achieved and maintained. This study undertakes a discursive analysis of world order: What is meant by 'order' and, more specifically, 'world order'? The alternative – realist and neo-realist, liberal and neo-liberal, Marxist and neo-Marxist, functionalist and neo-functionalist – perspectives on world order have also been examined, but the thrust of this work is essentially on a discursive analysis of a major transnational research enterprise, referred to as the World Order Models Project (WOMP), which was established in the heydays of the late 1960s. The normative and philosophical foundations of WOMP as well as its historical background have been discussed here in a comprehensive manner. The major and specific ideas of WOMP ideologues and scholars have been examined in the form of a thematic study.

The study has been divided broadly into three sections. The first section traces the genealogy of world order from the Vienna Congress in 1815 to the setting up of WOMP. The second section maps out the 'positivist' perspectives on world order emanating outside the parameters of WOMP. The final section delineates the themes of the seven different chapters, with a specific focus on WOMP.

I

Any chronological revision of world history will reveal that the question of world order is always contextualized as 'temporal' and 'spatial'. All international relations theories have also evolved in the same 'time-space' dimension. A cursory glance at events such as the American War of Independence (1776), the French Revolution (1789), the Russian Revolution (1905 and 1917) and World Wars I and II will reveal that wars have always brought in either 'temporal' or 'permanent' peace. However, peace apart, every war has redefined the notion of world order in its own way.

It was at the Vienna Congress that the first significant attempt to establish a world order was made. Underlying this endeavour was the assumption that world order could be maintained only if the great powers exercised special rights and responsibilities. The Concert of Europe, which emerged as a result in 1815, reflected the exclusive concerns of five great powers – Britain, France, Prussia, Russia and Austria – that acted as self-styled guardians of world order.[1] The Concert performed 'a variety of functions associated with contemporary international institutions: collective legitimization of new states, collective neutralization of certain areas, collective peacemaking and peacekeeping, collective enforcement of certain decisions, and collective rule making'.[2]

The question of world order was further postulated in the Treaty of Westphalia in 1648, which, for the first time, brought in the notion of 'sovereign nation-states'. Further, in the eighteenth and nineteenth centuries, European powers extended their colonial control in Asia, Africa and Latin America, thereby encompassing most of the world. World War I further consolidated European supremacy all over the world, 'whereby a handful of European states dominated the affairs of the world'.[3]

At the same time, World War I also witnessed the breakdown of the nineteenth century balance of power system, which had till then succeeded in maintaining peace among self-seeking sovereign states. In the wake of this massive failure, 'pacifists and legal scholars began to advance anti-sovereignty arguments and doctrines'.[4] The focus was on improving and reforming peaceful settlement procedures and on further developing and codifying international law. However, it was with the establishment of the League of Nations in 1920 that the first organized attempt was made to restructure the normative foundations of world order. States were believed to have the sovereign right to wage war before the League of Nations was established. Then, there was a renewed emphasis on natural law and just war. The covenant of the League of Nations restricted the right of a state to resort to war and it sanctioned only 'legitimate use of force'.[5]

The basis of the League of Nations was the collective security system, whereby the League could use military power to deter aggression and, if necessary, use a preponderance of power to enforce its decision. The Kellogg-Briand Pact of 1928 (also known as the Pact of Paris), which was ratified by sixty-two nations, was another step forward in the progressive delegitimization of war. Through this pact, all international conflicts, regardless of their origin or nature, were pledged to be settled through peaceful means, and war was denounced as an instrument of national policy.[6]

Requirements of world order seemed to gain further precedence over claims of sovereignty when the rights and responsibilities of individuals were sought to be redefined in a manner that would transcend moral and legal obligations to territorial states. The Treaty of Versailles, as a result of which the League of Nations was set up, introduced the concept of individual responsibility for war crimes. Moreover, new norms were defined on such matters as social welfare, slavery, the drugs and narcotics trade, and customs violations.[7]

While the League of Nations may thus be seen as an attempt to transcend the Westphalian state system, it could not remain unaffected by the malaise and malfunctioning of the existing world. The scope and success of the League of Nations was limited by autarky and unilateralism on the part of individual states. Many states, such as the United States of America, refused to join the League of Nations from its very inception. The colonial mentality of the founders of the League of Nations was revealed by the mandate system. Moreover, the League of Nations could not handle the Manchurian crisis in 1931, the Ethiopian crisis in 1935 and, most importantly, Hitler's decision to reoccupy the Rhineland in March 1936.

While the League of Nations eventually failed in overcoming the pitfalls of the sovereign state system, the Westphalian norms were brought into question on several other counts in the inter-war period. The Wilsonian advocacy of the right of national self-determination challenged imperialism indirectly. The Soviet revolutionary challenge was more direct because it sought to establish a new world order based on socialist internationalism and solidarity.[8]

The gradual emergence of the Wilsonian idealism of a 'peaceful world' not only laid down the basis of idealist theory, but also led to the formation of the League of Nations. Idealism was subsequently superseded by realism, which was guided by the basic axiom of power politics. The realist theory actually laid the ground for the occurrence of World War II. And the post-World War II period saw the dialectical interplay of both the idealist and realist paradigms in international relations theorizing and world order. While the Cold War power politics and the nuclear arms race can be explained by the realist paradigm, the evolution of the Third World and the Non-Aligned Movement (NAM) revived idealist thinking in international relations and world order.

Besides, the post-World War II period led to the worldwide acceptance of the principles of peace, national self-determination, and economic and political sovereignty – all principles that are intrinsically related with the notion of world order. It was also during this time that there was worldwide acceptance of the Keynesian theory of welfare economics (especially after the World Economic Depression of 1929–33) as the underlying economic basis of world order. Similarly, behaviouralism, which emphasized scientific objectivity and empiricism, was subsequently replaced by post-behaviouralism, which emphasized normative theorizing. So, the transition here was from 'what is' (empirical theory) to 'what ought to be' (normative theory).

Two obvious conclusions follow logically from the above discussion. The first, that the notions of war, peace, order and world order always follow the Weberian notion of ideal types. Second, there is always a binary construction in the evolution of world order – idealism-realism, traditional – scientific, behaviouralism – post-behaviouralism, colonialism – post-colonialism, liberalism-Marxism, modernism-postmodernism and positivism-post-positivism. In other words, there is always an intersectional analysis and 'dialectic' of the different schools of thought in the evolving nature of world order. One can even postulate the argument that there is a binary construction and dialectic even within a particular school of thought in theorizing about world order. Neither liberalism nor Marxism is a homogeneous school of thought in explaining and theorizing about international relations and world order. Accordingly, grand theorizing and construction of narratives and meta-narratives about world order discourses have flowed along different trajectories.

In retrospect, it may be said that the objective of every 'world order planning' since the Treaty of Westphalia has been to minimize the recurrence of a world war. Yet, as Samuel Kim pointed out, common to these attempts was a 'negative, retrospective and reactive mentality'.[9] They were products of 'condominial consensus or compromise among the great powers', and embodied 'a corporate oligopolistic structure with uneven distribution of values'.[10] They were 'designed more to manage inter-state relations than to satisfy global human needs'.[11]

The genesis of world order in the post-Cold War period can be located in the post-war political context of the Cold War, the nuclear arms race and neo-colonialism as well as in the academic traditions of peace research. On a different plane, this was also the period when the new left movement, the demand for a new international economic order as a counter-hegemonic struggle to the old Bretton Woods model of world order, and the anti-colonial and anti-apartheid struggle gained momentum. All these movements and developments propelled the need for an alternative[12] thinking and theorizing about world order.

World order studies refined and expanded the interdisciplinary approach of peace research by synthesizing the 'loose juxtaposition of concepts, paradigms and theories borrowed from various social science disciplines'.[13] Given their futuristic orientation, world order studies also formulated its own concepts and models suited to the purpose of designing sketches of a 'preferred world order' and working out feasible strategies of transition.[14]

Scholarly interest in world order studies received a major boost in the late 1960s when a group of eminent social science theorists from different continents came together under what came to be known as the World Order Models Project (WOMP), with active encouragement and support from the United Nations. WOMP drew scholars from Latin America, Africa, Japan, Europe, the Soviet Union, India and the United States, and had indirect representation from China. The scholars came from diverse fields, but more particularly from social sciences and law. What was new was the collaborative nature of their endeavour. The WOMP participants subscribed to a future world order based on four world order values: peace, economic well-being, social and political justice, and ecological balance. A direct offshoot of the legal-institutional approach, WOMP was sponsored by what was earlier known as the World Law Fund, which was later redesignated as the Institute for World Order. WOMP set out to draw a roadmap that would lead to a just and humane world order and, over the next two decades, published several normative, futuristic studies on what its members thought the 'preferred world for the 1990s'[15] could and should be.

WOMP gradually developed into an academic discipline, which was at once scholarly, scientific, predictive, inventive and critical. It did not confine itself to philosophical or speculative discussion of values; it tried to identify and address policy questions as well. Transformation was the key element in WOMP's approach in its search for a more humane and just world order.

Even in its rather brief history, WOMP went through several changing phases. The project was rather restricted in its aim and outlook when it started off. Order was conceived narrowly to mean only peace, peace was defined negatively as 'war prevention', and the approach adopted was legal-institutional. In subsequent years, however, the objectives and goals of WOMP came to be defined more comprehensively. Economic well-being, social and political justice, and ecological balance were included as integral ingredients of a desirable world. This broadened vision was the result of several non-Western theorists, such as Rajni Kothari and Ali A. Mazrui, joining the project, these theorists lent insights into Third World concerns and aspirations.

However, as the perspective widened, it also became more diffused. Internal differences showed up between the Northerners and the Southerners within WOMP, especially on strategies of economic development and the role of state and civil society institutions. Another area of disagreement was how the preferred world should ensure unity and cohesion without risking over-centralization and causing loss of autonomy to its constituents. This dilemma applied equally to the organization of the worldwide movement that had to be built in order to pursue WOMP's goal.

These differences were not easy to resolve and they were responsible, at least partly, for WOMP activities getting bogged down in the early 1980s. But what sent WOMP into near oblivion were the unanticipated events of the late 1980s and early 1990s. The disintegration of the Soviet Union, the end of bipolarity and the Cold War and the concomitant onset of unipolarity and United States hegemony, and the intensification of neo-liberal economic globalization forced fundamental changes in the very terms of world order discourse. The WOMP spirit tried to stage a return in the changed circumstances by redefining its aims, focussing now on issues of governance in a globalized world.

In the chapters to follow, my attempt is to assess WOMP's true worth. In doing so, I focus not on concrete and material changes, which the project naïvely hoped would be brought about within a stipulated time-frame, but the enduring relevance of the alternative ideas WOMP projected as a counterpoint to the scepticism of the dominant realist and neo-realist thinking in international relations studies.

Such attempts at recovering WOMP appear particularly worthwhile when we realize that contemporary literature on world order is unabashedly positivist in nature, not only ignoring, but even abhorring, normative concerns. It uncritically accepts that obsessive pursuit of material interests and power is normal and it rationalizes hegemonic 'universalization' of Western, predominantly American, norms. WOMP, too, must have had universalist aspirations, but its universalism was multicultural in nature. It explored the value frames of different cultures in the belief that within each of these cultures, there were some universalizable values. It banked on these universalizable values in the hope that conscious and consensual human effort could turn them into universal values.

This book not only undertakes a thematic study of WOMP, it also provides a critique of both WOMP and the contemporary world order discourses. It even further postulates an alternative world order based on the visions of the WOMP theorists. However, there are two fundamentally different ways in which the word, 'critical', can be used. The more common use implies an unsympathetic and negative assessment. For example, when a perspective is criticized, it is shown to suffer from serious flaws in its assumptions, analysis, inferences, implications and prescriptions. Often enough, such flaws are also shown to be irremediable. A case is then built that the perspective be altogether rejected and replaced with an alternative.

It is not in this negative sense that the term, critical, is used here. Rather, it is employed for the connotations it has in the critical theory[16] tradition. Here, the term, critical, is derived from 'critique' rather than criticism. Critiquing is primarily emancipatory in character. And emancipation can be conceptualized in terms of emancipation of individuals, states, nations, regions as well as the globe. This argument has been borrowed from one of India's eminent political theorists, Rajni Kothari, who redefined autonomy and self-reliance in terms of self-reliance of the individual, not just of the state. As Kothari pointed out, autonomy must be gained and maintained on the individual, national as well as global plane, but autonomy of the nation-state was particularly important, for it had to act 'both as a means to checking and defeating the existing structures of dominance and exploitation in the world and as a necessary condition of the autonomy and self-reliance of the individual'.[17]

This study makes a modest attempt to envisage a more humane, just and benevolent world order based on the vision of prominent WOMP theorists, such as Richard Falk, Rajni Kothari, Saul H. Mendlovitz, Samuel S. Kim and Ali A. Mazrui. Critiquing is done in the spirit of not merely sympathy, but also solidarity. When a perspective is critiqued, it is believed to be fundamentally sound and valuable. Critiquing only suggests how its strengths can be further strengthened and its shortcomings overcome. Critiquing seeks to enrich a perspective by bringing out its hidden potential. It is a form of collaboration.

It is in this spirit that the present study has tried to raise and seek answers to the following questions:

- What was the historical background of WOMP? What was its genesis and how and why did it develop in the late 1960s?
- What were the philosophical foundations of WOMP, which bound its theorists together?
- What were the universalizable values, according to the WOMP theorists? How could these be turned into universal values?
- What kind of processes did prominent WOMP theorists, such as Falk, Kothari, Mazrui, Mendlovitz and Kim envisage for making the transition from the real world to the preferred world?
- What kind of theoretical departures were made by theorists in the 1990s from the positions they held in the 1960s? What are the possible consequences of these departures for WOMP as a whole?
- What were the reasons for the marginalization and eclipse of WOMP? Was such an outcome inevitable?
- What are the prospects for the recovery and revival of WOMP, keeping in mind the geopolitical and geo-economic changes in the contemporary world?
- What kind of transformations and modifications are necessary for such a recovery? How can we achieve a humane world order, based on the four WOMP values, in the contemporary world?

II

Discourses on world order studies fall into two broad categories – normative and positivist. However, the bulk of the normative theorization comes from the WOMP theorists. This literature is the precise subject matter of this study. Separate chapters have been devoted to prominent WOMP theorists and their ideas and vision of a preferred world taken up thematically for detailed analysis and comment. In this section, the positivist perspectives on world order emanating outside the parameters of WOMP have been mapped, even though this literature bears no relation to the theme of my study, except as a study in contrast. However, I do not take up individual works separately, but construct a typology of this positivist literature to gauge its range.

A good starting point for this appeared to be a proposal made by Robert E. Harkavy. In his article, 'Images of the Coming International System',[18] Harkavy suggested that the literature on post-Soviet international relations appears to offer seven discrete images, models or paradigms. He lists them as:

- The three bloc neo-mercantilist thesis, or geo-economics.
- The multipolar balance of power model, hinged on the traditional realist and/or neo-realist frameworks.
- The controversial clash of civilizations thesis.
- The unipolar dominance model, related to the traditional geopolitical long cycle theory and to theories of hegemonic stability.
- The zones of peace versus zones of turmoil model, based on the apparently widening gulf between the developed and developing worlds.
- The global village model, based on the apparent shift of power and sovereignty from nation-states to international or non-governmental organizations, and the growth of functional global regimes.
- The bipolar redux model, anticipating either a future challenge to United States dominance by China, Russia, Japan or Europe, or a return to some sort of bipolar bloc structure.[19]

Harkavy's seven-fold classification can in fact be reduced to two more basic categories. The first category consists of realist and neo-realist studies. Common and central to them are questions of material interests, power and hegemony, not just as they obtain today, but also as they are likely to obtain in the foreseeable future. The Realist School would include the first, second, fourth and seventh types listed by Harkavy, suggesting, respectively, tripolarity, multipolarity, unipolarity and bipolarity as the basis of the emerging international system. Harkavy lists among contemporary realists, theorists such as Richard Rosecrance, Walter Russell Mead, Jeffrey Garten, Edward Luttwak, Lester Thurow, John Mearsheimer, Henry Kissinger, Charles Krauthammer, George Modelski, Richard Bernstein and Ross H. Munro.[20]

However, these are images of an international system and not of world order. This is a crucial distinction. This distinction in relation to realist and neo-realist theory has been analyzed and evaluated critically. The analysis led to the use of the term, system, in lieu of order.

The second basic category that emerges from Harkavy includes the third, fifth and sixth types on his list. Prospects of world order in these models depend on the possibility of creating an 'international society' in the present day circumstances. The creation of such a society depends, in turn, on compatibility between the religious, cultural and civilizational norms of the actors participating in the system.

Common to these socio-cultural perspectives is their focus on political and cultural values as a crucial factor in the making and unmaking of a world order. Yet, this should not be confused with a normative concern for the values found in WOMP. The orientation of these theorists is sociological. They are not interested in values per se, much less in their promotion. They are concerned merely with the presence or absence of values as a fact or as a factor that conditions the behaviour of socio-political actors.

What is equally common to all these models of an international system or society is their West centred orientation. Part of the reason, of course, is that almost all of this literature has emanated in the West. More crucially, however, this literature seems to have a myopic and prejudiced view of the non-Western world, treating it as the 'other'. The West views itself as rational, restrained and responsible, but considers the non-West to be either lacking in these qualities or possessing them in insufficient measure. The attitude towards this 'other' takes several forms, but even in its most benevolent form, it is still condescending. It adopts the stance of a missionary and a trustee. In the main, however, the non-Western world remains a source of constant misgiving, anxiety and threat. In no case is the West in need of learning anything from the rest of the world. The universalism of this literature is very sectarian.

III

Altogether, this study has been divided into seven chapters. In the Introduction, my attempt has been to briefly introduce the theme as well as the spirit in which the theme has been explored in the subsequent six chapters. Some background comments on mainstream world order studies are offered in order to indicate how WOMP marks a significant departure from the conventionally defined discipline.

The second chapter, 'Locating WOMP: Foundation Theories', explores in detail the larger philosophical context in which WOMP is to be located. This chapter is divided into seven sections. The first section attempts a brief survey of Western political thought in order to explore the notion(s) of order implicit in its various strands. The second section examines alternative meanings of world order found in different versions of liberal as well as realist theories of international relations by way of seeking the theoretical context of WOMP. The third section continues the discussion by referring to different forms of globalism. The next four sections take up successively the four values central to WOMP: peace, economic well-being, socio-political justice and ecology. In each case, the value is approached from alternative perspectives before an attempt is made to contextualize WOMP theorization.

While the second chapter explores the philosophical context of WOMP, the third chapter, 'Locating WOMP: History and Evolution', looks into the historical context of WOMP's genesis and development. It is divided into five sections. The first section traces the emergence of international society from the days of the Treaty of Westphalia. It seeks to tease out the notion(s) of world order implied in this society. The second section goes more directly into the genesis of WOMP, locating it in the post-war political context of the Cold War, the nuclear arms race and neo-colonialism as well as in the academic traditions of peace research. The next three sections sketch the evolutionary process of WOMP through different stages. The third section deals with the initial years of 1961–68, when the WOMP theorists were concerned almost exclusively with the issue of peace and displayed a shared faith in the adoption of a legal-institutional framework for war prevention. The fourth section deals with the years of 1968–78 when, thanks to the participation of non-Western scholars such as Rajni Kothari and Ali A. Mazrui, WOMP broadbased its concerns to include values of economic well-being as well socio-political justice. This was also the period in which WOMP became increasingly conscious of the need to work out the strategies of transition to the preferred world. The final section deals with what might be called the third and fourth stages of WOMP, in which interest shifted from governmental agencies to transnational social movements and grass roots initiatives. It also deals with the circumstances in which WOMP suffered from growing lack of internal cohesion and went into relative decline. The chapter ends with a reference to the newer forms of theorization in the age of globalization.

The next three chapters deal more directly with WOMP theorists. The fourth chapter, 'From Peace through Law to Humane Governance: The Ideas of Richard Falk', deals with the ideas of Richard Falk, by far the best known WOMP theorist. This chapter has been divided into six sections. The first section deals with Falk's delineation of the idea of peace and the role that international law and international organizations could play in bringing about and maintaining a peaceful world order. In the second section, Falk's views on security, the arms race, militarism and demilitarization are brought out. His views on other WOMP values such as economic well-being, socio-political justice and protection of environment are discussed in the third section. The fourth section deals with his views on the question of transition to a preferred world. The fifth section deals with the continuities and departures in Falk's thinking on WOMP. An overall evaluation of Falk is also attempted. The sixth section delineates Falk's newer theorizations on WOMP.

The fifth chapter, 'WOMP and the Third World: The Ideas of Rajni Kothari and Ali A. Mazrui', takes up Rajni Kothari and Ali A. Mazrui, the two most important Third World scholars associated with WOMP. This chapter is divided into nine sections. The first section introduces, in general terms, Kothari's Third World perspective and his emphasis therein on the values of autonomy and self-reliance. The second section contains a more detailed account of his discussion of peace as a prime WOMP value. The third section examines his notion of economic development as an alternative to Western theories of modernization. The fourth section takes up his discussion of issues related to socio-political justice and ecology. The fifth section discusses his perceptions on the transition to a preferred world. The sixth section analyzes Kothari's views on the success and failures of WOMP. The next two sections deal with the views of Mazrui. The seventh section deals with Mazrui's ideas on the importance of culture and traces the context of his principal contribution in the form of the World Federation of Cultures. The eighth section consists of a brief discussion of the values of peace, economic well-being and socio-political justice in Mazrui's writings. The final section relates the previously discussed ideas to the development of a world language and the role to be played by creative and egalitarian education.

The sixth chapter, 'The Ideas of Saul H. Mendlovitz and Samuel S. Kim', takes up the ideas of Saul Mendlovitz and Samuel Kim, two other WOMP theorists. Mendlovitz and Kim gave primacy to the politics of transition. These two WOMP theorists were concerned primarily with policy analysis and transformative politics. This chapter is divided into six sections. The first section deals with Mendlovitz's ideas on the origin, genesis and development of WOMP. The second section, which deals with Mendlovitz's ideas on peace and socio-political justice, is rather brief for two reasons: One, we find that his views on these two values closely resembled those of Richard Falk, which have been discussed already in the fourth chapter; two, Mendlovitz did not pay any notable attention to the two other values of economic well-being and ecological balance. The third section takes up Mendlovitz's ideas on the question of transition to a preferred world. The fourth section deals with Kim's methodology of WOMP. The fifth section takes up Kim's discussion of war and peace. The sixth section deals with Kim's analysis of economic well-being, while the seventh section deals with his views on socio-political justice, ecological balance and the question of transition to a preferred world.

The study ends with the chapter, 'Assessing WOMP: Towards a Critique', which sums up the earlier chapters and draws conclusions about the nature and relevance of WOMP. Given the cataclysmic changes that have swept the world ever since the 1990s, is WOMP relevant today? If we start critiquing WOMP, it would appear to have woven nothing but naïve and empty dreams. Even at the beginning of the 2010s, the conceptualization of a preferred world as visualized by the WOMP theorists seems no closer to reality. But that, however, does not make WOMP irrelevant, for all social and political philosophies, especially normative political philosophy, from time immemorial, end in a utopia. Therefore, rather than taking up any preoccupied notions of order and world order, we will try to demystify the existing paradigms and look for alternatives[21] – the notion that supposedly formed the basic argument and crux of the WOMP theorists.

The eighth chapter is an attempt to revisit WOMP in the contemporary world order. Our purpose in this chapter is to unravel the different images of the emerging positivist notions of world order, and also to examine how we can rejuvenate and restructure the WOMP spirit in the contemporary world order. Is it really possible to have such a world order as visualized by the WOMP theorists, or is it a too 'distant projected utopia', essentially given the fact that the contemporary world order reflects the dominance of neo-realist and neo-liberal theories and assumptions? I start with the basic assumption that it is indeed possible to have a more humane, benign and just world order, as visualized by the WOMP theorists, but we will definitely have to take into cognizance the contemporary nature of the social world as well as world order. The nature of the preferred world ought to be devised in such a manner that it should be all inclusive. Exclusion of individuals, communities, marginalized groups, states and social movements needs to be adequately addressed. An equally important question that needs to be addressed is the question of transformative politics to bring about the desired changes. There is a dire need, therefore, to reconceptualize the preferred world in such a manner that individuals and communities can realize their best self, as well as adequately address the voices of dissent emanating from below at the grass roots level within the broader liberal, left-liberal, Marxist as well as non-Marxist socialist paradigms. It will also try to evaluate how the WOMP spirit, based on the four world order values, can be best accommodated and tuned in with the contemporary world order. In doing so, I will explore the possibility of the extent to which the WOMP theorists' vision of a preferred world can be restructured, reoriented and rejuvenated in the contemporary world order, so that the world order becomes much more benign and humane, and the world becomes a better place for mankind to live in.

Notes

1. Samuel S. Kim, *The Quest for a Just World Order* (Boulder: Westview Press, 1984), 32.
2. Ibid., 36. For details, see Evan Luard, *Types of International Society* (New York: Free Press, 1976), 330–32.
3. Eric Hobsbawm, *The Age of Extremes: A History of the World 1914–91* (New York: Vintage Books, 1994), 32.
4. Ibid., 37.
5. Ibid., 37–8.
6. Ibid.
7. Ibid., 38.
8. Ibid., 37.
9. Ibid., 52.
10. Ibid.
11. Ibid.
12. Interview with Rajni Kothari by Sujit Lahiry on 1 and 2 June 2002.
13. Samuel S. Kim, *The Quest for a Just World Order*, 76.
14. Ibid.
15. *Preferred Worlds for the 1990s Series:* 1. Rajni Kothari, *Footsteps into the Future: Diagnosis of the Present World and a Design for an Alternative*, (New Delhi: Orient Longman, 1974); 2. Saul H. Mendlovitz, ed., *On the Creation of a Just World Order* (New Delhi: Orient Longman, 1975); 3. Ali A. Mazrui, *A World Federation of Cultures* (New York: The Free Press, 1978); 4. Richard Falk, *A Study of Future Worlds* (New Delhi: Orient Longman, 1975); 5. Johan Galtung, *The True Worlds: A Transnational Perspective*.
16. Stephen Hobden and Richard Wyn Jones, 'Marxist Theories of International Relations', in *The Globalization of World Politics: An Introduction to International Relations*, ed. John Baylis and Steve Smith (New York: Oxford University Press, 2001), 214–16. Also see Steve Smith, 'Reflectivist and Constructivist Approaches to International Theory', in *The Globalization of World Politics: An Introduction to International Relations*, ed. John Baylis and Steve Smith (New York: Oxford University Press, 2001), 233 and 234–36.
17. Rajni Kothari, *Footsteps into the Future: Diagnosis of the Present World and a Design for an Alternative* (New Delhi: Orient Longman, 1974), 113.
18. Robert E. Harkavy, 'Images of the Coming International System', in *Orbis: A Journal of World Affairs* (Fall 1997): 569–90.
19. Ibid., 570.

20. Richard Rosecrance, *The Rise of the Trading State* (New York: Basic Books, 1986); Walter Russell Mead, 'On the Road to Ruin', in *Harper's* (March 1990); Jeffrey Garten, *A Cold Peace* (New York: Times Books, 1992); Edward Luttwak, *The Endangered American Dream* (New York: Simon and Schuster, 1993); Lester Thurow, *Head to Head: The Coming Economic Battle among Japan, Europe and America* (New York: Morrow, 1992); John Mearsheimer, 'Back to the Future: Instability after the Cold War', in *International Security* 15, No. 1 (1990); Henry Kissinger, *Diplomacy* (New York: Simon and Schuster, 1994); Charles Krauthammer, 'The Poverty of Realism', *New Republic*, (17 Feb. 1986); George Modelski, *Transnational Corporations and World Order: Readings on International Political Economy* (San Francisco: Freeman, 1979); Richard Bernstein and Ross H. Munro, *The Coming Conflict with China* (New York: Knopf, 1997).
21. The word, 'Alternatives', was first propounded by Rajni Kothari. *Alternatives* is a journal brought out by WOMP and CSDS. Rajni Kothari was the first editor and he edited it for almost a decade. Currently, *Alternatives* is being jointly edited by R.B.J. Walker and D.L. Sheth. See in particular, Rajni Kothari, *State against Democracy: In Search of Humane Governance* (Delhi: Ajanta Publications, 1988); and Richard Falk, *On Humane Governance: Towards a New Global Politics* (London: Polity Press, 1995).

2 Locating WOMP

Foundation Theories

What do we mean by order and, more specifically, world order? What are the alternative perspectives on world order? Why did the WOMP theorists emphasize certain specific values like peace, economic well-being, social and political justice, and ecological balance? These are some of the questions addressed in this chapter. We try to examine the anatomy of the preferences behind WOMP's preferred world and relate them to the larger philosophical domains in which these preferences were embedded. We try to map the common theoretical ground of WOMP social theorists.

This chapter is divided into seven sections. The first section attempts a brief survey of Western political thought in order to explore the notion(s) of order implicit in its various strands. The second section examines the alternative meanings of world order found in different versions of the liberal and realist theories of international relations by way of seeking WOMP's theoretical context. The third section continues the discussion by referring to different forms of globalism. The next four sections take up successively the four values central to WOMP: peace, economic well-being, socio-political justice and ecology. In each case, the value is approached from alternative perspectives before an attempt is made to contextualize WOMP theorization.

I

The question what constitutes order has been asked by almost all political philosophers, but it has been answered in different ways. Making a thematic survey of Western political thought, John Morrow arrives at three alternative notions of order. To quote him:

> First, the issue of order has been related to the need for coercive regulatory agencies to repress behaviour that threatens the stability of society and jeopardizes beneficial human interaction. Secondly, order has been treated in more positive terms, and has been identified with establishing a basis from which human beings can reap the material, moral and psychological benefits of cooperation. Finally, one can identify a perspective on order that has played a prominent role in Marxist and anarchist political theory. Writers in these traditions view the state as an instrument of order, but they argue that it is necessary only because tensions between individuals and classes have resulted from oppressive and exploitative tendencies within modern societies. Marxists and anarchists believe that once the social and political structures of society have been transformed, a beneficial order based upon voluntary cooperation will emerge. This condition will be social, but it will not be political because it will lack both the state and the forms of coercive regulation that are central to politics.[1]

Classical political thinkers such as Plato, Aristotle and Cicero tended to focus on the polis or the city state, for they believed that a good order was possible only in a properly regulated polis that strived for the common well-being of all members of the community and helped them achieve ideals considered the foundation of human life. Plato's notion of order depended on a hierarchical, yet harmonious, relationship between the three principal social classes. The class of guardians ruled, the auxiliaries performed military and executive functions, and the producers engaged themselves in economic activities. Plato tightly separated the economic from the political, and made the non-involvement of the producers in political life a precondition of order.[2]

Aristotle differed with Plato on two counts. First, he looked not for an ideal, universally appropriate notion of order, but chose instead to examine the diverse forms that order could acquire depending on the socio-economic bases of various communities. Second, he believed that a judicious mix, rather than separation, of classes would produce order. Such a mix would reduce the risks of misuse of power on the one hand, and chronic disorder and revolution on the other. Common to Plato and Aristotle, nonetheless, was a positive conception of order and the centrality both accorded to structures and forms of politics in the creation of such an order.[3]

Medieval political theory contained both negative and positive conceptions of order. St Augustine's two cities theory postulated that timeless, rational order characterized the 'city of God' and provided 'a positive framework for the realization of the supreme end',[4] whereas the political order of the human existence, 'through which all must pass',[5] was necessarily incomplete and imperfect even when not repressive. Aquinas, on the other hand, did not look at the state as a repressive institution; he considered it the only institution that could promote effective cooperation among individuals. He believed that 'the order created by politics is directly related to the cosmic order that leads to God'.[6] Thus, Aquinas essentially laid the foundation of a positive conception of order.

Machiavelli, an early modern thinker, restored to secular politics the role that Christian thinkers had robbed it of in the establishment of positive order. He 'regarded participation in the political life of a republic as a way of both creating' a 'political order' and enjoying its benefits for 'human fulfilment'.[7] At the same time, Machiavelli postulated for its principalities a more restricted, or even negative, notion of order, which was established by a sovereign or supreme authority, unrestricted by the everyday demands of participatory ethics. In the sixteenth and seventeenth centuries, thinkers such as Bodin, Grotius and Hobbes carried forward the restrictive tradition of conceiving of order as a function of sovereignty.[8]

In the eighteenth, nineteenth and twentieth centuries, Rousseau, Kant, Hegel and Green visualized a positive relationship between politics and order, promoting cooperation which they regarded as fundamental to human well-being,[9] and yet ascribing 'a central role to the state in defining and maintaining such an order'.[10] Anarchists and Marxists, too, 'believed individual well-being to be materially, morally and psychologically dependent on social cooperation', yet they argued that such a 'cooperative order is an exclusively social phenomenon and political institutions, above all the state, are incompatible with it'.[11] A social order based on true sociability was possible only in a stateless society.

II

As our summary of the positions taken in Western political thought shows, negative and positive conceptions of order were often related to how individuals, groups, communities, classes and states were conceptualized and the way in which their interrelationship was understood. Some privileged the state, others the individual. To some, the organically constituted community came first, to others, freely formed associations. When a theorist thought of world order, his conception of world order too centred on the category he privileged. The major schools in the study of international relations – idealism, realism, neo-realism, neo-functionalism – all privileged states even if their conceptions did not match with why states did what they did. Liberals and certain kinds of functionalists, on the other hand, privileged individuals and free associations. Marxists and neo-Marxists privileged classes. Communitarians privileged communities.

Indeed, there were areas of overlap as well, but by and large, the basic divisions remained unbridgeable. The best course for us, therefore, would be to not search for one common notion of world order. It appears far more appropriate that we place the different conceptions parallel to one another in order to see which of these would most closely fit the WOMP notion of world order.

Within liberalism, we can identify three schools of thought – internationalism, idealism and institutionalism – which had different perceptions of order and world order.

The cornerstone of liberal internationalism was the idea that human beings were basically rational in their individual behaviour and reasonable in their interaction. Reason and reasonableness assured conditions of freedom. A natural order thus underpinned all human societies. 'A law-governed international society' could similarly emerge even without the formation of 'a world government'.[12] Kant, for example, argued that 'a federal contract between states to abolish war likened to a permanent peace treaty', could ensure 'perpetual peace'.[13]

Liberal idealists, on the other hand, said that international order did not exist, nor would it emerge spontaneously; it had to be constructed in order to prevent wars. This line of argument was put forward essentially by the likes of Woodrow Wilson, who advocated the formation of international organization(s) that would, in the fashion of a world government, regulate the behaviour of states in the world.[14]

Liberal idealists such as J.A. Hobson did not accept the laissez-faire view that free trade would deliver peace. Tim Dunne argued:

> Imperialism – the subjugation of foreign peoples and their resources – was becoming the primary cause of conflict in international politics. For Hobson, imperialism resulted from under-consumption within developed capitalist societies. This led capitalists to search for higher profits overseas, which became a competitive dynamic between states and the catalyst for militarism, leading to war.[15]

However, liberal institutionalists such as Ernst Haas believed that 'international and regional institutions were a necessary counterpart to sovereign states whose capacity to deliver welfare goals was decreasing'.[16] It was in the 1940s that liberal institutionalists presented the third form of liberalism. As the label itself suggests, they stressed the significance of transnational (non-governmental/ NGOs) organizations, rather than (government like) international organizations. This led to the integrationist theory, advocated by David Mitrany in Europe, and pluralism, which focused on interdependence, in the United States. The pluralists underlined the importance of new actors such as transnational corporations and NGOs on the one hand, and new patterns of interaction based on interdependence and integration on the other.[17] The most important theorists in this respect were Robert Keohane and Joseph Nye.[18]

On the other hand, realists such as Hedley Bull, Raymond Aron and Stanley Hoffman put forward a state-centric concept of world order. Bull pointed out that government was the principal source of domestic order, whereas a more primitive form of order was operative in what he regarded as the 'anarchical setting of international society'.[19] Generalizations about domestic society and politics could not be extrapolated to international society and politics. The realists accused the liberals of assuming a false continuity between the intra-national and inter-national domains. The nature of domestic order and world order had to be theorized entirely differently. Bull added, "The maintenance of order in any society presupposes that among its members, or at least among those of its members who are politically active, there should be a sense of common interest in the elementary goals of social life."[20]

He added, "For international society, which lacks governmental capacities and is composed of members with a weak perception for common interests, order is obtained primarily by such mechanisms as 'balance of power' and 'deterrence', encouraging mutual restraint in a manner compatible with the perceived separate interests of governments."[21]

Order would help us in our realization of other values, including the pursuit of justice. However, Bull held that 'the demands for justice were related in a profound way to the search for acceptable forms of order. If the parties could agree on just results, or if a consensus on an international level could be achieved, then order and justice could be reconciled'.[22]

Away from the endless debate between the liberals and the realists, there developed in the 1950s and 1960s what looked like quite another approach to world order. Martin Rochester contended that the liberals and the realists had been equally 'impressionistic and unstructured'[23] when they set out to 'speculate on how much progress has been made toward "world order" and how much progress can be expected in the future'.[24] The behavioural methodology sought more reliable answers to such questions by measuring the 'quantifiable elements of international politics'.[25] The central focus of Rochester's view was that if states were using judicial facilities, such as the Permanent Court of International Justice, which operated between World War I and World War II, and the International Court of Justice, which has been operating since World War II, 'more frequently and regularly to resolve their disputes with one another, then it is proper to conclude that a growth towards world order had taken place'.[26]

Considered more closely, this approach turned out to be different not so much in its philosophical content as in its methodological orientation. While it was certainly more empirical and, therefore, looked more scientific and objective, it was in fact no more than an 'extension of world government thinking on world order'.[27] It measured change in quantitative terms, but progress still meant only one thing – movement away from the dispersed state system towards convergence and consolidation of a single worldwide organizational system. Rochester simply assumed that the state system was 'incapable of qualifying as a world order system since it was insufficiently centralized'.[28]

A more sophisticated version of this perspective on world order preferred to measure the growth of interdependence rather than centralization. In this way, while 'the objectivity of analysis' and the 'behavioural criteria of assessment' were retained, the focus shifted to 'the rise of transnational phenomena of many kinds'.[29]

The WOMP perspective was unabashedly normative and prescriptive. WOMP theorists saw no value per se in objective and neutral analysis; whether quantitative or otherwise, analysis had to illuminate the path of efficacious transition from the highly unsatisfactory present to a desirable future. World order was defined thus: "The study of international relations and world affairs that focuses on the manner in which mankind can significantly reduce the likelihood of international violence and create minimally acceptable conditions of worldwide economic well-being, social justice, ecological stability and participation in the decision making process. In short, a student of world order seeks to achieve and maintain a warless and more just world to improve the quality of human life."[30]

WOMP theorists believed that normative and empirical approaches were not only complementary, but could also be synthesized:

> World order studies is postulated by the synthesis of normative and empirical analysis. Although the central objective is clearly normative in striving toward the realization of values, world order practitioners argue that the main global problems cannot be effectively explained, let alone projected or controlled, without first generating a vast amount of reliable empirical and behavioural data through rigorous empirical research. World order studies also adopts a holistic integrated approach to human conditions by conceptualizing and analysing the global problematique as a set of interlocking processes and relationships between and among the seemingly discreet global problems.[31]

Kim added:

> In short, world order studies does not so much reject the behavioural and social sciences, it attempts to refine, expand and synthesize a variety of concepts, paradigms and theories from different social science and humanities disciplines. The purpose is to develop concepts and theory suited to the world order modelling process. World order studies is designed to do what Saul H. Mendlovitz calls 'normative social research' and to develop a normative global paradigm for the study of the value shaping and value sharing process in a world that is becoming both increasingly interconnected and increasingly fragmented.[32]

Falk, probably the most eminent WOMP theorist, combined analytical, empirical, ideological and normative concerns in his definition of world order. He argued, "The set of human goals, or values, can be specified in a variety of testable and semi-testable ways. Past and future systems can be compared with the present system to the extent that relative goal realization can be determined in measurable terms."[33]

The WOMP theorists pointed out that world order inquiry was associated with both probable world modelling (that is, the linear projection of empirical, demographic, economic and social trends) and preferred world modelling (that is, the imaging or construction of an alternative framework of world order, sometimes called 'relevant utopias', capable of realizing world order values).[34]

WOMP theorists also distinguished between normative futurism and technocratic futurism:

> The former is 'based on the altered frameworks of comprehensive value realization', that is, a globalist approach to peace, social justice, economic well-being, ecological balance, while the latter finds 'fixes' (for example, space colonies, nuclear fusion energy) to solve the problems of human society within existing economic, cultural, political and ecological frameworks. Hence, the globalism which is 'normative futurism' and 'technocratic futurism' is further understood by what these propose to do – that is, how they would order the world: its politics, its economics, its social possibilities, its ecology, its culture. [35]

In short, a world order theory becomes relevant based on the following conditions: 'adoption of the instrumental view of theory; avoidance of all the common traps of theory building; affirmation of the centrality of values (normative theory) using scientific tools when necessary or useful; and acknowledgement that theory building is a continuous, cumulative and self-correcting process'.[36]

WOMP believed that the preferred world was attainable only when the concerned actors made a combined effort. Samuel Kim argued, "The quest for a just world order is a collective, transnational struggle in which individuals and groups at different systemic levels join hands, actively participating in ongoing social, political, economic and cultural processes that embrace all of humanity."[37]

No doubt, states were commonly obsessed with outdated notions of sovereignty, territoriality and militarized security. As such, they often acted in conservative and reactionary ways. But states should not necessarily be seen as a hurdle, for there could exist within them forces of progress. However, since there was a general depreciation of the state as an instrument, non-state actors, ranging from international institutions to multinational corporations, had come to play an important and active role in system change and transformation.

III

The spirit and style of WOMP can be grasped better if we were to place it against four contending world order images in the form of global models, which Falk and Kim have enumerated as 'system diminishing, system maintaining, system reforming, and system transforming'.[38]

System diminishing globalism was "essentially imperial in conception. It premises prospects for order upon global unification through the domination of a single centre of power or through some kind of allocation of imperial authority arising out of unresolved rivalries. The basis for this globalism is military power forged into tight alliance systems."[39] Falk enumerates some of its modern day manifestations thus:

> In general, system diminishing attitudes include abandoning concern about human rights, renouncing efforts to complete negotiations on a new law of the sea, eroding support fòr the United Nations, diminishing support for programmes designed to help poorer Third World countries, and avoiding procedures for the peaceful settlement of disputes.[40]

The system maintaining image of world order had a realist perspective. It sought to prevent the breakdown of existing patterns of order based on a hierarchical or hegemonic structure of power and authority in the face of rapid change and disruption. It drew sustenance from the propensities of principal governments and the elite. It avoided normative political questions and preferred to seek technical solutions. It attached priority to coordination of economic policy as the basis for an improved world order.[41]

The system maintaining approach was primarily defensive and status quoist in nature, but in order to maintain stability and the status quo, it was prepared to make marginal adoptions and accommodations that were perceived to be essential. Advocated by realists such as Daniel Bell, Hedley Bull and Stanley Hoffman, the system maintaining perspective on world order was reflected in the Trilateral Commission, founded in 1973 at the initiative of David

Rockefeller, in Jay Wright Forrester's *World Dynamics* (1971) and in the Club of Rome report, 'The Limits to Growth' (1972).[42] The governing groups and their supporting elites in the most powerfully constituted states essentially supported the system maintaining approaches to world order.

As Richard Falk observed:

> The organizing objective is to assume efficient economic performance, as measured by economic growth and calculated by GNP increases. Whatever means facilitate such growth are positive and should be encouraged; whatever means interfere, even if it is the exercise of democratic rights themselves, are negative and should be curtailed. The international distribution of power, wealth and prestige is relevant only to the extent that it poses managerial challenges. The state system, with its reliance on war as the ultimate arbiter of conflict, is accepted as inevitable, and the ecological dangers engendered by industrial technological pressures are viewed as containable.[43]

The system reformers built their theories on the reform tradition of John Hobson, John Maynard Keynes and David Mitrany. They demanded that the global political economy should be efficiently and equitably managed through a series of institutional reforms. Their proposals for global reform were primarily with regard to inter-state social and political justice and inter-state economic well-being. However, the structural modifications they advocated would not alter the basic order of international relations pivoted around the role and predominance of the sovereign state.[44] The system reformers 'believe that greater international efficiency can be combined with greater international equity, greater international protection of national autonomy with greater international cooperation, greater international justice with greater international law and order'.[45]

The system reforming image of world order was linked to the liberal internationalist approach based on the notion of complex interdependence. Subsumed under this category are neo-realists, functionalists and neo-functionalists.[46] One of the most influential works on regime research was *Power and Interdependence* by Keohane and Nye.[47] The prime mover for system reform was the Third World caucus on global developmental strategy popularly known as the Group of 77 (G-77). Through the UN General Assembly and the UN Conference on Trade and Development (UNCTAD), it put forward the demand for a new international economic order. Other good examples of the system reforming image of world order are *Rio: Reshaping the International Order* and *North-South: A Program for Survival*.[48]

Whereas the system reforming image of world order did not challenge the legitimacy or viability of the Westphalian state system, the system transforming image was based on the belief that, dominated by inter-state rivalries, this system was inadequate in serving the interests of humanity in the present age. The neo-Marxist world system approach is one of the glaring examples of the system transforming image of world order. Elaborated upon by Immanuel Wallerstein, it envisioned 'a disintegration of the world capitalist system brought about by accelerating contradictions on the one hand, and the coalition of the world's anti-systemic forces – or what he calls 'real worldwide inter-movement links' – on the other'.[49]

However, the most apt example of a system transforming perspective was the World Order Models Project (WOMP). Samuel Kim pointed out that whereas the 'world system image of system transformation is grounded upon too narrow a value base' in Marxist theory,

> The WOMP approach relates 'oppression' to a broader category of social reality than the adverse effects of the international division of labour, placing greater emphasis on what it means to be treated as 'a nuclear guinea pig' or as ecologically expendable. This world order theory also clarifies the preferred future by postulating values rather than by conceiving of the oppressed as autcmatic bearers of the normative content of the politics of transformation. World order theorists are more concerned than world system theorists with mapping structural alternatives to either world government or statism. The world system approach is essentially a depiction of the rise and fall of capitalism as a world force in the aftermath of the breakdown of feudalism; the WOMP approach is more concerned about discerning challenges and devising responses in short term as well as long term spans.[50]

Kim defined world order transformation as 'a series of long term and largely irreversible changes and trends in the established values, norms and structure of international society, resulting in a new pattern of relationship between its constituent units (actors)'.[51] Falk, Kim and Mendlovitz further clarified that:

> System change does not necessarily mean political integration or centralization at the supranational level, much less 'world

> government'. It means a fundamental rearrangement of structure so that a different configuration of actors with different orientations towards power, security, well-being and governance will emerge.[52]

IV

In *The Quest for a Just World Order*, Samuel Kim defined WOMP's tasks as clarification of assumptions, diagnosis of the state of the world, exploratory forecasting of trends, normative forecasting of preferred futures, mapping transition strategies, and review and evaluation.[53]

The WOMP participants wanted to build a preferred world based on the four world order values accepted by all of them even though the primacy accorded to these values varied from scholar to scholar. These four world order values were: peace, economic well-being, social and political justice, and ecological balance.

In this section, we will analyze the anatomy of the preferences behind WOMP's preferred world and relate them to the larger philosophical domains in which these preferences were embedded. Any political theory is implicitly or explicitly based on certain epistemological and normative assumptions. While epistemological assumptions set the limits within which political inquiry takes place, normative assumptions provide the basis for the criteria of relevance and significance of choosing research paths.

The notion of peace is one of the central concepts in political theory. However, theorists of different persuasions have defined peace differently.

Defining it negatively, the realist and neo-realist schools of thought saw peace as prevention of war. Realists believed that the state was both immutable and irreplaceable as the principal actor in international relations. States were primarily preoccupied with questions of material interests, power and hegemony. The realists, including the structural realists (such as Morgenthau) and historical or practical realists (such as Machiavelli and Carr) believed that a perennial struggle for power among states made permanent peace in international relations a virtual impossibility. Realists saw the best chance for peace in balance of power. Contemporary neo-realists such as Kenneth Waltz[54] and John Mearsheimer,[55] too, believed in this general framework of international relations. Huntington's clash of civilizations thesis considered the emergence of positive peace, based on legitimacy and authority, improbable because notions of what is legitimate vary from one civilizational area to another and a cross-cultural consensus on the question is impossible.[56] However, as Tim Dunne and Brian C. Schmidt argued:

> At the margins of realism, we find a form of liberal realism, which rejects the pessimistic picture of historical and structural realists, believing that the state of war can be mitigated by the management of power by the leading states in the system and the development of practices such as diplomacy and customary international law.[57]

From the sixteenth century onwards, liberal theorists proposed various plans for peace. However, the liberals disagreed on whether collective security, commerce or world government should be employed to establish peace. We have already noted the need to distinguish three different strands of liberalism – liberal internationalists, idealists and liberal institutionalists.

The liberal internationalists assumed that a natural order underpinned human society. They expected natural harmony to deliver peace. They believed that natural order had been corrupted by undemocratic state leaders and their outdated policies, balance of power being among them. The two leading liberal internationalists of the Enlightenment (in the eighteenth century) were Immanuel Kant and Jeremy Bentham. Bentham famously argued that 'between the interests of nations, there is nowhere any real conflict' and showed that many federal states 'were able to transform their identity from one based on conflicting interests to a more peaceful federation'.[58] Liberals based their optimism on 'an extension of the idea of social contract between individuals in domestic society to states in the international system, subjecting the states to a system of legal rights and duties'.[59] They 'believed that a law governed international society could emerge without a world government'.[60] They believed also that a more pacific form of international relations would evolve through commerce or travel between the peoples of the world.[61]

Idealism, the second strand of liberalism, believed that states could never settle their disputes by themselves. Idealists such as Woodrow Wilson believed in collective security. They underlined the need for the construction of an international order to be managed by an international organization. States must be bound by the rules and norms of such an international organization, he said.

These liberal idealist policies led to the formation of the League of Nations in the 1920s and the United Nations in 1945.[62]

The period of liberal idealists gradually came to a close with the collapse of the League of Nations. Liberal idealism gave way to liberal institutionalism in the 1940s. The liberal institutionalists emphasized the growing importance of the international institutions. The core concept was ramification: "Cooperation in one sector would lead governments to extend the range of collaboration across other sectors. As states become more embedded in an integration process, the 'cost' of withdrawing from cooperative ventures increases."[63] Peace would be the natural fallout of integration.

Neo-liberalism can also be differentiated into three strands: neo-liberal internationalism, neo-idealism and neo-liberal institutionalism. The neo-liberal internationalists advanced the thesis of democratic peace in the late 1980s and early 1990s. This thesis emphasized that liberal states do not go to war with other liberal states.[64] This indicated that democracy was a major source of peace. Michael Doyle and Bruce Russett were the main exponents of the democratic peace theory. Doyle pointed out:

> Democratic representation, an ideological commitment to human rights and transnational interdependence provide an explanation for the 'peace prone' tendencies of democratic states. Equally, the absence of these attributes, he argues, provides a reason why non-democratic states tend to be 'war prone'. Without these domestic values and restraints, the logic of power replaces the liberal logic of accommodation.[65]

Further, the 'supporters of democratic peace ideas do not reject the insights of realism, but they reject "vulgar realisms" and its preoccupation with the idea of war of all against all. They argue that internal norms and institutions matter.'[66]

The argument was taken further by a hypothesis put forward by Francis Fukuyama in 1989. In an article titled 'The End of History' (1989) and later in the book, *The End of History and the Last Man* (1992),[67] Fukuyama contended that liberalism had become the dominant ideology with the collapse of the socialist bloc. Since most East European countries had opted for liberal democracy and market economies, it meant the beginning of a new phase in history, 'where liberal economic values would prevail globally'.[68] Fukuyama's theory was based on three concrete arguments: 'one about the pacific character of democracies; another about the integrative role played by multilateral institutions; and a third about the benign security consequences of global capitalism'.[69]

According to Tim Dunne:

> Neo-idealists have responded to globalization by calling for a double democratization of both international institutions and domestic state structures. Radical neo-idealism is critical of mainstream liberalism's devotion to 'globalization from above', which marginalizes the possibility of change from below through the practices of global civil society.[70]

Neo-liberalism, referred to as neo-liberal institutionalism, emerged primarily in response to Kenneth Waltz's theory of neo-realism as elaborated in his *Theory of International Politics* (1979). Leading neo-liberal institutionalists such as Axelrod, Keohane and Oye were specifically concerned with how cooperation could be initiated and maintained under conditions of anarchy. They suggested the creation of regimes in order to facilitate cooperation.[71]

It is in this context that we can best understand the WOMP position on the value of peace. Most WOMP theorists conceptualized peace as 'absence of violence' in the initial period. Richard Falk discussed international law, nuclear disarmament and international organization in the context of war prevention. However, from the early 1980s, WOMP scholars conceptualized the social, economic, cultural and environmental dimensions of peace. Going beyond the narrow notion of military security, they discussed varied aspects of social security, economic security, cultural diversity and environmental stability. Falk believed that the problems of poverty, underdevelopment, repression and the escalation of large scale violence in many parts of the world were intrinsically related to militarism.[72] This argument was echoed by Rajni Kothari, who also pointed to 'non-military threats to peace arising out of the socio-economic and political process'.[73] Kothari believed that the concept of peace should be conceived as a new conception of life itself and not in a negative sense as the negation of war.[74] He added that ensuring a more peaceful world had two major preconditions:

> The first of these is the achievement of a world consisting of autonomous states that are in a position to enjoy a much more meaningful equality of status than today; the second is the ability of these states

to provide minimum living conditions for their peoples, which also entails a certain minimum of equality among them.[75]

Ali Mazrui added a cultural dimension by pointing out that:

> The problem of world peace is, in the initial stages, a problem of domestic cultures and of relations between social groups in individual countries and of values governing those groups. It could be said that all international wars have been, so far, externalized civil deficiencies, both cultural and social. To solve the problem of international conflict, therefore, necessitates an attempt to tackle the causes of domestic tensions and domestic pathologies.[76]

Mazrui pointed out that denial of social justice and economic welfare were more basic social determinants of social violence.[77]

V

All political philosophers and all major political ideologies – liberalists, neo-liberalists, Marxists and neo-Marxists as well as the liberal normative theorists of WOMP – assume the value of economic well-being, but their interpretations differ widely from one another.

Liberals such as J.S. Mill were the first to stress the need for a welfare state. Mill did not defend unqualified laissez-faire, but argued that just and orderly economic development was possible only if trade unions were allowed to operate, for that would ensure a balance between the bargaining powers of the capitalists and their employers.[78] It was Keynes, however, who built a comprehensive case for welfarism. He argued that capitalism had to be given a humane form in order to ensure its survival. Such a crucial thing as employment generation could not be left to the whims of market forces. The state must ensure that levels of employment were satisfactorily maintained. If workers were unemployed, they must be given unemployment allowances. Keynes contended that full employment led to higher growth rates. If workers were provided better wages, they would wish to consume more and demand would increase, and both the capitalists and the workers would decide appropriate wages to maintain such economic growth.[79] The state must also undertake welfare oriented activities in the fields of health and education.

After the disintegration of the USSR, liberalism was increasingly replaced by neo-liberalism. For the neo-liberals, free markets and free trade were of paramount importance in international politics for these promoted both peace and prosperity.[80] Major trading states, such as the United States and its Group of Eight (G-8) partners, global financial institutions and multinational corporations had widely promoted the neo-liberal ideology in the underdeveloped countries of the Third World.

World system and dependency theorists, on the other hand, pointed out the imbalanced nature of the international political economy. They divided the world into core, periphery and semi-periphery and believed that the core had drained away all the wealth from the periphery and semi-periphery in an exploitative relationship. This had resulted in the core regions becoming richer, while the peripheral and semi-peripheral regions became increasingly poorer.[81] The Marxists and neo-Marxists thus saw economic well-being only in the defeat of global capitalism.

Initially, the WOMP theorists did not give primacy to the value of economic well-being. It was only in the 1970s that this value also emerged as a priority concern for the WOMP social theorists. Underlying Falk's discussion of issues such as the gap between the rich and the poor, income thresholds: minima and maxima, profitability versus minimum standards of human dignity, national economic development, etc. underlined this shift.[82] In the 1990s, Falk advocated a people-centric economic approach to globalization. He counter posed globalization from below against globalization from above in order to eliminate global poverty and to secure the economic well-being of the peoples of the world.[83]

Rajni Kothari focussed on economic well-being, especially of the peoples of the Third World. He advocated genuine democratization of economic structures at the national and transnational levels and proposed that the world be restructured into economically self-reliant federations of nation-states.[84]

Kothari raised some fundamental normative questions with regard to the theory of development. Conventional theories of development rationalized policies that served the structures of state security and promoted the exclusive lifestyle of the ruling elites, while the basic aim of economic development ought to be removal of poverty and ensuring basic minimum living standards for all. Kothari proposed an alternative model of development to achieve the socially approved minima of health, education, drinking water and public transportation for all. He emphasized agriculture and rural development in order to remove unemployment and to bridge the gap between the city and the countryside. He also called for an ethic, both of production and consumption.[85]

Ali Mazrui believed that the process of modernization, especially the modernization of economic culture, would be the key to ensuring economic well-being. There was a need to restructure economic relationships in such a manner that there would not be any violent revolution. Rather than altogether abolishing classes, increased mobility ought to be promoted among the various domestic classes.[86]

Samuel Kim talked about two dimensions of global inequities – human and national. He pointed out the failure of the liberal capitalist international order, evident in the facts that global interdependence and global inequality continued to persist. The integration of the Third World into the capitalist world economy had resulted in its pauperization and peripheralization. He argued that the Bretton Woods post-war economic order had perpetuated the established pattern of overdevelopment-underdevelopment, dominance-dependence, and centre-periphery relations.[87]

Kim argued that distributive justice could not be realized unless the poorest countries and the worst off groups participated in the national decision making process at the global level.[88] The movement built around the demand for a new international economic order had forcefully 'highlighted the national dimensions of global inequities in access to capital, markets, resources and technology'.[89] Kim believed that the state was the only organization that could promote general economic well-being and fulfil basic human needs. However, sometimes, the state promoted only urban centred class interests. There were also some systemic structural constraints[90] in the establishment of an equitable economic order.

VI

The value of socio-political justice was expounded by the liberals, neo-liberals, communitarians, Marxists and eminent WOMP social theorists.

The liberal notion of political justice demands first and foremost 'the establishment of democratic institutions in the political life of the community so that these institutions represent and take care of the interests of the people, not of any privileged class'.[91]

Political justice entailed the establishment of representative institutions – the legislature and executive – on the principle of universal adult franchise and maintaining the independence of the judiciary. 'In the second place, political justice implies a full guarantee of the liberty of thought and expression, especially the right to criticize the government and its policies. Finally, there should be complete freedom for forming associations and interest groups to enable the citizens to articulate their interests through the normal channels of communication and through political parties, as well as to express their approval or disapproval of particular measures, to organize peaceful protests against harmful measures, and to pressurize the working of the government through democratic channels and procedures. In a nutshell, political justice postulates a universal availability of the mechanism for resolving the conflicting claims of different interests in society.'[92]

The classical liberals attacked absolute state and arbitrary authority. Constitutional restraints, representative government and individual rights were some of their major demands. The Glorious Revolution in England was the first liberal revolution that resulted in the victory of the idea of popular sovereignty over royal sovereignty. It resulted in the establishment of a limited constitutional monarchy. John Locke was the first to formulate the principle of a constitutional government.[93] Others, such as Bentham and James Mill, wanted to abolish distinctions and discriminations based on race, ethnic origin or gender, and ensure equal dignity for all individuals. They advocated the idea of universal suffrage. Possession of property as a condition for political rights was sought to be removed.[94] Modern liberals such as Green, Hobhouse and Laski wanted the state to play a positive role in protecting the interests of the poor and deprived sections of society. They envisaged the welfare state as a way of ensuring social justice.[95]

Within the liberal tradition itself, there were variations in the interpretation of socio-political justice. The libertarians, or the neo-liberals, tried to revert to the laissez-faire philosophy. Libertarians such as Hayek, Friedman and Nozick believed that a free market was the only way to ensure the full autonomy and freedom of the individual. They believed that laissez-faire capitalism would ensure social progress.[96] Nozick argued that 'a libertarian society, which allows all individuals and groups to shape their life according to their wishes, fulfils the most plausible definition of a utopian social order'.[97] The neo-idealist liberals did not accept that the market could be relied upon for either allocation of resources or for generation of employment opportunities. They, therefore, emphasized not just macro institutional democratic reforms, but also grass roots democratization.[98]

The value of social and political justice was also embedded in Marxist political theory. Marx believed that these values could be realized only in a classless and stateless society. Justice of any kind was impossible in a class divided society, where relations of only domination and subordination could exist between antagonistic classes. Class struggle was the only means to ensure social progress.

Antonio Gramsci, an early twentieth century Marxist thinker, focussed on subtler forms of class domination because of which consent for a particular social and political system was produced and reproduced. The ruling classes often managed to so disperse their moral, political and cultural values throughout society that subordinate groups and classes would also accept these values as their own. Dominant ideologies got so entrenched in the institution of civil society that the subordinate group would never question their authority. Gramsci called such subtle forms of domination 'hegemony' and emphasized that a 'counter hegemonic struggle' had to be initiated in order to challenge the ruling class.[99]

The critical theory that emerged out of the work of the Frankfurt School dealt with issues of emancipation.[100] In this regard, its theorists – Max Horkheimer, Theodor Adorno, Herbert Marcuse and Jurgen Habermas, among them – made penetrating analyses of 'culture, bureaucracy, social basis and nature of authoritarianism and the structure of the family'.[101]

The WOMP theorists followed a liberal approach. Where Western scholars such as Richard Falk stressed issues such as human rights, others such as Rajni Kothari looked at the value of social and political justice from a Third World perspective.

In his later writings, Falk raised a crucial question: 'How do we balance the greater economic and social equity of socialist polities with the greater cultural and intellectual openness of capitalist nations?'[102] He outlined five categories of rights for the purposes of inquiry, reflection and policy recommendation: basic human needs; basic decencies; participatory rights; security rights; and humane governance.[103] He argued that even materially advanced societies suffered from 'normative regression' and 'invisible oppression' in the areas of environment and culture.[104] Falk lamented that in most Asian countries, the native groups allied with the colonial exploitation had 'held onto political power, stifling social progress and economic reform'.[105] Therefore, a post-independence revolutionary struggle was required for 'wresting political control from the traditional ruling classes and instituting a mass based programme of land reform, education, public hygiene, social equality and radical consciousness'.[106]

In the post-Cold War era, Falk started emphasizing the role of new social movements. He identified the two contradictory and antagonistic forces within globalization. While globalization from above was led by powerful states and transnational businesses,[107] globalization from below required 'an array of transnational social forces animated by environmental concerns, human rights, hostility to patriarchy, and a vision of human community based on the unity of diverse cultures seeking an end to poverty, oppression, humiliation and collective violence'.[108]

Falk used the concept of 'humane governance' to stress the need to achieve comprehensive rights for all peoples. Humane governance, Falk pointed out:

> emphasizes people centred criteria of success, as measured by declines in poverty, violence and pollution and by increasing adherence to human rights and constitutional practices, especially in relation to vulnerable segments of society as well as by axiological shifts away from materialist or consumerist and patriarchal conceptions of human fulfillment.[109]

Falk concluded that democracy was both a means to humane governance as well as a feature of its embodiment.[110]

Rajni Kothari stressed the need for autonomy and self-reliance in order to realize justice in a world where there existed extremes of disparity and inequality both between and within nations.[111] In order to create a just society, we need to move 'towards a pluralist, decentralized polity with a humane technology and a relatively self-reliant economy, self-reliant for the people and not just for the state, as has been the thinking on self-reliance till recently'.[112]

Both governmental and non-governmental actors would provide the basis of a new coalition of interests, which would be engaged in the politics of global transformation.[113] New grass roots social movements had gradually emerged to reflect the viewpoint of the deprived and marginalized sections. These movements, Kothari added, could produce a macro challenge, a general transformation through a non-party political process.[114]

Kothari pointed out that if the Third World countries adopted the Western model of development and modernization, they would lose their autonomy and not be able to provide political justice to their citizens.[115] He suggested an alternative approach and outlined some major policy initiatives in it. Some of the major imperatives were:

> Economic self-reliance, national (or regional) security, distributive economic policy (with special reference to the agricultural hinterland), institutionalization of social democracy for achieving the integration of centre and periphery, and establishing the authenticity of the national political culture.[116]

Ali Mazrui also elaborated on political justice, but from a cultural perspective. He examined the 'postcolonial tensions of political and cultural adjustment, especially as illustrated in Africa'.[117] There was a need to address the violence that accompanied processes of convergence in situations of asymmetry between cultural donors and cultural recipients. Problems of fragile institutions and of fragmented identity had been responsible for much of the political upheaval in Africa.

VII

It was only in the 1970s that theorists took into cognizance the increasing menace of environmental degradation. Thus, it is only in recent times that ecological balance has become one of the key issues in international relations.

The 1960s witnessed the first general concern for the human environment and the 'limits to growth' thesis gained acceptability. However, environmental issues entered into the agenda of global politics only after the UN Conference on the Human Environment held in Stockholm in 1972. Thereafter, there were many UN conferences on environment related issues, but the last and the most effective summit was the Rio de Janeiro Earth Summit held in 1992.

Dennis Pirages elaborated an eco-political theory of international relations. The epistemological and normative implications of this eco-political revolution could be compared with those of the earlier agricultural and industrial revolutions. "Highlighting all the anomalies and dilemmas, as well as the irrelevance of the prevailing realist school, Pirages advanced an eco-political paradigm as an 'alternative model of reality' for describing, explaining and projecting shifts in world politics. Because of its planetary scope, survivalist ethics, functional approach and futurist time dimension, this eco-political paradigm is congenial to world order studies."[118]

Kothari pointed out that there were two schools of ecologists. The first school was 'the ecodevelopment school of ecologists who are concerned with making development both environmentally viable and socially equitable'.[119] The second school of ecologists believed in pure and simple conservation 'with little or no regard either for the cause underlying today's runaway technology and its ravaging of the environment, or for the need for planning for the future which, while providing for the basic necessities of all, would ensure an ecologically sustainable strategy of growth'.[120]

It was gradually realized that there existed a mutually complementary relationship between the two world order values of economic well-being and ecological balance. Elaborating on this aspect, Kothari argued:

> This symbiotic relationship between environmental and socio-economic goals is becoming increasingly recognized by world order advocates, and is leading to the formulation of new development strategies that are ecologically sustainable as well as more economically and politically just.[121]

In 1972, Falk, for the first time, discussed at length the ecological perspective of world order. He tried to show the contradiction between statist and ecological imperatives. The world system had been dominated by territorially organized sovereign states ever since the Treaty of Westphalia. In competitive pursuit of power and wealth, states had recklessly exploited the resources located within their territories. Colonial exploitation had worsened the situation even more. Wars, population explosion, poverty and ever rising material aspirations had lead to an unbearable environmental overload.[122]

Falk designed a new ecological perspective on world order to achieve three main ends: peace and equity among humans; harmony between humans and nature; and regard for the future of the earth and future generations of men.[123] He was mostly concerned with the international setting of the planetary crisis and concentrated upon the changes that were needed in the structure of the world society to maintain the harmony of the planet.

Falk proposed and developed the idea of 'ecological politics, whose essence is a political embodiment of man-in-nature, as the ideological underpinning for an adequate conception of world order'.[124] 'Pluralism, zones of autonomy, diversity of lifestyle, culture and ideology are all values that could be emphasized in a system of world order suitable for the ecological age.'[125]

Samuel Kim pointed out that the global environment consisted of two separate, but closely intertwined and interacting, sub-systems – the natural environment and the social environment. While the natural environment included 'the atmosphere, marine and terrestrial environments', 'the environmental impacts of such human activities as population growth, resource use and militarization constituted the social environment'.[126] He argued, "The ecological crisis is much more than a crisis of external ecospheric limits."[127] The exploitative and unjust social structures of domestic and international societies were the root cause of the ecological crisis.[128]

Kim identified the anti-ecological use of modern technology to exploit and consume scarce resources as one of the principal cause of the ecological crisis. He added:

> There are two kinds of socioecological pollution: the pollution of overdevelopment (affluence) and the pollution of underdevelopment (poverty). The latter is also caused by unjust social structures, for peasants, whose land has been pre-empted for cash crops, end up cultivating marginal soil, contributing to further deforestation and soil erosion. Both forms of socioecological pollution are linked by the invisible hands of the global dominance or dependence system.[129]

Thus, the quest for a just world order obviously included the quest for a more decent environment. Kim observed:

Ecological thinking and world order thinking converge in their transnational and transdisciplinary framework of inquiry informed by values, holism, futurism and humanism, and in their prescriptive commitment to social transformation for survival and solidarity with future generations.[130]

Notes

1. John Morrow, *History of Political Thought: A Thematic Introduction,* (London: Macmillan Press Ltd, 1998), 19.
2. Ibid., 19 and 22–23.
3. Ibid., 23–24.
4. Ibid., 27.
5. Ibid., 26.
6. Ibid., 28.
7. Ibid., 29.
8. Ibid., 29–30.
9. Ibid., 42.
10. Ibid., 46.
11. Ibid.
12. Tim Dunne, 'Liberalism', in *The Globalization of World Politics: An Introduction to International Relations*, ed. John Baylis and Steve Smith (New York: Oxford University Press, 2001), 166.
13. Ibid., 165–66.
14. Ibid., 167.
15. J.A. Hobson, quoted in Tim Dunne, 'Liberalism', op. cit., 167.
16. Haas, quoted in Tim Dunne, 'Liberalism', in *The Globalization of World Politics: An Introduction to International Relations*, ed. John Baylis and Steve Smith, 169. For details, see E. Haas, *The Uniting of Europe* (Stanford: California University Press, 1958), 154–58.
17. Tim Dunne, 'Liberalism', in *The Globalization of World Politics: An Introduction to International Relations*, 169–71.
18. Keohane and Nye, quoted in *The Globalization of World Politics: An Introduction to International Relations*, ed. John Baylis and Steve Smith, 170. For details, see Robert Keohane and Joseph Nye, eds, *Transnational Relations and World Politics* (Cambridge, Mass.: Harvard University Press, 1971).
19. Hedley Bull, quoted in Richard Falk, 'Contending Approaches to World Order', in *Toward a Just World Order: Studies on a Just World Order,* Vol. 1, ed. Richard Falk, Samuel S. Kim and Saul H. Mendlovitz (Boulder: Westview Press, 1982), 151.
20. Hedley Bull, *The Anarchical Society: A Study of Order in World Politics* (New York: Columbia University Press, 1977), 53.
21. Hedley Bull, quoted in Richard Falk, 'Contending Approaches to World Order', in *Toward a Just World Order: Studies on a Just World Order, Vol. 1,* ed. Richard Falk, Samuel S. Kim and Saul H. Mendlovitz, 151.

22. Richard Falk, 'Contending Approaches to World Order', 151.
23. Ibid., 153.
24. Ibid., 152.
25. Ibid.
26. Ibid., 153.
27. Ibid.
28. Ibid.
29. Ibid.153. See also Robert Keohane and Joseph Nye, *Power and Interdependence: World Politics in Transition* (Boston: Little Brown and Co., 1977); Merriam Camps, *The Management of Interdependence: A Preliminary View* (New York: Council on Foreign Relations, 1974); Richard Rosecrance and Others, 'Whither Interdependence', *International Organization* 31 (Summer 1977).
30. Mendlovitz and Weiss, quoted in Richard Falk, 'Contending Approaches to World Order', in *Toward a Just World Order: Studies on a Just World Order,* Vol. 1, ed. Richard Falk, Samuel S. Kim and Saul H. Mendlovitz, 154. For details, see Mendlovitz and Weiss, 'The Study of Peace and Justice: Toward a Framework for Global Discussion', in *Planning Alternative Futures*, ed. Louis Rene Beres and Harry Targ (New York: Praeger, 1975).
31. Samuel S. Kim, *The Quest for a Just World Order* (Boulder: Westview Press, 1984), 6.
32. Ibid., 6–7.
33. Richard Falk, 'Contending Approaches to World Order', in *Toward a Just World Order: Studies on a Just World Order, Vol. 1*, ed. Richard Falk, Samuel S. Kim and Saul H. Mendlovitz, 155.
34. Richard Falk, Samuel S. Kim and Saul H. Mendlovitz, 'Alternative Images of the Future – Introduction', in *Toward a Just World Order,* op. cit., 499.
35. Falk and Kim, quoted in Norman K. Swazo, 'The 'Ontological' Meaning of the World-Order Movement', in *Alternatives* X (1984): 269. For details, see Richard Falk and Samuel S. Kim, 'An Approach to World Order Studies and the World System', *WOMP Working Series, No. 22* (New York: Institute for World Order, 1982).
36. Samuel S. Kim, *The Quest for a Just World Order,* 60–61.
37. Ibid., 301.
38. Falk and Kim, quoted in Norman K. Swazo, 'The 'Ontological' Meaning of the World-Order Movement', in *Alternatives* X (1984): 269.
39. Richard Falk and Samuel S. Kim, 'World Order Studies and the World System', in *Contending Approaches to World Systems Analysis,* ed. William R. Thompson, (London: Sage Publications, 1993), 221.

40. Ibid., 221.
41. Richard Falk, 'Contending Approaches to World Order', 38. Also see Samuel S. Kim, *The Quest for a Just World Order*, 63.
42. Ibid., 38.
43. Richard Falk, 'Contending Approaches to World Order', in *Toward a Just World Order*, ed. Richard Falk, Samuel S. Kim and Saul H. Mendlovitz, 159.
44. Ibid., 159–60. Also see Samuel S. Kim, *The Quest for a Just World Order*, 64.
45. Samuel S. Kim, *The Quest for a Just World Order*, 64.
46. Ibid., 65.
47. Robert Keohane and Joseph Nye, *Power and Interdependence: World Politics in Transition* (Boston: Little Brown and Co., 1977), 242.
48. Samuel S. Kim, *The Quest for a Just World Order*, 65. For details, see Jan Tinbergen, coordinator, 'Rio: Reshaping the International Order', a report to the Club of Rome (New York: E.P. Duttan and Co., 1976); and 'North-South: A Program for Survival', a report of the Independent Commission on International Development Issues under the chairmanship of Willy Brandt (Cambridge, Mass.: MIT Press, 1980).
49. Ibid., 67. For details, see Immanuel Wallerstein, 'Friends and Foes', in *Foreign Policy*, No. 40, (Fall 1980) 119–31.
50. Samuel S. Kim, *The Quest for a Just World Order*, 67–68.
51. Ibid., 17.
52. Richard Falk, Samuel S. Kim and Saul H. Mendlovitz, 'General Introduction', in *Toward a Just World Order*, 3.
53. Samuel S. Kim, *The Quest for a Just World Order*, 309.
54. Kenneth Waltz, quoted in Tim Dunne and Brain Schmidt, 'Realism' in *The Globalization of World Politics: An Introduction to International Relations*, 153. For details, see Kenneth Waltz, *Theory of International Politics*, (Reading, MA: Addison Wesley, 1979).
55. John Mearsheimer, 'Back to the Future: Instability after the Cold War', in *International Security* 15, No. 1 (1990), 5–56.
56. Samuel P. Huntington, 'The Clash of Civilizations', in *Foreign Affairs* 72, No. 3 (1993), 22–169. For details, see Samuel Huntington, *The Clash of Civilizations and the Remaking of the World Order* (New York: Simon and Schuster, 1996).
57. Tim Dunne and Brian Schmidt, 'Realism', in *The Globalization of World Politics: An Introduction to International Relations*, 149.

58. Bentham, quoted in Tim Dunne, 'Liberalism', in *The Globalization of World Politics: An Introduction to International Relations,*166.
59. Ibid.,166.
60. Ibid.
61. Ibid., 170.
62. Ibid., 167–71.
63. Ibid., 169.
64. Ibid., 171.
65. Doyle, quoted in John Baylis, 'International and Global Security in the Post-Cold War Era', op. cit., 263. For details, see M.W. Doyle, 'On the Democratic Peace', in *International Security* 19, No. 4 (1995), 164–84.
66. John Baylis, 'International and Global Security in the Post-Cold War Era', op. cit., 263.
67. Francis Fukuyama, 'The End of History', *The National Interest* 16 (1989). Also refer Francis Fukuyama, *The End of History and the Last Man* (London: Hamish Hamilton, 1992).
68. Francis Fukuyama, quoted in Michael Cox, 'International History since 1989', in *The Globalization of World Politics: An Introduction to International Relations*, 113. For details, see Francis Fukuyama, 'The End of History', in *The National Interest*, 16 (1989).
69. Francis Fukuyama, quoted in Michael Cox, 'International History since 1989', in *The Globalization of World Politics: An Introduction to International Relations*, 114.
70. Tim Dunne, 'Liberalism', op. cit., 177.
71. Ibid., 176–77.
72. Richard Falk, 'Normative Initiatives and Demilitarization: A Third System Approach', in *Toward a Just World Order,* ed. Richard Falk, Samuel S. Kim and Saul H. Mendlovitz, 624–26. Also refer Richard Falk, Samuel S. Kim and Saul H. Mendlovitz, 'Introduction – Orientations to Transition', in ibid., 562–63.
73. Rajni Kothari, *Transformation and Survival: In Search of a Humane World Order* (London: Aspect Publications, 1990), 43.
74. Ibid., 46.
75. Ibid., 59.
76. Ali A. Mazrui, *A World Federation of Cultures: An African Perspective* (New York: Free Press, 1978), 245.
77. Ibid., 246.
78. Subrata Mukherjee and Sushila Ramaswamy, *A History of Political Thought: Plato to Marx* (New Delhi: Prentice Hall of India, 1999), 322.

79. J.M. Keynes, *The Economic Consequences of the Peace* (London: Macmillan, 1919).
80. Steven L. Lamy, 'Contemporary Mainstream Approaches: Neo-Realism and Neo-Liberalism', in *The Globalization of World Politics: An Introduction to International Relations*, 188.
81. Stephen Hobden and Richard Wyn Jones, 'Marxist Theories of International Relations', in *The Globalization of World Politics: An Introduction to International Relations*, 205–08.
82. Richard Falk, *A Study of Future Worlds* (New Delhi: Orient Longman, 1975), 17–22.
83. Richard Falk, *On Humane Governance: Toward a New Global Politics* (London: Polity Press, 1995), 172–7. Also refer Richard Falk, 'The Making of Global Citizenship', in Jeremy Brecher, John Brown Childs and Jill Cutler, eds, *Global Visions: Beyond the New World Order* (Boston: South End Press, 1993), ix and 39–40.
84. Rajni Kothari, quoted in Thomas Pantham, *Political Theories and Social Reconstruction: A Critical Survey of the Literature on India* (New Delhi, Sage, 1995), 152.
85. Rajni Kothari, *Rethinking Development: In Search of Humane Alternatives* (London: Aspect Publications, 1990), 8–21. Also refer Rajni Kothari, 'Toward a Just World', in *Toward a Just World Order*, 579–601; Rajni Kothari, *Transformation and Survival: In Search of a Humane World Order* (London: Aspects Publications, 1990), 146–50.
86. Ali A. Mazrui, *A World Federation of Cultures: An African Perspective*, 243, 271 and 303.
87. Samuel S. Kim, *The Quest for a Just World Order*, 137–50 and 190–91.
88. Ibid., 193.
89. Ibid., 150.
90. Ibid., 193.
91. O.P. Gauba, *An Introduction to Political Theory* (New Delhi: Macmillan, 1995), 281.
92. Ibid., 281.
93. Ibid., 328–9.
94. Ibid., 329.
95. Ibid., 337.
96. Ibid., 337–8.
97. Robert Nozick, quoted in O.P. Gauba, op. cit., 338.
98. Tim Dunne, 'Liberalism', in *The Globalization of World Politics: An Introduction to International Relations*, 175.
99. Stephen Hobden and Richard Wyn Jones, 'Marxist Theories of International Relations', op. cit., 210–11.

100. Stephen Hobden and Richard Wyn Jones, 'Marxist Theories of International Relations', op. cit., 214–16.
101. Ibid., 214.
102. Richard Falk, quoted in Richard Falk, Samuel S. Kim and Saul H. Mendlovitz, 'Social Justice – Introduction', in *Toward a Just World Order*, 368.
103. Richard Falk, 'Comparative Protection of Human Rights in Capitalist and Socialist Third World Countries', op. cit., 424–25.
104. Richard Falk, 'On Invisible Oppression and World Order', op. cit., 43–46.
105. Richard Falk, *A Global Approach to National Policy* (Cambridge: Harvard University Press, 1975), 72.
106. Ibid.
107. Richard Falk, 'The Making of Global Citizenship', in *Global Visions: Beyond the New World Order*, ed. Jeremy Brecher, John Brown Childs and Jill Cutler (Boston: South End Press, 1993), ix and 39.
108. Ibid., 39.
109. Richard Falk, *On Humane Governance: Toward a New Global Politics*, 14.
110. Ibid., 116 and 239.
111. Rajni Kothari, *Footsteps into the Future: Diagnosis of the Present World and a Design for an Alternative* (New Delhi: Orient Longman, 1974), 113.
112. Rajni Kothari, *State against Democracy: In Search of Humane Governance* (Delhi: Ajanta Publications, 1988), 70.
113. Rajni Kothari, 'Towards a Just World', in *Toward a Just World Order*, 601.
114. Rajni Kothari, *State against Democracy: In Search of Humane Governance* (Delhi: Ajanta Publications, 1988), 2–7. Also refer Rajni Kothari, *Rethinking Development: In Search of Humane Alternatives*, 66–70.
115. Rajni Kothari, *State against Democracy: In Search of Humane Governance*, 111–17.
116. Ibid., 131–32.
117. Ali A. Mazrui, *A World Federation of Cultures: An African Perspective*, 191.
118. Dennis Pirages, quoted in Richard Falk, Samuel S. Kim and Saul H. Mendlovitz, 'Ecological Balances – Introduction', in *Toward a Just World Order*, 437.
119. Rajni Kothari, *Rethinking Development: In Search of Humane Alternatives*, 107.
120. Ibid., 108.
121. Rajni Kothari, 'Environment and Alternative Development', in *Alternatives* 5, No. 4 (1980).

122. Richard Falk, *This Endangered Planet: Prospects and Proposals for Human Survival* (New York: Vintage Books, 1971), 21–23, 37–43, 104–213.
123. Ibid., xiii.
124. Ibid., 21.
125. Ibid., 35.
126. Samuel S. Kim, *The Quest for a Just World Order,* 251.
127. Ibid., 245.
128. Ibid., 250.
129. Ibid., 250–51.
130. Ibid., 250–51.

3 Locating WOMP

History and Evolution

In the previous chapter, we explored the philosophical context of WOMP. This chapter looks into the historical context of its genesis and development. It is divided into five sections. The first section traces the emergence of international society from the days of the Treaty of Westphalia. It seeks to tease out the notion(s) of world order implied in this society. The second section looks more directly into the genesis of WOMP, locating it in the post-war political context of the Cold War, the nuclear arms race and neo-colonialism as well as in the academic traditions of peace research. The next three sections sketch the evolutionary process of WOMP through its different stages. The third section deals with the initial years of 1961–68, when WOMP theorists were concerned almost exclusively with the issue of peace and displayed a shared faith in the adoption of a legal-institutional framework for war prevention. The fourth section deals with the years, 1968–78, when, thanks to the participation of non-Western scholars, WOMP broadbased its concerns to include values of economic well-being as well as socio-political justice. This was also the period in which WOMP became increasingly conscious of the need to work out strategies of transition to the preferred world. The final section deals with what might be called the third and fourth stages of WOMP, in which interest shifted from governmental agencies to transnational social movements and grass roots initiatives. It also deals with the circumstances in which WOMP suffered from growing lack of internal cohesion and went into relative decline. The chapter ends with a reference to the newer forms of theorization in the age of globalization.

I

Most conventional notions of world order presume or postulate an international society. This society is defined as a 'group of states', which are 'conscious of certain common interests and common values'; they are 'bound by a common set of rules in their relations with one another' and participate in 'common institutions'.[1] The core constituent of such a society is thus the sovereign state. It should be appropriate, therefore, to trace back historically the concept of world order since the formation of the modern sovereign state system.

It is generally agreed that the transition from the medieval to the modern state system took place with the Treaty of Westphalia (1648). The Thirty Years' War (1618–48), which preceded it, destroyed the medieval order that had been shaped in the image of a Eurocentric Christian commonwealth dominated and held together by imperial and/or papal hierarchies.[2] The Treaty created instead a world in which sovereign states competed with one another in the pursuit of power and material interests, but also had to learn to coexist and interact. This marked the starting point for the development of 'new norms applicable to the behaviour of new sovereigns'[3] and resulted eventually in the formation of 'the first completely explicit international society with its own diplomatic institutions, formal body of law, and enunciated practices of prudential statecraft, including the balance of power'.[4]

Practices such as conciliation, mediation and arbitration were introduced in this period, as was 'international congress' 'as an ad hoc system of communication and conflict resolution'.[5] A multipolar balance of power moderated power clashes. Yet, sovereign states waged wars as often as they entered into alliances and treaties. The logic of sovereignty often triumphed over the need for international consonance. The dominant mood of the classical period was separation rather than integration, and autarky rather than interdependence. As a result, social integration in the system was quite low.[6] William Penn, Abbé St Pierre, Rousseau, Bentham and Kant[7] made pleas for world order through institutional reforms, but these pleas were 'all dismissed as incompatible with the realities of the states system'.[8]

The first significant attempt to establish a world order was made only at the Vienna Congress in 1815. Underlying this attempt was the assumption that world order could be maintained only if the great powers exercised special rights and responsibilities. The Concert of Europe, which emerged as a result, reflected the exclusive concerns of five great powers, Britain, France, Prussia, Russia and Austria, which acted as the self-styled guardians of world order.[9] The Concert of Europe performed 'a variety of functions associated with contemporary international institutions: collective legitimization of new states, collective neutralization of certain areas, collective peacemaking and peacekeeping, collective enforcement of certain decisions, and collective rule making'.[10]

It was also during this period that the European powers extended their colonial control in Asia, Africa and Latin America, thereby encompassing most of the world. World War I, 'whereby a handful of European states dominated the affairs of the world',[11] further consolidated European supremacy all over the world,

At the same time, World War I also marked the breakdown of the nineteenth century balance of power system, which had thus far succeeded in maintaining peace among self-seeking sovereign states. In the wake of this massive failure, 'pacifists and legal scholars began to advance anti-sovereignty arguments and doctrines'.[12] The focus was on improving and reforming peaceful settlement procedures and further developing and codifying international law. The first organized attempt to restructure the normative foundations of world order was made with the establishment of the League of Nations in 1920. Before the League of Nations was established, states were believed to have the sovereign right to wage war. Now, there was a renewed emphasis on natural law and just war. The covenant of the League of Nations restricted the right of a state to resort to war and sanctioned only 'legitimate use of force'.[13]

Central to the League of Nations was the collective security system, whereby the League could use military power to deter aggression and, if necessary, use a preponderance of power to enforce its decision. Another step forward in the progressive delegitimization of war was the Kellogg-Briand Pact of 1928 (also known as the Pact of Paris), which was ratified by sixty-two nations. Through the Kellogg-Briand Pact, all international conflicts, regardless of their origin or nature, were pledged to be settled through peaceful means, and war was denounced as an instrument of national policy.[14]

The requirements of world order seemed to gain further precedence over claims of sovereignty when rights and responsibilities of individuals were sought to be redefined in a manner that would transcend moral and legal obligations to territorial states. The Treaty of Versailles introduced the concept of individual responsibility for war crimes. New norms were defined also on such matters as social welfare, slavery, the narcotics and drugs trade, and customs violations.[15]

While the League of Nations may thus be seen as an attempt to transcend the Westphalian state system, it could not remain unaffected by the malaise and malfunctioning of the existing world. Autarky and unilateralism on the part of the various states restricted its scope and success. From the very beginning, many states such as the United States refused to join it. The mandate system revealed the colonial mentality of the founders of the League of Nations. Further, the League was unable to handle the Manchurian crisis of 1931, the Ethiopian crisis of 1935 and, most important, Hitler's decision to reoccupy the Rhineland in March 1936.

While the League of Nations failed eventually to overcome the pitfalls of the sovereign state system, the Westphalian norms were brought into question on several other counts in the inter-war period. The Wilsonian advocacy of the right of national self-determination challenged imperialism indirectly, while the Soviet revolutionary challenge was more direct. The latter sought to establish a new world order based on socialist internationalism and solidarity. Yet, these challenges were rather short lived. As Samuel S. Kim pointed out:

> The Soviet Union and the United States both abandoned their initial revisionist challenges and retreated into the cocoon of state sovereignty. The Marxist notion of the state as a coercive instrument of exploitation that would eventually wither away was transformed (or rather deformed) into the Stalinist notion of a garrison super state.[16]

Nonetheless, anti-colonial nationalism did gather force and momentum in the inter-war period. On another plane, the economic depression of 1929 shattered the world economy. This crisis of

> unprecedented depth brought even the strongest capitalist economies to their knees and seemed to reverse the creation of a single universal world economy, which had been so remarkable an achievement of nineteenth century liberal capitalism.[17]

The 1930s also witnessed the rise of totalitarian regimes in Italy and Germany. While Mussolini established a fascist state in Italy, Hitler established a Nazi state in Germany. This was accompanied by the crisis in the Far East, especially the Japanese occupation of Manchuria between 1931 and 1933.

World War II brought about fundamental changes in world politics. The European domination of world politics came to an end. The United States and the former USSR emerged as the two key players in world politics. Three major political, ideological and technological developments took place in the wake of the war. These were the collapse and end of the colonial empires in Asia, Africa and some parts of Latin America; the beginning of the Cold War, which reflected the political, military and, most importantly, ideological confrontation between the United States and the USSR; and the development of weapons of mass destruction – the atomic bomb, the hydrogen bomb, nuclear weapons, chemical weapons, biological weapons, the means of their delivery as well as their control over them by the developed countries.[18]

The period saw unprecedented and dramatic expansion of the international society. Newly independent Third World countries wanted to pursue independent foreign policies and desired to establish their own distinct identity in international relations. Most did not want, therefore, to be part of the Cold War politics or be associated with the military pacts led by the United States and the USSR. Another major development was the establishment of the United Nations in 1945 to promote global peace and prevent the outbreak of another world war.

World War II also witnessed the emergence of a new liberal world economic order. At the Bretton Woods Conference in 1944, policy makers sought to ensure that the economic depression did not recur. They also sought to rebuild the war torn economies of Europe. The Bretton Woods Agreements of 1944 set up the International Monetary Fund (IMF) and the International Bank for Reconstruction and Development (now known as the World Bank). The former 'was created to ensure a stable exchange rate regime' and provide 'emergency assistance to countries facing a temporary crisis in their balance of payments regime'.[19] The World Bank 'was created to facilitate private investment and reconstruction in Europe. The Bank was also charged with assisting "development" in other countries, a mandate which later became the main reason for its existence. Finally, the

General Agreement on Tariffs and Trade (GATT) was signed in 1947 and became a forum for negotiations on trade liberalization.'[20]

In retrospect, it may be said that the objective of all world order planning since the Treaty of Westphalia was to minimize the recurrence of another great war. Yet, as Samuel Kim pointed out, common to these attempts was a 'negative, retrospective and reactive mentality'.[21] They were products of 'condominial consensus or compromise among the great powers' and embodied 'a corporate oligopolistic structure with uneven distribution of values'.[22] They were 'designed more to manage inter-state relations than to satisfy global human needs'.[23]

II

Wishing to avert a repetition of the horrors of World War II, the UN found itself caught up in the Cold War calculations of the rival superpowers. The Cold War was at once military, economic, political and ideological. Its military manifestations were strategic alliances, the arms race, the nuclear build-up and proxy wars. The world economy stood divided into two parallel streams once the Soviet bloc opted out of the Bretton Woods agreements and set up a socialist commonwealth in the form of the Council for Mutual Economic Assistance (CMEA). Economic aid and trade as well as capital and technology transfer among the states of the CMEA were driven by the Cold War rivalry.

While the two power blocs sold different paths of economic development to the newly independent countries, most were lured into adopting the Western path of capitalist modernization with varying doses of Keynesian welfarism. However, even after several decades, the promise of fast and comprehensive growth remained unfulfilled, causing widespread dissatisfaction and resentment. The Third World countries discovered that they were slipping deeper and deeper into a relationship of dependency on the advanced Western economies, while the gap between the rich North and the poor South widened rather than narrowed.

The Cold War, underdevelopment and poverty combined to stir a critical consciousness amongst people against the growing disorder and anarchy. Institutions of civil society, the academic community, and the political elite of the different countries started demanding an alternative world order, though the tone and temper of their arguments often set them apart.

Besides the political context sketched above, the intellectual origins of WOMP can also be traced back to the peace research movement of the 1950s and 1960s. The movement arose out of disenchantment with the intellectual self-isolation of traditional international relations studies. Peace research sought to be more interdisciplinary. "In fact, it served as a rendezvous point for various disciplines concerned with human conflict behaviour."[24] Peace research was also 'more value oriented', questioning 'the feasibility as well as desirability of value neutral' inquiry. It was 'broader in its scope' since it studied violence in all forms, domestic or transnational. It probed conflicts in a comparative framework.[25]

World order studies refined and expanded the interdisciplinary approach of peace research by synthesizing the 'loose juxtaposition of concepts, paradigms and theories borrowed from various social science disciplines'.[26] Given their futuristic orientation, world order studies also formulated their own concepts and models suited to the purpose of designing sketches of a preferred world order and working out the strategies of transition.[27]

Scholarly interest in world order studies received a major boost in the late 1960s when a group of eminent social theorists from different continents came together under what came to be known as the World Order Models Project (WOMP). WOMP drew scholars from Latin America, Africa, Japan, Europe, Soviet Union, India and the United States and also had indirect representation from China. Over the next two decades, these scholars published several normative futuristic studies on what they thought the preferred world for the 1990s[28] could and should be. The WOMP participants subscribed to a future world order based on four values: peace, economic well-being, social and political justice, and ecological balance. A direct offshoot of the legal-institutional approach, WOMP was sponsored by what was earlier known as the World Law Fund and later redesignated as the Institute for World Order.

The values upheld and projected by the WOMP writings have truly universal relevance and appeal, yet the perspectives brought to bear on these issues by the theorists belonging to different continents were refreshingly different from one another. The universalism of WOMP was thus multicultural. Its assumption was that even though different cultures had different values, they also had some values that were universalizable. The hope was that such universalizable values could, with conscious effort, be turned into universal values.

WOMP gradually developed into an academic discipline that was at once scholarly, scientific, predictive, inventive and critical. It did not confine itself to a philosophical or speculative discussion of values. Rather, it tried to identify and address policy questions as well. Transformation was the key element in WOMP's approach, but there was no room in it for violent or revolutionary transformation. WOMP theorists believed that a more just and humane world order would emerge in a gradual, non-violent and evolutionary manner within a broad liberal paradigm.

Richard Falk and Saul Mendlovitz, two pioneering WOMP theorists, believed that WOMP values could be best promoted if an academic and pedagogic discipline was developed around them. Their programme was designed to 'spread among professional and graduate schools, and ultimately permeate college and pre-college years'.[29] The WOMP theorists believed that such intellectual interventions would go a long way in achieving the desired change.

Within WOMP, there were discernible differences between the views of the Western scholars and the Third World scholars. While Western scholars such as Falk and Mendlovitz adopted a perspective that emphasized the role of world level institutions, Third World scholars such as Rajni Kothari feared that such institutions would encourage excessive centralism. Kothari's perspective was of a pluralist and decentralized world order in which grass roots activism played a significant role.[30] As he put it, "From the idea of world unity, the whole idea of a world federation was evolved."[31]

III

The WOMP approach went through various stages of evolution from its inception. Although the more basic values and features remained constant, there were significant shifts in conceptual focus and methodological orientation.[32] One can see at least four distinct stages in the development of WOMP.

The period from 1961 to 1968 constituted the first stage in the development of WOMP, marked by the efforts of a group of concerned United States scholars such as Falk and Mendlovitz to establish an academic discipline devoted specifically to study prevention of wars and other forms of large scale collective violence.

Rejecting the prevalent notion that conflicts and violence were integral to the anarchical inter-state system, these scholars proceeded on the premise that international law and institutions could be developed into credible and effective means of maintaining peace. These scholars were greatly influenced by the publication of *World Peace through World Law*,[33] a plan conceived of and elaborated by two international lawyers, Grenville Clark and Louis B. Sohn, who proposed that the United Nations Charter be amended 'to transfer some functions, capabilities and resources from national governments to a rearranged set of global institutions'.[34] Falk and Mendlovitz did not postulate any organizational alternative to the state system, but they expected states to rise above narrow geopolitical calculations. They believed that it was possible within the existing framework to demilitarize international relations, promote interdependence, and resolve issues such as human rights and the nature of developmental assistance. A variety of structural reforms could be ushered in by augmenting the United Nations and strengthening regional institutions and specialized regimes to handle the growing complexity of international relations.[35]

The group actively thought of involving the academic community in different parts of the world to build strong intellectual support for a global peace movement. Aspiring to turn their project into a transnational research enterprise, it was decided that scholars worldwide would be invited to pursue nationally or regionally based inquiries into problems relevant to war prevention.

Quite soon, these theorists realized that war prevention could not be discussed in isolation. Poverty and social injustice were so inextricably interwoven with the outbreak of international violence that they had to be included in an integrated framework for defining measures for war prevention. While the advanced economies had largely solved the problems of mass poverty and grave injustices and could, therefore, afford to give almost exclusive priority to peace, it was felt that the Third World countries had to give much higher priority to economic well-being and social justice.[36]

This initial stage of WOMP suffered from several limitations. A major flaw in its framework was that 'it appealed to the enlightened self-interest of the privileged to take the initiative in transition polities, basing the appeal on the uncritical transference of liberal reform politics to the international scene'.[37] A second flaw was its excessively American orientation. As Samuel S. Kim pointed out:

> Its conceptual origin, key participants and pedagogic materials were all American. Its legal and structural design for world order reflects the rather unique historical experience of the United States with its largely successful transition from the relatively decentralized condition of 'state' sovereignty under the Articles of Confederation to a 'more perfect union' under a new federal system.[38]

More severe critics charged that it was no more than a mask to disguise the 'neo-imperial motive of the Pax Americana'[39] Many condemned it as an exercise in constitutional or legal engineering, while still others thought of it 'as a kind of intellectual utopianism through which world order scholars could escape the 'messy and uncivilized' political struggles of forging an actual new order'.[40] 'Finally, this world order approach was considered conceptually inadequate' because it 'abstracted the question of system transformation in a manner unresponsive to the broader world order agenda of the non-Western peoples of the world'.[41]

IV

World order studies reached their zenith with the formal establishment of the World Order Models Project in 1968. WOMP was sponsored by what was then known as World Law Fund and later redesignated as the Institute for World Order. It was during this phase (1968–78) that participation of scholars from Latin America, Japan, India and Africa made WOMP a truly broadbased movement. Falk described this as a phase of 'transnational collaboration'.[42] Since values were stated in general terms and could therefore be subjected to a variety of interpretations, WOMP became genuinely pluralistic in its vision. Participants were free to propose additional values. There was also a general consensus in favour of including a much broader range of actors. These could be world institutions, transnational actors, international organizations, regional arrangements, sub-national movements, local communities and individuals.[43]

The research group agreed on a series of enterprises to promote research, education and a transnational social movement to realize world order values. The first major venture was the publication of a genuinely transnational journal called *Alternatives*, with Rajni Kothari as its first editor and two dozen distinguished scholars on its editorial board. It was decided to bring out an annual 'State of the

Globe' Report to track local, regional and global trends and evaluate the extent to which world order values had diminished or been realized during the preceding year. The report would also make suggestions and recommendations about what ought to be done.[44] In addition, WOMP decided to hold a series of transnational seminars for scholars and public figures. It also 'set out to create the basic instructional materials needed for a worldwide educational movement, whose ultimate thrust would be global reform'.[45]

Nine meetings of WOMP were held during this period in different parts of the world. The first meeting was held in New Delhi in February 1968, with participants drawn from Western Europe, Latin America, Japan, India and North America. In the subsequent years, participants from Africa, the USSR and Scandinavia joined the deliberations, as did at a still later date, a Chinese and a West Asian scholar. Jagdish Bhagwati of MIT organized one meeting with a group of economists in order to provide an economic perspective. This meeting resulted in the first WOMP book, called *Economics and World Order: From the 1970s to the 1990s*.[46] The African research group organized a conference that resulted in the second WOMP book, edited by Ali Mazrui and Hasu Patel, called *Africa and World Affairs*.[47] The collaborative research culminated in a series of five books under the umbrella title of *Preferred Worlds for the 1990s*.[48]

Participants were selected for their intellectual credentials and generally progressive orientation, and not because all of them had the same vision on global reform. There was a great diversity of views among the theorists. One participant, Foujad Ajami, pointed out:

> Non-Western participants in that project assaulted and challenged its Western ethnocentrism; 'non-lawyers' enhanced and broadened its concerns and pushed it in the direction of political harmony and culture. Those concerned with socio-economic justice drew attention to the fact that peace, unless rooted in socio-economic justice, can be meaningless, stultifying and perhaps repressive; the strong have always sought peace as a means of ensuring that their order would be unchallenged and undisturbed. The intrusion of concern for justice into world orderism was to profoundly change its thrust and essence. The hitherto legal emphasis of the movement was increasingly modified to be more self-consciously political.[49]

However, one should not exaggerate these differences. Despite this diversity, the WOMP theorists shared a common commitment to the broader value framework of democracy, human rights and anti-imperialist politics.[50] For most of the theorists, WOMP became a lifelong scholarly and political vocation. But, as we shall see, the circumstances and experiences of the later years led to considerable dilution of these differences. The result was that whereas, in the first phase, WOMP had placed almost exclusive emphasis on war prevention, in the second phase, it placed much greater emphasis on economic well-being and socio-political justice. Ecological issues, however, were yet to occupy its theorists as a major concern.[51]

Differences surfaced yet again when, towards the end of the 1970s, WOMP developed a major concern for the transformation of the state. First World participants tended to see the state as a vehicle of militarist ambitions and the arms race and, therefore, regarded a strong state as the chief obstacle to global reform. They wanted the state to become more responsive to the aspirations generated within civil society. In contrast, the Third World participants were greatly concerned about neo-colonial exploitation as well as First World domination in the political and cultural domains. They reposed greater faith in the potential of Third World states to safeguard their independence. They were worried that weak states could be penetrated easily.[52] This faith in the progressive role of the state was shaken as many Third World states became increasingly militaristic in their outlook and actions, while their leaders squandered and plundered national resources. 'The experience of the emergency in India during 1976–77' and the militarization of sub-Saharan Africa and the Southern core of South America during the 1960s and 1970s were prime examples of these negative trends.[53] As a result, there was a new thrust on human rights and democracy. The Third World scholars no longer regarded constitutionalism as a luxury for which they should aspire only after the 'basic needs' of the poor were satisfied.

The result was that the sharp differences between the Northern and Southern participants once again gave way to a new convergence. A more balanced and variegated perspective now combined issues of peace, democracy, human rights, poverty alleviation and justice. For example, WOMP displayed a strong affinity during the early 1970s with the demand for a New International Economic Order, which had been raised by Third World countries in forums such as the United Nations General Assembly and the United Nations Conference on Trade and Development (UNCTAD).[54]

It was also during this phase that WOMP developed a more policy oriented approach. Theorists realized that utopian pictures of the preferred world would not make a material difference by themselves; the real challenge was to work out viable strategies of transition. They had to develop an ordered agenda, for which operational strategies and policies could then be formulated. Intellectual and conceptual tools needed to be developed for operationalizing values. More data was required on their interrelationship. Reliable indices had to be developed for measuring change. In this endeavour, the behavioural sciences approach was likely to prove more relevant than the speculative style that most WOMP theorists had adopted in the past.[55]

Theorists were asked to be 'as explicit as possible' about the constitutive order and authority structures needed during the period of transition and at the ultimate end.[56] Thanks to this methodological reorientation, the term, 'preferred world', came to have a more rigorous meaning, 'stated in fairly precise behavioural detail, including a behavioural description of the transition process from the present to the new system'.[57]

Since an operational definition of goals was of crucial importance, it was necessary that precise priority setting rules be laid down for handling instances of conflict among values. In thinking about transition, some participants tended to accord primacy to reforms in national societies.[58] They argued that such reforms must precede global social change, particularly so within the major countries. "Others argued for the primacy of the global agenda and the critical role of transnational functional political movements and institutions."[59] The issue, therefore, was how much centralization or decentralization was appropriate in different substantive arenas and the criteria relevant for deciding the appropriate level. A unified approach demanded that theorists moderate the values emanating from their specific cultural or geographic backgrounds with values of greater universal relevance.[60]

These were tricky issues and WOMP did not prove too successful in sorting them out. Samuel Kim, himself a prominent WOMP theorist, admitted, "The *Preferred Worlds* series has not provided either a satisfactorily systematic or substantive treatment of transition politics by way of prescribing behavioural guidance for world order activists."[61] In addition, Kim pointed out, "WOMP was unable to achieve sustained participation of scholars from the Soviet Union or, more generally, from the Communist world."[62] He was also of the view that while 'Third World participation symbolized the transnationalization of world order inquiry', it did so "without achieving any corresponding cohesion in research purpose, modelling design or an integrated world order vision. Instead, it entailed a constant questioning of WOMP's premises."[63]

At the same time, Kim pointed out that 'generating a strong and cohesive political will toward normative goals of system transformation' was difficult, 'if not impossible', in the given 'global conditions of fragmentation'.[64] Also, there was still a 'virtual monopoly of the realist school in defining what is real and feasible'.[65]

V

The third stage of WOMP began in 1978 when it adopted a more diverse and diffused approach. Reflected in a number of its projects, including a multivolume series called *Studies on a Just World Order*,[66] this approach distinguished between three intersecting systems of politics. The first consisted of the territorial states with their supporting infrastructure of corporations, banks and knowledge industries. The second was made up of international organizations, global as well as regional, including the United Nations. The third consisted of the popular sector, with people acting individually and collectively through voluntary social movements and associations of all kinds.[67]

In its two earlier phases, WOMP had focussed on the first and second systems of politics. In this latest phase, it shifted its attention emphatically to a third system, focussing on the role of social movements and grass roots initiatives as forms of struggle of the oppressed. At the same time, however, WOMP embarked on a series of studies that were more in the nature of a continuation of the earlier phases. Addressing governmental leaders and others who shaped public opinion, these studies were more business-like in their approach and dealt with global policy issues such as nuclear non-proliferation, human rights, basic human needs and the demand for a New International Economic Order.[68]

WOMP slowed down considerably in the late 1980s. It lacked official backing of any sort anywhere, so funding for its transnational conferences and research programmes became a major area of concern. There was also a growing feeling that the areas of consensus were shrinking among the WOMP participants and there was very little hope of a coherent vision emerging in the foreseeable future.[69] Falk listed the basic issues that remained unresolved:

> Was it useful to set forth visions of global scale reform? Did such visions go beyond a new round of reformist constitutionalism, even if in the mild form of a strengthened United Nations? Was centralization feasible and desirable at a regional level? At a global level? What were the economic features of a positive ideology of global reform?[70]

WOMP was never formally suspended, but most of its participants began to focus their energies on activities within their own countries. Some WOMP theorists, including Richard Falk, got 'involved in two follow-on collaborative undertakings: the Peace and Global Transformation Project of the United Nations University and the Committee for a Just World Peace'.[71] Some WOMP activities, like the publication of *Alternatives*, continue, expanding dialogue across boundaries and providing educational material in world order studies.

As events actually unfolded in the 1990s, their harsh reality seemed to expose the 'hollowness' of the philosophical and normative foundations that had informed the WOMP preferences. The theorists realized that their capacity to exert influence on governmental policy or even public opinion was marginal. They were kept away from all structures of decision making. First World policy makers were interested only in maintaining a status quo that favoured the privileged position of their countries.

The result was a near eclipse of the WOMP spirit. It was against this background of declining expectations, hopelessness and grim failure that its activists initiated a programme called The Global Civilization: Challenges for Democracy, Sovereignty and Security Project (Global Common Project, or GCP)[72] in order to move away from their earlier predicaments and to reassert normative concerns of world community in a market driven global economy. The GCP emerged out of the conversations and dialogue held in the fall of 1986 between the WOMP group and Georgi Shakhnozarov, the then vice-president of the International Political Science Association and a special assistant to Russian President Mikhail Gorbachev.[73]

A steering committee – composed of scholars, diplomats, media persons and religious leaders – held two meetings in mid-1987 and in the spring of 1988 (in Nyon, Switzerland). Five workshops were organized over a period of five years, each devoted to a principal theme of the project. These were: 'The Coming Global Civilization: What Kind of Sovereignty?' (Moscow, 1988); 'Deepening and Globalizing Democracy' (Yokohama, 1990); 'Global Political Economy: Trends and Preferences' (Cairo, 1990); 'Shaping Global Polity' (South Bend, 1991); and 'Toward a Just World Order for the Twenty-First Century' (Harare, 1993).[74]

The results from these workshops were published in part through public education and dissemination programmes, but more especially through a wide range of WOMP inspired publications in the form of books and papers. GCP rapporteur Richard Falk brought out a volume titled *On Humane Governance: Toward a New Global Politics* (Falk, 1995), in which he tried to crystallize ideas on some of the 'enduring concerns' of both WOMP and the GCP.[75] He argued that globalization and the consequent gradual erosion of the state-centric system had led to the decline of geopolitics and the rise of what he called geo-governance. Falk was interested in exploring the extent to which such geo-governance could 'be made more humane, more people oriented, more focused on human rights, and global demilitarization'.[76] Geo-governance in this preferred form is what Falk called 'humane governance'.[77]

We should note in the end that the four stages in the development of WOMP were all interrelated. Even though there had been shifts in focus and methodological orientation, its basic concerns remained unchanged throughout: 'emphasis on system transformation; depiction of preferred world order systems; avowal of explicit values; concern about transition politics; and, a holistic conception of global human interests and needs'.[78]

Notes

1. Hedley Bull, *The Anarchical Society: A Study of Order in World Politics* (London: Macmillan, 1977), 13.
2. Samuel S. Kim, *The Quest for a Just World Order* (Boulder: Westview Press, 1984), 27.
3. Ibid., 27.

4. Robert H. Jackson, 'The Evolution of International Society', in *The Globalization of World Politics: An Introduction to International Relations*, ed. John Baylis and Steve Smith (New York: Oxford University Press, 2001), 44.
5. Samuel S. Kim, *The Quest for a Just World Order*, 30–31.
6. Ibid., 30–31.
7. Ibid., 31. For details, see William Penn, *Essay Towards the Present and Future Peace of Europe by the Establishment of a European Diet, Parliament or Estates (1693)*; Abbé St Pierre, *Project for Perpetual Peace (1712)*; Jean Jacques Rousseau, *Lasting Peace Through the Federation of Europe (1761)*; Jeremy Bentham, *Plan for a Universal and Perpetual Peace (between 1786 and 1789)*; Immanuel Kant, *Thoughts on Perpetual Peace* (1795).
8. Ibid., 31.
9. Ibid., 32.
10. Ibid., 36. For details, see Evan Luard, *Types of International Society* (New York: Free Press, 1976), 330–32.
11. Eric Hobsbawm, *The Age of Extremes: A History of the World – 1914–91* (New York: Vintage Books, 1994), 32.
12. Samuel S. Kim, *The Quest for a Just World Order*, 37.
13. Ibid., 37–38.
14. Ibid.
15. Ibid., 38.
16. Ibid., 37.
17. Eric Hobsbawm, *The Age of Extremes: A History of the World – 1914–91*, 7.
18. Len Scott, 'International History 1945–90', in *The Globalization of World Politics: An Introduction to International Relations*, ed. John Baylis and Steve Smith, 75.
19. Ngaire Woods, 'International Political Economy in an Age of Globalization', in *The Globalization of World Politics: An Introduction to International Relations*, 278.
20. Ibid., 278.
21. Samuel S. Kim, *The Quest for a Just World Order*, 52.
22. Ibid., 52.
23. Ibid.
24. Ibid., 76.
25. Ibid.
26. Ibid.
27. Ibid.

28. *Preferred Worlds for the 1990s Series:* 1. Rajni Kothari, *Footsteps into the Future: Diagnosis of the Present World and a Design for an Alternative* (New Delhi: Orient Longman, 1974); 2. Saul H. Mendlovitz, ed., *On the Creation of a Just World Order,* (New Delhi: Orient Longman, 1975); 3. Ali A. Mazrui, *A World Federation of Cultures* (New York: The Free Press, 1978); 4. Richard Falk, *A Study of Future Worlds* (New Delhi: Orient Longman, 1975); 5. Johan Galtung, *The True Worlds: A Transnational Perspective.*
29. Harold D. Lasswell, 'Foreword', in *The Strategy of World Order: Toward a Theory of War Prevention,* Vol. I, ed. Richard Falk and Saul H. Mendlovitz (New York: World Law Fund, 1966), iii.
30. Rajni Kothari, *Memoirs: Uneasy is the Life of the Mind* (New Delhi: Rupa, 2002), 33.
31. Interview with Rajni Kothari by Sujit Lahiry on 1 and 2 June 2002 (see Appendices).
32. Samual S. Kim, *The Quest for a Just World Order,* 83.
33. Grenville Clark and Louis B. Sohn, *World Peace through World Law,* III Edition (Cambridge, Mass.: Harvard University Press, 1966).
34. Samuel S. Kim, *The Quest for a Just World Order,* 83.
35. Richard Falk, *The Promise of World Order: Essays in Normative International Relations,* (London: Wheatsheaf Books, 1987), 17.
36. Saul H. Mendlovitz, 'Introduction', in Rajni Kothari, *Footsteps into the Future: Diagnosis of the Present World and a Design for an Alternative* (New Delhi: Orient Longman, 1974), xi-xii.
37. Samuel S. Kim, *The Quest for a Just World Order,* 84.
38. Ibid.
39. Ibid.
40. Ibid.
41. Ibid.
42. Richard Falk, *The Promise of World Order: Essays in Normative International Relations* (London: Wheatsheaf Books, 1987), 18.
43. Saul H. Mendlovitz, 'Introduction', in *On the Creation of a Just World Order,* ed. Saul H. Mendlovitz (New York: The Free Press, 1975), xii-xiii.
44. Ibid., xi.
45. Ibid., x.
46. Jagdish Bhagwati, *Economics and World Order: From the 1970s to the 1990s* (New York: Macmillan, 1972).
47. Ali A. Mazrui and Hasu Patel, eds, *Africa and World Affairs* (New York: The Third Press, 1973).

48. *Preferred Worlds for the 1990s Series:* 1. Rajni Kothari, *Footsteps into the Future: Diagnosis of the Present World and a Design for an Alternative* (New Delhi: Orient Longman, 1974); 2. Saul H. Mendlovitz, ed., *On the Creation of a Just World Order* (New Delhi: Orient Longman, 1975); 3. Ali A. Mazrui, *A World Federation of Cultures* (New York: The Free Press, 1978); 4. Richard Falk, *A Study of Future Worlds* (New Delhi: Orient Longman, 1975); 5. Johan Galtung, *The True World: A Transnational Perspective*.
49. Foujad Ajami, 'World Order: The Question of Ideology', in *Alternatives* 6 (Winter 1980–81), 474.
50. Richard Falk, *The Promise of World Order: Essays in Normative International Relations*, 19.
51. Samuel S. Kim, *The Quest for a Just World Order*, 84. Also refer Saul H. Mendlovitz, ed., *On the Creation of a Just World Order*, xi.
52. Richard Falk, *The Promise of World Order: Essays in Normative International Relations*, 19–21.
53. Ibid., 21.
54. Ibid., 20.
55. Saul H. Mendlovitz, 'Introduction', in *On the Creation of a Just World Order*, xii-xiii.
56. Ibid., xiv-xv.
57. Ibid., xiii.
58. Ibid., xv.
59. Ibid.
60. Ibid., xv-xvi.
61. Samuel S. Kim, *The Quest for a Just World Order*, 85.
62. Ibid., 85.
63. Ibid.
64. Ibid., 86.
65. Ibid.
66. For details, see Richard Falk, Samuel S. Kim and Saul H. Mendlovitz, eds, *Studies on a Just World Order*, Vol. 1: *Toward a Just World Order* (Boulder: Westview Press, 1982); Richard Falk, Friedrich Kratochwil and Saul H Mendlovitz, eds, *Studies on a Just World Order*, Vol. II: *International Law and a Just World Order* (Boulder: Westview Press, 1982); Richard Falk, Samuel S. Kim and Saul H. Mendlovitz, eds, *Studies on a Just World Order*, Vol. III: *The United Nations and a Just World Order* (Boulder: Westview Press, 1983).
67. Samuel S. Kim, *The Quest for a Just World Order*, 86.

68. Ibid., 86. Also see Richard Falk, 'Contending Approaches to World Order', in Richard Falk, Samuel S. Kim and Saul H. Mendlovitz, eds, *Toward a Just World Order: Studies on a Just World Order,* Vol. I (Boulder: Westview Press, 1982), 161.
69. Richard Falk, *The Promise of World Order: Essays in Normative International Relations*, 21–22.
70. Ibid., 22.
71. Ibid.
72. Saul H. Mendlovitz, 'Preface', in Richard Falk, *On Human Governance: Toward a New Global Politics* (London: Polity Press, 1995), vii.
73. Ibid., vii.
74. Ibid., viii.
75. Richard Falk, *On Human Governance: Toward a New Global Politics* (London: Polity Press, 1995). See therein also the Preface by Saul H. Mendlovitz, viii.
76. Richard Falk, *On Human Governance: Toward a New Global Politics,* ix.
77. Ibid., 9.
78. Samuel S. Kim, *The Quest for a Just World Order,* 86.

4 From 'Peace through Law' to 'Humane Governance'

The Ideas of Richard Falk

Richard Falk, decidedly one of the more eminent theorists of the World Order Models Project (WOMP), was the Albert Milbank Professor of International Law at Princeton University, in Princeton. He is currently professor at the University of California, Santa Barbara. He wrote numerous books, articles, monographs and research papers in the hope of laying down the normative bases of a more just and benevolent preferred world order.

Although Falk started writing on the different aspects of world order as early as in 1966, the most succinct definition of world order is to be found in one of his writings of 1975, wherein he used the term world order 'to mean the aggregation of norms, procedures and institutions that give shape and structure to international society at a particular time'.[1] He added, "World order is an analytic concept, although world order analysis usually centres upon normative issues such as the extent to which preferred norms are followed and chosen values are realized in particular international settings."[2]

As with most WOMP theorists, Falk's preferred world order was based on the four values of peace, economic well-being, social and political justice, and ecological balance. Although he paid attention to all of them, he focused in particular on the value of peace. Here too, he directed his attention primarily to the legal aspects. In fact, Falk began by accepting as his basic model the proposal put forward by Granville Clark and Louis B. Sohn[3] – establishing world peace through world law.

A strong believer in the utmost necessity of bringing about a peaceful world, nonetheless, Falk did not believe in forced change.

He had greater faith in the ultimate effectiveness of persuasive action when it was undertaken in a concerted manner by all the concerned actors, whether these were states, non-state organizations, institutions or groups. He was of the view that there could grow within the state system itself some non-state actors and organizations that would convince the state to make moves in a more just and humane direction. Some of these might prefer the change to be gradual, but there would also be others who might well persuade the state system to carry out drastic reforms.

A prerequisite of such concerted action was widespread education in the value of peace. Therefore, Falk especially underlined the role of such education, which was needed by people in both the developed and developing worlds.

This chapter has been divided into six sections. The first section deals with Falk's delineation of the idea of peace and the role that international law and international organizations could play in bringing about and maintaining a peaceful world order. In the second section, we study his views on security, the arms race, militarism and demilitarization. His views on other WOMP values such as economic well-being, socio-political justice and environment protection are discussed in the third section. The fourth section deals with Falk's views on the question of the transition to a preferred world. The fifth section deals with the continuities and departures in his thinking on WOMP. An overall evaluation of Falk is also attempted here. The sixth section delineates his newer theorizations on WOMP.

I

Falk believed that real progress towards peace could be made only when we adequately understood the nature of what he called the 'war system'. Widely spread, this system was also deeply embedded in the very structures of the present world order. Its range was manifested through several indicators. The principal ones among these were 'the number of battle deaths per year and per conflict, and the amount of money devoted to the national maintenance of war fighting capabilities, computed both in absolute terms and as a proportion of GNP'.[4] Progress towards peace could, therefore, be measured in concrete and operational terms. The most significant indices of such progress were: 'decline in the frequency of wars', 'reduction in casualties' (military and civilian) per war, 'reduction in the geographical scope of war', reduction in the 'duration of wars', 'reduction in the threats of war', and reduction in the 'assertion of military capability, ranging from reprisals to showing the flag'.[5]

Richard Falk focused primarily upon the transition techniques that could most effectively be used to shift the pattern of inter-state relations from a dominantly threat and war system to a dominantly reconciliation and peace system. He tried to review the contribution of general international law to the control of international violence.[6] He argued that international relations had undergone a series of transformations. He tried to deal with both the problems of diverse perspectives and the problems of system change as they affected the international legal order. He classified the national actors into modernizing, revolutionary and status quo nations. The most central transformation that Falk wanted to bring about involved the effort to bring a warless world into being.[7]

Since Falk's conception and analysis of peace were multidimensional, he covered several interrelated themes in his writings. The two most prominent among these were the role that international law and international organizations could play in the prevention of war, and the significance of disarmament, especially nuclear disarmament. Falk believed that the prospects of a peaceful world order depended largely on the extent to which states were prepared to minimize their reliance on war and violence in the pursuit of national security. This, in turn, required a shift away from the military concept of security.[8]

Falk's academic training in legal studies led him to emphasize, in particular, the role of international law in bringing about a peaceful world. His optimism in this regard stemmed from his understanding that the international legal order itself had gone through successive evolutionary stages. Historically, five alternative conceptions of the international legal order could be observed to have existed at different points of time. Falk called these the Westphalia conception, the Charter conception, the geopolitical conception, the rules of the game conception, and the decentralized modes of implementation.[9] But all these conceptions also competed among themselves. Traces of these conceptions continue to exist as strains in contemporary thinking on international law. Falk argued that normative tension prevailed to a large extent between the Westphalian conception (state centred international law premised on sovereign consent) and the Charter conception (community centred international law premised on the existence of global public interests, morality and will, and expressed in such documents as the United Nations Charter). Neither conception had had a chance to prove satisfactory by itself.

This was particularly the case during periods such as the present one, which are marked above all by transition and transformation. We are witnessing the gradual decline and erosion of the state system and increased roles for non-territorial actors.[10] A new kind of globally constituted system, encompassing new identities and actors, is emerging. It is a world at once more localized and more globalized than the authority patterns associated with states that could grasp and grapple with.[11]

A new synthesis was, therefore, awaited if international law was to remain relevant and effective. Falk labelled the postulated arrival of such a synthesis 'the Groatian moment'.[12] Falk's allusion to Grotius was significant because, undoubtedly, the latter had been the greatest international legal theorist of transitional times. With this allusion, Falk was suggesting that international legal theorists needed to take the longer historical view and he raised two fundamental questions: 'What can we learn from the prior transition process, which culminated in the birth of the state system? How can international law and lawyers help ensure the emergence of a new post-state system that is relatively more peaceful and just?'[13]

Falk argued that although a Groatian-type synthesis was still awaited, some kind of globally constituted system, encompassing new identities and actors, seemed to be emerging. He suggested several plausible forms now being pursued by this emergent globalism.[14] The four plausible forms and options that he depicted were: Option A: World Government (illustrated by the Clark-Sohn model); Option B: Concert of Great Powers (illustrated by Nixon's Geopolitical Management Scheme); Option C: Concert of Multinational Corporate Elites (illustrated by the Trilateral Commission); and Option D: Global Populism (illustrated by WOMP). Falk believed that a value oriented and decentralized globalism such as WOMP was the best alternative and to be chosen over all the other alternatives for a movement of global reform. Such an altered world order would be at once more localized and more globalized than the authority power patterns associated with states and superpowers.[15]

He made an appeal to international lawyers to work for the emergence of the preferred globalism.[16]

- Falk believed that international law and lawyers would be able to play a significant role only when they became sensitive to the wider process of change under way in international society and, also more pointedly, when they gave self-conscious support to a set of explicit world order goals that structured both the means and ends of transition.[17] Falk then elaborated on how international lawyers could contribute to the cause of global peace and help in the movement towards his preferred world.
- International lawyers needed to direct more of their energies to the challenge of emergent globalism, as well as to that of mastering the workings of law within the traditional system of sovereign states.
- International lawyers should distinguish among the main plausible forms of emergent globalism by reference to value consequences.
- International lawyers could contribute best to the successful solution of the transition problem by strengthening support for a new framework of authority built around a mixture of territorial and non-territorial actors and a blend of local, regional and global identities. The normative underpinnings of such a system were to be founded on the realization of peace, economic well-being, human rights, ecological balance and human scale and ideologies of governance.[18]

Intimately connected to the role of international law was the role of international organizations such as the United Nations. Falk was worried that there was an increasingly negative perception about the role of the United Nations in international society. The legitimacy and authority of the UN was under question because a huge gap separated the goals proclaimed in its charter and its observable actual behaviour. Falk attributed this gap to the highly unequal distribution of power among nations and the competitive logic of state sovereignty.[19] This logic was most manifest in the character of superpower diplomacy, whereby the professed goals were frustrated by the Cold War calculations. Falk contemplated the adoption of a new charter based on the Clark-Sohn plan and the Chicago proposals. These were designed to shift capabilities from states to international institutions.[20]

II

When dominant states accorded primacy to the logic of sovereignty and gave precedence to calculations of power, they ended up not only sabotaging international organizations such as the United Nations, but also creating other sorts of problems for peace. The arms race, particularly the nuclear arms race, was one such problem. The issue was bound to draw the attention of a scholar like Falk.[21] In drawing the contours of international law responsive to the nuclear age, Falk, therefore, stressed on three goals: avoiding nuclear war, minimizing instability, and scaling down the arms race. The success of such a legal regime depended on the values, beliefs and commitment shown by political leaders, military bureaucracies and the public.[22]

What goes particularly to Falk's credit, however, is that he went beyond the manifest forms of the arms race and raised the much larger issue of militarism: "The main dangers to world peace arise from four complementary structures of militarism that set the security agenda for the governments of the world."[23] These four structures were:

- The strategic arms race, reflecting and fuelling East-West rivalry for predominance;
- The closely associated gamut of arms sales and hegemonic intervention in the internal affairs of weak states;
- Proxy wars, conflicts related to state building and regional rivalries; and
- Internally repressive tendencies.[24]

Falk thus dramatically broadened the traditional understanding of war by including in the scope of discussion militarism and militarization, hegemonic domination and internal repression. Moreover, he argued that militarism was intrinsically linked also to problems such as poverty, underdevelopment, repression and escalation of large scale violence in many parts of the world. So long as the militarist behaviour of the statist elites retained legitimacy, peace would elude domestic societies as well as the international system. Transition towards a peaceful world order, therefore, necessitated delegitimizing militarism and reversing the current tendencies towards it.[25]

Falk attempted to identify and explore the 'creative space' available for the struggle against militarism. He looked for normative initiatives that could challenge the underlying assumptions of militarism. He then went on to see how these initiatives could be linked to actual social forces. In the process, he examined the structures and restraints of different kinds of polities.[26]

Falk distinguished between three systems of politics in the contemporary global situation. The state and its supporting infrastructure, such as corporations, banks and media, constituted the first system. The politics of this system was 'supportive of the underlying logic of militarization'. The second system, comprising the United Nations and regional international institutions, was 'mainly a dependency of the first system' and, therefore, 'unable to implement demilitarization initiatives'. The third system, 'represented by people acting individually and collectively through voluntary institutions' and associations, including churches and labour unions, could 'promote normative initiatives' relevant to demilitarization at this stage. Such normative initiatives undertaken in the third system could help in mobilizing 'effective opposition to militarization in all three systems by altering the normative climate, thereby producing a new creative space for political innovation'.[27]

Falk's understanding of the relationship between militarism, demilitarization and what he called 'genuine security' can be summarized as follows. He categorized the entire process of demilitarization into four distinct categories. In the first category, militarism necessitated the strategic arms race, while demilitarization required stabilization, détente and defensive postures and the corresponding distinct from militarism and demilitarization demanded disarmament, peacekeeping and resistance training.

Similarly, in the second category, hegemonic politics supported militarism; respect for sovereign rights, including self-determination, enhanced demilitarization, and the genuine security encouraged a world community of diverse peoples. In the third category, a peripheral war system encouraged militarism, procedures for peaceful settlement helped demilitarization and regional communities of diverse peoples ensured genuine security. In the fourth and last category in the demilitarization process, internal militarism sustained militarism, while human rights, civilian rule and a reduced defence sector helped in demilitarization; in this category, humane governance would secure genuine security.[28]

By the middle of the 1990s, Falk's growing concern with globalization had led him to the use of a fairly different vocabulary in theorizing on world order. The key terms now were geo-governance and humane governance. He argued that with the gradual erosion of the state system, an integrated economic, cultural and political world was fast emerging. Consequently, geo-politics was being replaced by geo-governance. Falk was mainly interested in exploring the extent to which such geo-governance could be made more humane, more people oriented and more focused on human rights, so that it led to democratic decentralization. This preferred form of geo-governance was to be called humane governance.[29] Falk now looked at the value of peace in the larger perspective of humane governance. Security would thus mean human security. A systematic critique of political violence and war had to be built around this key concept.

III

Richard Falk's ideas on the value of economic well-being could be summed up more simply. These ideas were based on an assumption and a prescription.

The assumption was that even though economic demands and aspirations were believed to be 'elastic' and could therefore be manipulated to become virtually infinite, it was nonetheless possible to define the range of real economic needs of a people. At one end of the spectrum were what Falk called minimum economic needs, which had to be satisfied for a society to be just and humane. At the other end were the maximum justifiable needs beyond which ownership and consumption became criminally wasteful. The narrower the range of minimum-maximum needs, the more harmonious was the society. The ultimate goal, therefore, should be to achieve, in practice, such a narrowed range in ownership and consumption patterns. This was crucial for ending both poverty and exploitation of the poor by the rich.[30]

The prescription was that a country's national wealth should be so distributed as to provide all citizens with basic minimum needs such as food, housing, health care, education, and employment and cultural opportunities. Falk, however, does not share with us any details of how such a distribution was to be actually achieved. Was the economy to be essentially a free market, while the state was highly welfarist, so that inequities of income were compensated for? Or was the economy to be so planned and regulated that desirable income distribution was achieved automatically? One thing is abundantly clear from Falk's discussion: He rejects the simplistic notion of economic development in which an abstract notion of per capita income is projected as the key index.

As a Western liberal theorist, Falk is much more forthcoming on the question of social and political justice. The main concern here is to 'assure conditions for the realization of individual and group dignity within national societies'.[31] At one level, Falk seems to equate social and political justice with what are called first generation human rights: the rights of self-expression and meaningful political participation, equality of treatment regardless of race, sex, age, religion or ethnic differences, and elimination of all forms of torture and cruelty. On the transnational plane, human rights are brought to bear upon questions of colonialism, racialism and genocide, as also on issues related to mobility and migration.[32] At another place, Falk identified his conception of human rights in terms of basic human needs, basic decencies, participatory rights, security rights and humane governance.[33]

Falk made a comparative assessment of the protection of human rights in capitalist, socialist and Third World countries. In a socialist country, human rights practice was caught in a contradiction between the theory of a classless and stateless society on the one hand, and a bureaucratic, centralized dictatorship in the form of a super-state on the other. Yet, in many Third World countries, the socialist model for the realization of human rights values was still seen as appropriate. This was so because in Third World countries, too, capitalism had led to some form of repressive rule.[34]

Falk argued that we were victims of an oppressive world system and that was a threatening factor for each of us. As he argued, the special circumstances of those societies that were in a sense materially privileged had resulted in 'normative regression' and 'invisible oppression' in its many environmental and cultural forms.[35] Falk enumerated three types of what he called invisible oppression even in the so-called free societies. Just as slavery had been accepted as inevitable for centuries, even now, a few persons had delegated to themselves the right to decide when and under what conditions nuclear war would be waged. Slow poisoning of land and water by the dumping of low level radioactive wastes and other hazardous toxic chemicals continued in a similar fashion. In other words, he argued that the extent to which our awareness of the present predicament penetrated our social consciousness would help in mobilizing the movement for a just world. A powerful social force (although passive) that was a catalyst for social change might already be present in the existing world society. It needed to be activated more vigorously. Here, Falk cited the example of the transnational anti-nuclear movement, present in all democratic, industrialized societies, as well as the growing movement for nuclear disarmament in Western Europe.

Falk also highlighted the issue of political justice. He emphasized the need to learn some lessons from the Vietnam War. The desire to maintain a pro-West, anti-communist government in control of South Vietnam had been the policy of five American presidents since 1950. The containment of the world communist movement, mainland China and revolutionary nationalism were the three principal objectives of the American policy in Vietnam, which also ensured the continued division of Vietnam into two sovereign states. In the concluding phases of the American military involvement in the region, Falk argued that the debate over the consequences of the Vietnam conflict had three different interpretations. The first position, associated with liberal internationalism and endorsed by most professional military men and the American right wing, saw the war as a qualified success. The second principal position, associated with the espousal of Machiavellian notions of state interest, regarded it as a failure of a sense of geopolitical proportion. The third main position, advocated by President Nixon and foreign policy advisors such as Henry Kissinger, William Rogers and Melvin Laird, regarded the Vietnam War as a qualified failure of tactics. All these three positions showed the continuation of two American objectives in Asia – to prevent Chinese expansion and to prevent any anti-communist regime from being toppled by internal revolutionary forces. He, however, favoured the excluded fourth position, which repudiated the United States' objectives in Vietnam on moral and political grounds.[36]

Asia had undergone a two-phase revolution. The first phase was concerned with the struggle against colonialism and thereby reacquiring national control over the government apparatus. But in most Asian countries, the native groups allied with the colonial system (such as Britain) had held on to political power, stifling social progress and economic reform. Therefore, the second post-independence phase of the revolutionary struggle involved wresting political control from the traditional ruling classes and instituting a mass based programme of land reform, education, public hygiene, social equality and radical consciousness. The fourth position accepted this analysis of political conflict in Asia and sought to adjust American policy accordingly.[37]

Falk also dealt with the counterinsurgency warfare conducted in Vietnam between 1962 and 1973, in which the methods and tactics used by the United States were in contravention of both the customary law as well as the treaty rules governing the conduct of international warfare and, therefore, a crime under international law. Falk mounted an argument against counterinsurgency policies and tactics on the basis of moral, legal and political considerations, and linked it to the more general case for global reform. The refusal to abide by the dynamics of national self-determination was the most fundamental wrong of American intervention in Indo China. These dynamics would have led to political independence for the three Indo Chinese countries and a drastic kind of social transformation, somewhat similar with the outcome in China. The economies of the resulting societies would have been built around egalitarian, if austere, principles.[38]

Falk argued that discrimination, proportionality, necessity and humanity were the methods and tactics through which the general mandates of the law of war were not directly violated. The most characteristic method of large-scale counterinsurgent warfare in Vietnam was massive reliance on air power.[39] The United States used anti-personnel weaponry, initiated kill ratios and body counts and the Phoenix Programme, destroyed crops and poisoned wells, and committed atrocities and torture in Vietnam. Falk discussed the role of international law in such counterinsurgency warfare.

Falk also dealt with the Nuremberg judgement in relation to the atrocities committed during the Vietnam war. A Nuremberg perspective was given by Falk on the Pentagon Papers trial. He focused primarily on the issue of state crime in a time of war. The Nuremberg judgement, rendered after World War II, was based on the view that individuals, whatever their station in society, must heed the claim of universal norms, as embodied in the Nuremberg Principles, even in defiance of the legal mandates of their own governments.[40] In 1971, the United States government released, against the domestic opponents of the Vietnam war, major portions of the so-called Pentagon Papers by Daniel Ellsberg and Anthony Russo. The Pentagon Papers showed that the fundamental obligations embodied in international law, and which were therefore binding on national governments, were not being followed by the United States government. International law had been violated by the United States in at least three respects: 'by failing to respect international agreements seeking to secure international peace; by failing to seek peaceful settlement of international disputes; and by intervening in the internal affairs of a foreign state'.[41] The promises made by the victors of World War II at Nuremberg and Tokyo were thus largely unfulfilled. In formal bodies such as the United Nations, these promises were repeated by the world community as a whole, but they are yet to be implemented, even if only through the process of self-restraint.[42]

Falk provided a Nuremberg perspective on the trial of Karl Armstrong as well. The Armstrong case raised the question of how we really felt about the Nuremberg precedent as operative law when its teachings were turned inward. These questions went to the essence of global reform, for what was at stake was whether the non-violent processes of the law would at least give a hearing to individuals engaged in conscientious acts of resistance designed to curb the war waging propensities of a sovereign state. Armstrong's violent act had anarchic potential and that violence always posed threats to bystanders. Falk argued that Armstrong's act of exploding bombs should not be granted complete legal exoneration, although the Nuremburg argument was persuasive enough for leniency in the case.[43] Therefore, he concluded that at this stage in world history, nothing could be more revolutionary than a militant non-violent movement for drastic global reform in which the adherents exhibited discipline, courage and tactical ingenuity.[44]

It became apparent from both these trials that the United States' involvement in Indo China and Vietnam was in violation of the Nuremberg Principles. At Nuremberg, crimes against peace, war crimes and crimes against humanity were the three categories of offences that were regarded as punishable crimes under international law. 'Aggressive war' was regarded at Nuremberg both as illegal in itself and as entailing individual criminal responsibility for its principal planners.[45] The United States violated the Nuremberg Principles both with regard to the use of its military power against a foreign society and with regard to the attitudes toward individual responsibility. Though the United States had committed war crimes, crimes against peace and crimes against humanity, no effort was being made to hold its policy makers responsible for the moral consequences in Vietnam. Moreover, because of the non-availability of a proper adjudicating tribunal, the perpetrators could not be prosecuted according to the Nuremberg Principles. Falk, therefore, suggested that the promises of Nuremberg could not be kept by governments, but only by popular forces, who were committed to building a new world order in which tenderness toward nature and fellow men was the basis of organization and action.[46]

Falk thus wanted us to keep the Nuremberg tradition alive and draw lessons from it. After World War II, the decision to prosecute German and Japanese leaders as war criminals, although flawed as a legal proceeding, created a precedent that leaders of governments and their subordinate officials were responsible for their acts and could be brought to account before an international tribunal. It also affirmed the reality of crimes against humanity and crimes against peace, as well as the more familiar crimes arising from violations of the laws of war. The Nuremberg judgement also generalized the occasion of prosecution so as to make it an ingredient of international order.[47] The Nuremberg Principles (originally endorsed by unanimous vote at the United Nations General Assembly and later on by the International Law Commission) provided authoritative legal criteria to assess official behaviour and thus became part of international law. But it was apparent that no willingness was shown to carry forward the Nuremberg Principles as a practical check on sovereign discretion.

Falk pointed out that though the Russell Tribunal was established later in 1967, serious crimes against humanity continued to be perpetuated in Latin America, Asia and Africa against the people of these countries. The Algiers Declaration further supplemented the Universal Declaration of Human Rights (1948) of the United Nations. But none of these resulted in the desired objective. It was in July 1976 at Algiers that the International League for the Rights and Liberation of Peoples gave the Algiers Declaration institutional backing. The most ambitious project of the League was to launch an International People's Tribunal that would investigate, assess and report on allegations of violations of people's rights.[48] An International People's Tribunal, even though it offered only one dimension, kept the Nuremberg idea alive, and it compensated to some extent for the failure of governments and international institutions to uphold the rights of people. Its success depended upon the support it could generate as a means of carrying on the anti-imperial struggle in a variety of contexts.[49]

Falk thus highlighted how the United States involvement in Indo China and Vietnam constituted 'crimes against humanity'; yet, there was no trial conducted as per the Nuremberg Principles, which required that individuals, whatever their station in society, must heed the claim of universal norms even in defiance of the legal mandates of their own government.[50] There were serious violations of a similar nature in other parts of Asia, Africa and Latin America. In all such cases, the citizens were either ignorant or remained passive.

Falk emphasized the need to awaken people to the realities of invisible oppression. Instead of hoping for state sponsored trials, popular forces had to organize themselves against war crimes.[51] He foresaw the emergence of some groups that would take up the task of fighting such oppression. Since then, numerous active groups have actually built up influential anti-nuclear movements. The green movements in various countries[52] have taken up the cause of spreading awareness about the need for environment protection.

In his later writings, Falk subsumed all these issues under the nomenclature of humane governance. An integral part of humane governance was sensitivity to ecological issues. Falk argued that the fight against global environmental pollution and the conservation of the earth's depleting resources were inalienable parts of his world order value system.

A major crisis the world faced today was ecological disequilibrium. Herbicides, deforestation, bombardment and artillery fire, and weather modification were the major forms of warfare waged directly against the environment. Falk outlined several problem areas in maintaining the ecological balance. He drew a typology of ecological disasters as follows:

- Type A: Ecological disasters of a sudden, dramatic character, such as the breakup of a large oil tanker on the seas or a collision between a nuclear submarine and a merchant vessel;
- Type B: Gradual deterioration of environmental quality by cumulative processes (for example, carbon dioxide build-up in the atmosphere or in the oceans);
- Type C: Various risks and injuries associated with the handling, storage, disposal and generation of ultra-hazardous materials (for example, nuclear explosions, ocean dumping of nerve gas, storage valves for radioactive wastes);

- Type D: Infringement on the heritage of mankind as a consequence of deliberate policy or negligence with respect to the preservation of cultural or natural wonders (for example, Abu Simbal, Murchison Falls) or with regard to the conservation of endangered animal species (for example, the blue whale);
- Type E: Failure to conserve scarce resource stocks for the benefit of future generations or to satisfy the development requirements of the poorer sectors of the world;
- Type F: Use of scarce resources for unproductive, wasteful and destructive purposes (for example, arms spending, consumer advertising);
- Type G: The control of environmental warfare and the prohibition of ecocide (for example, herbicides, systematic ploughing); and
- Type H: The control of weather modification capabilities and policy in times of peace and war.[53]

In many ways, these disasters were interrelated. For example, the threat to the survival of the planet originated from the 'war system' and population pressure, which equally caused environmental overload. Falk's whole purpose was to encourage awareness and induce action so as to address the challenges posed by the endangered planet.[54] He emphasized the need for adequate and critical planning. That would involve accumulation of data and time bound action plans to be undertaken by state and non-state actors. He proposed the idea of ecopolitics, whose essence would be the 'political embodiment of man-in-nature'.[55] Politics of pluralism, autonomy and diversity were needed to build a world order suitable for the ecological age.[56]

IV

In his approach to reform of the world order, Falk emphasized two orienting imperatives – the methodological and the normative approaches. He focused on the system transforming approaches to world order and acknowledged that a minimum realization of normative goals on a planetary scale required profound changes in political culture and structure. He stressed on the task of establishing humane patterns of governance at all levels of social interaction, from the self to the world.[57] In other words, he argued that world order studies should be given a transdisciplinary orientation.

Falk pointed out that world order studies not only sought to depict and gave an explanatory analysis of current international behaviour, but also sought to establish a framework of thought and action for shaping the future in a more just and humane direction. He considered how to think and what to do about the future of world order. He offered constructive ideas and directions for global reform. He set forth elements of non-utopian vision that drew their inspiration from several sources: 'the non-territorial central guidance of medieval Europe; the checks and balances of constitutional order; ideas about man and nature long prevalent in the Orient; notions of human solidarity manifest in the main cultural traditions of the past; concepts of peace and justice in the political and moral traditions of non-violence; humanism and socialism; and a distrust of government found in such diverse sources as philosophical anarchism and populist politics'.[58]

Richard Falk attempted to evolve a comprehensive framework for studying global reform. His objective was twofold. In the first instance, it was educational – to encourage disciplined inquiry into the future of international relations from an avowed and explicitly normative perspective. He argued against a value neutral approach to this subject matter as ethically misleading, politically irresponsible and historically irrelevant. At the same time, he tried to understand and present the state system as it operated at that time. He believed that drastic types of global reform were both possible and necessary, but that their success depended upon our ability first to comprehend and then to institute a credible politics of transformation.[59]

Falk's second objective was to move the domains of feeling and action closer to the domain of thought. There was a need for a new conception of knowledge that encompassed the processes of man's material, social and spiritual development. We needed a broadly based transnational movement for global reform that sought both to influence public opinion and to encourage responsiveness from centres of power and wealth.[60] The central question that Falk posed in this work was: 'Can we devise human means to fashion a new system of world order from which a decent form of global society can evolve? Put differently, in this period, when the state system is eroding and rapidly being superseded, can we facilitate the transition to a system of world order that is an improvement upon what now exists?'[61]

Falk sought to develop appropriate ways of thinking seriously (as opposed to sentimentally or cynically) about the political prospects of global society, and put forward a set of proposals for accomplishing global reform within a period of several decades. He outlined a world order system responsible for and stemming from global humanism. He believed that its pursuit was the highest priority for people everywhere, and that the shape of global reform was too important to leave in the hands of statesmen, generals or businessmen.

Falk tried to put forward a vision of a new, improved system of world order to be achieved by the end of the nineteenth century. How to think, what to hope and what to do were the three sorts of issues emphasized in moving towards the preferred world. He attempted to depict a futuristic dimension of world order studies. Falk outlined his concept of a preferred system of world order in consonance with WOMP values, which was sought to be brought about by 2000 or shortly thereafter, without relying on violence or intimidation. In setting forth a new world order, he emphasized structural reforms and outlined its three principal features – systematic scope, normativity and orientation towards the future. He emphasized world order reform and reformers and outlined a new system of world order.[62]

Falk discussed eight different images of the preferred world – the existing system; the five power variant of the existing world order system; the regionalist modification of the existing world order system; transnational corporate modifications of the existing world order system; functionalist order in the world order system; world government modifications of the existing world order system; world empire or world state modifications of the present world order system; and preferred world alternatives to the existing world order system.[63] He also provided some illustrations, some consciousness raising tactics and programmes, mobilization contexts and transformation contexts while discussing the challenges to transition toward the preferred world. All this would need a spontaneous mass movement for world order reform that would be committed to promote the four world order values of peace, economic well-being, environmental quality, and social and political justice.[64] He raised a central question of world order inquiry: "Who will hold power and exercise authority?" At the same time, he challenged us to inquire to what extent the world order values could be achieved by incremental reforms of the present system.[65]

The need, therefore, Falk felt, was for increased central guidance in world affairs, including some increase in coercive authority. Central guidance implied a unified capacity for policy formation, coordination and implementation, especially with issues closely related to WOMP values. The shape of the central guidance system was determined by the posited need to diminish the role of the sovereign state in world affairs and the emergence of a substantial number of non-governmental actors to assure the protection of world community priorities. Simultaneously, new symbols of popular global identity and allegiance would gain precedence over nationalistic ones for a sizeable portion of mankind.[66]

Falk divided the entire period of world order activities into three phases: comprehensive humanist reform, transnational collaboration, social movements and the struggle for peace and democracy.[67] He believed that the destiny of life on earth could be shared across boundaries of race, class, nation and gender. He tried to identify a framework appropriate for a period of structural transition.[68]

Falk pointed out that the world order movement was guided by a kind of affirmative thought and action – that is, to both to understand and change the existing world. He attempted to do two main things: set forth a design perspective that should influence the presentation and understanding of our preference model for the 1990s; and highlight the main world order building blocks that existed within the present world order system. Falk envisaged an open system of world order. The basic design for a new world order system was founded upon a synthesis of ordering structures that had been or were in being at that time, as well as reliance upon institutional and procedural innovation. He discussed the elements of structure in past, present and future world order systems. He pointed out the objectives and presented a structural outline of the present system of world order. Falk also gave illustrations of past systems of world order – the 1890, 1920 and 1950 world order systems. Lastly, he outlined the principal types of world order that seemed relevant to the future. In this regard, he talked about nine different types of images in the world order systems. These were the images of an enhanced state system, world government, a regionalist nexus of power/authority, a functionalist nexus of power/authority, a world empire nexus of power/authority, a power/authority nexus based on a concert of principal actors, a condominium nexus of power/authority, a small state nexus of power/authority, and an anarchist power/authority nexus. Falk concluded that these images were both weak countertendencies in the current world order system and building blocks for the future. Their relevance to the present was to help structure a feasible vision of a world order solution and to provide an intellectual basis for the preference model.[69]

Falk depicted the world order building blocks and considered the basic orientations towards structural reform in the political realm. He set forth a specific preference model that was designed to maximize the prospects of feasibility and the realization of values. He argued that the preference model of WOMP USA was the most viable one for a global movement committed to a programme of drastic reform by the end of the country, without recourse to violence and without the sort of systemic shock that might be administered by global warfare, pandemic, widespread famine, or major ecological collapse. He set forth the main elements of structural reorganization that seemed to be desirable to realize the four WOMP values. However, along with structure, changes in attitude and behavioural tendencies were likely to be important features of a transformed world. Falk outlined the structural attributes of the preferred model of world order. This presentation of the preference model would be focused upon the general purpose and functional actors at the global level – that is, the universal structural elements in the central guidance system.[70]

At the same time, Falk attempted to describe the transition process, provide some thoughts on method, and offer some ideas on transition tactics and strategy. The concept of transition was defined as planned and value directed change that would deliberately facilitate the shift from one system of world order to another. The transition problem would, therefore, involve the specific effort to describe the process by which the preferred world might be brought about beneficially by the end of the 1990s, or more realistically, by a sequence of changes stretched out over a time span that could not be associated with definite, chronological intervals. Implicit in WOMP's idea of transition was the need for inter-systemic transformation, making the transition process eventuate in a new system of world order; the transition tactics and strategy involved accelerating the process and devising ways to assure its completion in accordance with our specified value preferences.[71]

On these bases, Falk essentially outlined a new kind of transnational functionalist world order. The idea of world order should include within it ecological, demographic and technological developments. It should also protect and promote dignity, safety and security for individuals and groups. Therefore, the primary task was to keep the existing system under some degree of reasonable control during the period of transition to a more centralized system.

V

Falk had visualized in the early 1970s that his preferred world order would be realized by the 1990s. His optimism was based on historical experience, which showed that world order underwent structural changes roughly every thirty years. He identified 1890, 1920 and 1950 as the years of such significant restructuring in recent history.

By the end of the 1980s, however, it was clear that WOMP had managed to achieve very little concrete success. Falk had considered three elements necessary for structural reform. These were structural change, change in attitude and change in behavioural tendencies.[72] None of these elements appeared notably active. Also missing was the 'institutional and procedural innovation' that was expected to synthesize with the existing structures.[73]

Falk's assumption was that the states themselves would be a key actor in the transition to a preferred world. This was a seriously flawed assumption insofar as a large number of the countries in Asia, Africa and Latin America were concerned, for they had no effective state authority or the regimes were altogether too conservative and reactionary. They would have no interest in promoting the kind of values that were dear to WOMP. What is worse, these regimes were non-democratic and repressive. They would not allow forces of change to emerge or become active. Even in the case of those countries where the regimes were liberal, democratic and progressive, the effectiveness of the state in playing a positive role was seriously undermined when globalization, which had already been under way, gathered unprecedented momentum. With neo-liberalism becoming the dominant ideology after the demise of the Soviet bloc, positive liberalism and the concept of a welfare state took a back seat. It was perhaps recognition of these facts that led Falk to minimize the role of the state in his later writings. He expressed his sense of disappointment when he wrote:

> I have devoted most of my professional time over the past several years to an exercise of this kind, known as the World Order Models Project. It is itself a non-trivial social fact that such an undertaking is conceived and carried forward at this historical moment. The impact of such consciousness raising is disappointing on the level of action.[74]

Did this mean that WOMP was a complete failure? Falk himself did not think so. In an email communication to this author, he wrote:

> it depends upon how success is measured. As a project to change the world, it failed. As a project to influence the climate of opinion and elites, it is hard to say: There were indications of influence in the early period of Gorbachev leadership in the Soviet Union, and possibly in the approaches taken by some Latin American countries; also, the challenge in academic circles to realism was definitely helped by WOMP and its plea for a normative approach to the study and practice of international relations. It is also true that for the scholars involved, the project was a success in shaping their own evolving outlook and research agenda. It continued for more than 30 years, despite the logistical problems of organizing global meetings on low budgets and raising the funds needed.[75]

Nor did Falk believe that WOMP had no future. He wrote:

> There is a current attempt to bring WOMP back to life under the leadership of John Fousek at Rutgers University. The objective circumstances of near nuclear war in South Asia and the global war on terror, as well as persisting poverty and global warming, suggest the importance of alternative thinking at this time. Maybe WOMP is not the right label. Probably, a new generation should rise to the challenge. We need visions of a humane future and transition strategies to bridge the gap from here to there.[76]

It was clear then that Falk had given up none of his idealism or humanism. It is only that by the 1990s, the world had gone through unexpected dramatic changes. Falk began to focus on new issues that demanded attention. Global citizenship and what he called geo-governance were two such issues. He switched over to theorizing about what he called humane governance. He began to argue that there should be 'globalization from below' rather than 'globalization from above'.[77]

VI

The disintegration of the Soviet Union and the consequent end of the Cold War gradually resulted in the decline of both WOMP and the normative values associated with it. In the post-Soviet world, normative values were increasingly questioned and they began to be interpreted in accordance with the new issues and problems of the whole world. It was in this context that Falk emphasized the new issues in WOMP such as sovereignty, globalization and global citizenship, geo-governance and humane governance.

Falk tried to redefine political communities taking into account the contending sovereignties all over the world.[78] He emphasized the continuing role of states in the modern world and the different strategies through which some political actors, including states, had managed to participate in other forms of political community.[79] He sketched a pattern of 'evasions', which referred to a locus of action distinct from the state, but not necessarily in opposition to it. The proper assessment of a particular evasion depended on a convincing interpretation of its project for the future and its actual role in relation to the state as well as some judgement of its relation to world order values.[80]

Falk discussed three principal patterns of evasions – evasions across boundaries (transnational), evasions within boundaries (internal) and evasions beyond boundaries (supranational) – that, while being ambiguous in character, were producing new allegiances and political identities and establishing nascent political communities of local, transnational, regional and global scope.[81] He concluded that an emergent global civilization (of indefinite normative contour) did not imply that the territorial state or the state system was becoming extinct; rather, it appeared to be challenging the earlier statist monopoly over the symbols and practices of sovereignty that had existed for the past several hundred years.[82]

It was through a global citizenship that Falk wanted to evolve a more humane, benevolent and just world order.[83] Citizenship, in general, expressed membership and the quality of participation in a political community. People all over the world had different experiences of citizenship. Citizenship could be understood both formally as a status and, more adequately, existentially as a shifting set of attitudes, relationships and expectations (with regard to privileged and underprivileged classes) with no necessary territorial delimitation.[84] Falk argued that this complexity was further compounded by the two very different sorts of globalization that were impinging on the life experiences of individuals and groups – one he called globalization from above, against which he pitted and supported the other, globalization from below, as the basis of humane governance.

After discussing the two different types of globalization, Falk discussed the various forms and varieties of global citizenship. He concluded that 'the gropings of global civil society encourage a human rights and democracy orientation towards global citizenship – the world as delightfully heterogeneous, yet inclusive of all creation in an overarching frame of community sentiment, premised on the biological and normative capacity of the human species to organize its collective life on foundations of non-violence, equity and sustainability. This reality imaginatively already exists – and hence, politically, a one world community is an emergent possibility.'[85]

Richard Falk pointed out that the contemporary political discourse of WOMP had gradually moved from geo-politics to geo-governance. He tried to assess the achievements of WOMP over the past quarter century and to explore the likely contours of the global order, which seemed to be emerging. He distinguished WOMP from the more popular metaphor, 'new world order', and also debated and discussed the postmodern features of WOMP. He pointed out that cognitive pessimism, the metaphors of chaos and a sensitivity to concealed social forces were the three clusters of ideas that had become methodologically associated with the WOMP outlook.[86] He himself raised the question of whether WOMP was a Western undertaking.[87]

Over the years, Falk pointed out, WOMP had emphasized three interactive types of learning experiences: the internal dynamic of criticism and response; the external dynamic of criticism and response; and the hermeneutical dynamic associated with assessing prospects for historical interaction (the interplay of values, ideas and acts within domains of political engagement).[88]

Falk argued that in the 1990s, the WOMP agenda should also include the issues of human rights, democracy and views from civil society. There was a need to evolve a more acceptable and democratized global framework and institutional arrangements to address security, environment and development. Moreover, a fresh interpretation should be given to the world order values in light of the changing contexts and perceptions; normative questions should be raised to serve human interest.[89]

In the mid-1990s, Falk brought into use new terms such as geo-governance and humane governance in theorizing and analyzing WOMP. He also became part of a programme called the Global Civilization: Challenges for Democracy, Sovereignty and Security Project (GCP) initiated by WOMP. Throughout its work, the GCP and its global consortium of institutional affiliates maintained the need for alternative policies that would promote the world order values of peace, economic well-being, social and political justice, ecological balance and positive human identity.[90]

Falk tried to crystallize the ideas on some of the enduring concerns of WOMP and the GCP. He argued in particular that with the gradual erosion of the state system, geo-politics was being replaced by geo-governance. He pointed out that a more integrated economic, cultural and political world was emerging, a set of circumstances identified here as geo-governance.[91] The quest here was for a transition to humane governance, that is, a preferred form of geo-governance. Falk was mainly interested in exploring the extent to which such geo-governance could be made more humane, more people oriented and more focused on human rights so that it led to democratic decentralization.

The achievement of comprehensive rights for all peoples on earth was emphasized by humane governance. Humane governance 'emphasizes people centred criteria of success, as measured by decline in poverty, violence and pollution and by increasing adherence to human rights and constitutional practices, as well as by axiological shifts away from materialist/consumerist and patriarchal conceptions of human fulfillment'.[92] Falk made an appeal to all sane and intelligent persons to enlist their energies and resources in fulfilling this mission of achieving humane governance.

Falk pointed out that the old geo-politics of power politics, especially in the North-South settings was still evident, even though the Cold War was over, in relation to the structures and practices of bipolarity. However, the end of the Cold War, the disintegration of the former USSR and the subsequent formation of the Commonwealth of Independent States (CIS) had produced some important benefits in relation to the quality of world order. For example, the menace of strategic nuclear war had certainly receded on the global level, but there were still many unresolved tensions within civil society. Globalization from above was taking the form of cultural homogenization, franchise capitalism and centrally guided media. These should be contrasted with globalization from below, which embodied the spirit and substance of humane governance, as it was more oriented towards nature and its human inhabitants.[93]

Falk also discussed the relationship between realism, reality and normative opportunity. He argued that the growing relevance of realist theory had led to a politics of bounded conviction, rooted in the quest for humane governance. The 'call here is for "global constitutionalism" within a political atmosphere that could follow upon a successful movement to strengthen transnational democracy'.[94]

The two major features of the new world order at the sub-strategic level were warfare and anarchy. Falk elaborated on the triple indictment of humane governance. He described the first indictment using the metaphor, 'global apartheid', and the second indictment as 'avoidable harm'. The first indictment implied structure, the second indictment was related to policy failure in matters of normative concern. This indictment insisted that the policies being pursued by those in authority, whether as officials or agents of civil initiatives, were causing harm to humanity.[95] Falk described the third indictment as 'drifting toward eco-imperialism'. The political consequences of the two interactive processes – the worsening of environmental conditions and the persistence of dominant growth oriented economic priorities were included in the third indictment.[96] Humane governance presupposed overcoming the triple indictment.

In order to be realistic, humane governance would have to address the economic and environmental policy agenda by adopting appropriate procedures and establishing institutions of a magnitude capable of overcoming global apartheid and thereby avoiding human suffering, and arresting environmental decay. Along with human governance, Falk also felt the need for a rethinking of sovereignty, democracy and development.[97] He sought to achieve humane governance on a state by state basis, including the distribution of authority between different levels of social organization.[98] He raised the question of whose democracy and democracy for whom.[99] Humane governance within the structure of the states system of world order could thus be assessed by degrees of realization of individual and group rights across the spectrum of economic social, cultural, civil and political concerns.[100]

Falk also discussed the state of democracy after the Cold War. Increasing support had been generated for democratization in various geographical areas and in many distinct cultural and political circumstances in the post-Cold War period. The emergent forms of capital driven geo-governance deformed democratization and problematized the relationship between democracy and humane governance.[101] He concluded that democracy was both a means to humane governance as well as a feature of its embodiment. Humane governance implied movement toward a reasonably fair world economy and would improve the life prospects of future generations.[102]

Notes

1. Richard Falk, *A Global* Approach *to National Policy* (Cambridge: Harvard University Press, 1975), 2.
2. Ibid.
3. Granville Clark and Louis B. Sohn, *World Peace through World Law* (Cambridge: Harvard University Press, 1956).
4. Richard Falk, *A Study of Future Worlds* (New Delhi: Orient Longman, 1975), 13.
5. Ibid.
6. Richard Falk and Saul H. Mendlovitz, 'Toward a Warless World: One Legal Formula to Achieve Transition', in *The Strategy of World Order,* Vol. I, Richard Falk and Saul H. Mendlovitz, eds (New York: World Law Fund, 1968), 12–6.
7. Richard Falk, 'Historical Tendencies, Modernizing and Revolutionary Nations and the International Legal Order', in *The Strategy of World Order,* Vol. I, op. cit., 172.
8. Richard Falk, *A Study of Future Worlds*, 11.
9. Richard Falk, 'The Interplay of Westphalia and Charter Conceptions of International Legal Order', in *International Law: A Contemporary Perspective: Studies on a Just World Order,* Vol. 2, Richard Falk, Friedrich Kratochwil and Saul H. Mendlovitz, eds (Boulder: Westview Press, 1982), 116–35.
10. Richard Falk, 'A New Paradigm for International Legal Studies: Prospects and Proposals', in *International Law: A Contemporary Perspective: Studies on a Just World Order,* Vol. 2, 651.
11. Ibid., 637 and 673–86.

12. Richard Falk, 'The Interplay of Westphalia and Charter Conceptions of International Legal Order', in *International Law: A Contemporary Perspective*, 112.
13. Richard Falk, 'A New Paradigm for International Legal Studies: Prospects and Proposals', in *International Law: A Contemporary Perspective*, 653–54.
14. Ibid., 637.
15. Ibid., 637 and 673–86.
16. Ibid., 637.
17. Ibid., 636–37 and 651–52.
18. Ibid., 637.
19. Richard Falk, *A Global Approach to National Policy*, 169–75.
20. Ibid., 194.
21. Richard Falk, *The Promise of World Order: Essays in Normative International Relations* (Great Britain: Wheatsheaf Books, 1987), 234.
22. Richard Falk, 'Toward a Legal Regime for Nuclear Weapons', in *International Law: A Contemporary Perspective*, 463–66.
23. Richard Falk, *The Promise of World Order: Essays in Normative International Relations*, 234.
24. Ibid.
25. Richard Falk, 'Normative Initiatives and Demilitarization: A Third System Approach', in *Toward a Just World Order: Studies on a Just World Order*, Vol. I, Richard Falk, Samuel S. Kim and Saul H. Mendlovitz, eds (Boulder: Westview Press 1982), 626; Also see section, 'Introduction – Orientations to Transition', ibid., 562–63. A useful reference is there also in Richard Falk, 'Unravelling the Future of World Order', in *The War System: An Interdisciplinary Approach*, Richard Falk and Samuel S. Kim, eds (Boulder: Westview Press, 1980), 636–7.
26. Ibid., 626–30. Also see in the same book, the section, 'Introduction – Orientations to Transition', 563.
27. Richard Falk, 'Normative Initiatives and Demilitarization: A Third System Approach', op. cit., 626–30.
28. Richard Falk, *The Promise of World Order: Essays in Normative International Relations*, 234.
29. Richard Falk, *On Humane Governance: Toward a New Global Politics* (London: Polity Press, 1995), 9–46. See especially the Preface, ix.
30. Richard Falk, *A Study of Future Worlds* (New Delhi: Orient Longman, 1975), 17–22.
31. Ibid., 23.
32. Ibid., 23–26.

33. Richard Falk, 'Comparative Protection of Human Rights in Capitalist and Socialist Third World Countries', in *Toward a Just World Order,* Richard Falk, Samuel S. Kim and Saul H. Mendlovitz, eds, 424–25.
34. Ibid., 405–30.
35. Richard Falk, 'On Invisible Oppression and World Order', in *Toward a Just World Order,* Richard Falk, Samuel S. Kim and Saul H. Mendlovitz, eds, 16 and 43–46.
36. Richard Falk, *A Global Approach to National Policy,* 57–71.
37. Ibid., 72.
38. Ibid., 7.
39. Ibid., 79–80.
40. Ibid., 7.
41. Ibid., 115.
42. Ibid., 7–8.
43. Ibid., 144.
44. Ibid., 144–45.
45. Ibid., 149–50.
46. Ibid., 154–56.
47. Richard Falk, 'Keeping Nuremberg Alive', in *International Law: A Contemporary Perspective: Studies on a Just World Order,* Vol. 2, Richard Falk, Friedrich Kratochwil and Saul H. Mendlovitz, eds (Boulder: Westview Press, 1982), 494.
48. Ibid., 494–500.
49. Ibid., 500.
50. Richard Falk, *A Global Approach to National Policy,* 133–44.
51. Ibid., 149–50 and 154–56.
52. Richard Falk, 'On Invisible Oppression and World Order', in *Toward a Just World Order,* 43–47.
53. Richard Falk, *A Study of Future Worlds,* 27–28.
54. Richard Falk, *A Global Approach to National Policy,* 16–28. Also refer Richard Falk, *This Endangered Planet: Prospects and Proposals for Human Survival* (New York: Vintage Books, 1971), 27 and 448.
55. Richard Falk, *This Endangered Planet,* 21.
56. Ibid., 35.
57. Richard Falk, 'Contending Approaches to World Order', in *Toward a Just World Order,* 171.
58. Richard Falk, *A Global Approach to National Policy,* 9–10.
59. Richard Falk, *A Study of Future Worlds,* Preface, xxix.

60. Ibid., xxix.
61. Ibid., xxx.
62. Richard Falk, 'Toward a New World Order: Modest Methods and Drastic Visions', in *On the Creation of a Just World Order – Preferred Worlds for the 1990s*, Saul H. Mendlovitz, ed. (New Delhi: Orient Longman, 1975), 211–19.
63. Ibid., 219–41.
64. Richard Falk, 'Toward a New World Order: Modest Methods and Drastic Visions', 241–57.
65. Richard Falk, 'What New System of World Order?', in *Toward a Just World Order*, Vol. I, Richard Falk, Samuel S. Kim and Saul H. Mendlovitz, eds (Boulder: Westview Press, 1992), 503.
66. Richard Falk, *A Study of Future Worlds*, 11–52.
67. Richard Falk, *The Promise of World Order: Essays in Normative International Relations*, 13–24.
68. Ibid., 27 and 252.
69. Richard Falk, *A Study of Future Worlds*, 11–52.
70. Ibid., 1–80.
71. Richard Falk, *A Study of Future Worlds* (New Delhi: Orient Longman, 1975). Falk initially emphasized the relation between time (designated either as t_1, t_2, t_3, $t_{4...}$ t_n, or as t_{1974}, t_{1984}, t_{1994}, t_{2004}, etc.) and arena (A^n = national arenas, A^r = regional arenas, A^g = global arenas, A^{tn} = transnational arenas). The transition process was to be completed by 2004, at which time S_2 exists, a new transitional process would be projected in relation to S_3. The broad pattern of development over the time interval, t_1 –t_3, was considered in relation to both political action and political arenas. In the 1970s (t_1), it would be political consciousness and the domestic imperative. In the 1980s (t_2), it would be political mobilization and the transnational imperative. In the 1990s, it would be political transformation and the global imperative. Falk also emphasized critical arenas of change and action. He projected the following sequence of critical arenas: Domestic arena (t_1) – Transnational and Regional Arenas (t_2) – Global Arena (t_3).
72. Richard Falk, *A Study of Future Worlds*, 275. At a certain time, around the mid-1970s, Richard Falk became deeply engaged in the WOMP project, so much so that he desired the realization of the four normative values of WOMP within a specified time scale (i.e., by 2004; t_{1974} – t_{1984} – t_{1994}– t_{2004}). As any programme in social and political science, where any time-frame is fixed for realizing the objective, is fraught with failures

and non-realization, so also was Falk's 1975 writing on the realization of WOMP by 2004. We do not present it here.

73. Richard Falk, *A Study of Future Worlds*, 157.
74. Richard Falk, *The Promise of World Order*, 272.
75. Richard Falk's email communication on 18 June 2002.
76. Ibid.
77. Richard Falk, 'The Making of Global Citizenship', in *Global Visions: Beyond the New World Order*, Jeremy Brecher, John Brown Childs and Jill Cutler, eds (Boston: South End Press, 1993), ix and 39–40. In the 1990s, Falk started talking about two different types of globalization – globalization from above and globalization from below. While globalization from above – also known as the New World Order – was based on the leading states and transnational business and political elites, Falk identified another, less widely recognized type of globalization – globalization from below. It consisted of 'an array of transnational social forces animated by environmental concerns, human rights, hostility to patriarchy, and a vision of human community based on the unity of diverse cultures seeking an end to poverty, oppression, humiliation and collective violence'. Globalization from below, instead of inclining toward a new world order, moved towards a 'one world community'. It was an 'expression of the spirit of democracy without frontiers, mounting a challenge to the homogenizing tendencies of globalization from above'. It was based in a 'global civil society', which sought 'to extend ideas of moral, legal and environmental accountability to those now acting on behalf of state, market and media'.
78. Richard Falk, 'Evasions of Sovereignty', in *Contending Sovereignties: Redefining Political Community*, R.B. J. Walker and Saul H. Mendlovitz, eds (Boulder: Lynne Rienner Publishers, 1990), 8–9.
79. Ibid., 8–9.
80. Ibid., 70.
81. Ibid., 9 and 70–71.
82. Ibid., 77.
83. Richard Falk, 'The Making of Global Citizenship', in *Global Visions: Beyond the New World Order*, 1–40.
84. Ibid., 39.
85. Richard Falk, 'The Making of Global Citizenship', 50.
86. Richard Falk, 'From Geopolitics to Geo-governance: WOMP and Contemporary Political Discourse', in *Alternatives* 19, No. 2 (Spring 1994), 145–48.
87. Richard Falk, *On Humane Governance: Toward a New Global Politics* (London: Polity Press, 1995), 148.

88. Ibid., 148–53.
89. Ibid., 153.
90. Ibid., vii (Preface by Saul. H. Mendlovitz, co-director, WOMP).
91. Ibid., 2.
92. Ibid., 14.
93. Ibid., 22–36.
94. Ibid., 37–44
95. Ibid., 47–55.
96. Ibid., 75.
97. Ibid., 78.
98. Ibid., 108–112.
99. Ibid., 113.
100. Ibid., 114.
101. Ibid., 116.
102. Ibid., 240.

5 WOMP and the Third World

The Ideas of Rajni Kothari and Ali A. Mazrui

In this chapter, we will examine the ideas of Rajni Kothari and Ali A. Mazrui, the two most important Third World scholars associated with WOMP. The first section introduces, in general terms, Kothari's Third World perspective and his emphasis therein on the values of autonomy and self-reliance. The second section contains a more detailed account of his discussion of peace as a prime WOMP value. The third section examines his notion of economic development as an alternative to Western theories of modernization. The fourth section takes up Kothari's discussion of issues related to socio-political justice and ecology. The fifth section discusses his perceptions on the transition to a preferred world. The sixth section analyzes his views on the successes and failures of WOMP. The next two sections deal with the views of Mazrui. The seventh section deals with his ideas on the importance of culture and traces the context of his principal contribution in the form of the World Federation of Cultures. The eighth section consists of a brief discussion of the values of peace, economic well-being and socio-political justice in Mazrui's writings. The final section relates the previously discussed ideas to the development of a world language and the role that could be played by creative and egalitarian education.

I

One of the most prominent theorists of Indian politics, Professor Rajni Kothari was associated with the World Order Models Project

(WOMP) for more than two decades. His writings on a just world order, written from what might broadly be called a Third World perspective, bring out the common concerns and aspirations of marginalized nations and peoples. He passionately argues their case for autonomy, development and self-reliance. He underlines the role of the Third World in the democratization of world order, but equally underlines the need for greater democracy within the Third World itself. Kothari also displays great faith in grass roots initiatives. These must take over as and when states fail in transforming themselves. We now reproduce here Kothari's ideas on world order, and how he became associated with WOMP:

> The idea of world order, which is today seen as a strategy of global dominance, was for long an offshoot of Western progressivism in the form of liberal internationalism, arising from the growing disappointment with the states system following the end of the 'balance of power' phase of world politics with the First World War. It got a further fillip after the experience of fascism on the one hand and communism on the other. This drew in particular upon a branch of the discipline of international law that thought of promoting 'world peace through world law' as a model of both conceptualization and research. A book of that name by Grenville Clark and Louis B. Sohn (Harvard University Press, first published in 1956) had a considerable influence in the United States and in the world federalist circles in some countries in Europe. An institute called the World Law Fund was established in the 1960s, and leading experts in international law, Saul Mendlovitz and Richard Falk among them, launched a research project called the World Order Models Project in which scholars from various parts of the world (Ali Mazrui, Johan Galtung, Yoshikazu Sakamoto and the present author among them) were invited to participate. This led to a series of publications which provided a variety of regional 'models' of world order.[1]

Kothari argued that there was a broad theory of WOMP, which was based on world unity. It was based on the premise that the world should get united since there were arms being amassed everywhere, and especially since an intense nuclear arms race had started between the two superpowers, thereby increasing manifold the possibilities of a nuclear world. The beginnings of WOMP could be located in the growing militarization and nuclearization of the whole world. Thus, from the idea of world unity, the idea of a federation was evolved. WOMP was conceived as 'a movement for reforms that must be thought of in macro terms and bring about socio-economic change, bring about a truly federal structure of the world, and try to have cultural roots in the Third World also'.[2]

Kothari was deeply concerned that the conventional view of world order was Western in both its origin and content. More specifically, it was 'an offshoot of Western progressivism in the form of liberal internationalism'.[3] He believed that WOMP theorization had been unable to free itself of this legacy. In their desire to move towards one world[4] and create a 'one world political community', theorists such as Falk and Mendlovitz had emphasized the role of world level institutions. But, unless consciously checked, such institutions were very likely to turn out to be nothing but a replication of Western liberal values and institutions. Kothari thought such 'universalism' to be seriously suspect.

World order designs such as offered by Falk and Mendlovitz entailed uniformity and centralization. However, Kothari was committed to a decentralized perspective on world order. He laid stress on the role of the 'lower tiers of the global polity'.[5] He pointed out, 'The poor and the oppressed and the 'stateless' simultaneously need a global framework that is democratic and representative and a decentralized "political" structure within and across nation-states, both together responding to the demands of civil society, ethnic identity, constitution of the state, political-cultural movements, and together providing a "world order" that emanates from the very stirrings of civil society and the peoples of the world.'[6]

Kothari was aware that the Third World states were weak and heterogeneous. Most of them were also tied in a neo-colonial relationship to the metropolitan centres in the North. As such, they did not have enough clout to make significant changes in the global distribution of power. Nonetheless, Kothari believed that diffusion of transformatory ideas, no matter how slow, would eventually bear results in 'restructuring world politics to remove conditions that perpetuate inequality and dependence and devising institutions – at various levels – that will consolidate a world based on the principles of autonomy and equality'.[7]

WOMP tried to identify the basic values that had to be the source of these transformatory ideas. Kothari expanded on these values: 'The basic objective of WOMP was the maximization of certain values, that is, the values of peace, economic well-being, social and political justice, and ecological balance in order to realize a just world. I added the value of democratic self-reliance.'[8]

Kothari's principal theme was the need for autonomy – both for individual human beings and for states and nations. Autonomy must be gained and maintained on the individual, national and global planes, but autonomy of the nation-state was particularly important for it had to act 'both as a means to checking and defeating the existing structures of dominance and exploitation in the world and as a necessary condition of the autonomy and self-reliance of the individual'.[9]

While emphasizing on the autonomy of the nation-state, Kothari was particularly concerned with the autonomy of nations in the Third World. He was concerned that the poor and formerly colonial territories should consolidate their independence and he asserted that the world of autonomous nation-states should not merely be accepted as a reality, but as a 'preferred reality'. The objective was to make the autonomy of states more real than it was during this period, in which there was a division between super, intermediate and marginal states.[10] The world system during that period was not divided simply between dominant and dependent states, there were also deep divisions within the latter. He observed:

> The basic issue in restructuring world reality is to establish the autonomy of nations in the Third World and on that basis to promote a sense of collective self-regard among them so that we can realize the values of individual freedom and dignity, justice in the distribution of worldly goods, and opportunity for participation in decision making structures at various levels.[11]

To make autonomy, self-reliance and equality more sustainable, Kothari postulated major changes in the territorial structure of the world map. The preferred world would have twenty to twenty-five states, each large in size and strong enough to be self-reliant, which would maximize the goals of power; power would be distributed equally between nations and this would also minimize the dominance of a few powers.[12]

Along with the values already mentioned, what should be developed was the larger ethic of behaviour, or what Kothari called the ethic of self-control.[13] Whereas in the poor countries, autonomy was frustrated by underdevelopment, exploitation and structural violence, he observed that in the rich countries, autonomy was frustrated by overdevelopment and waste of resources.[14] He argued, 'The economic system entailed in our preferred world must be changed from the present growth based model aimed at an aggregate production target to a need based model defined by the principles of individual autonomy, social justice and non-violence.'[15]

Kothari believed that the world had been witnessing major changes in recent history. Some of these were conducive to the creation of a preferred world order, while others posed challenges. On the positive side were the new developments in science and technology, the demystification of the laws of economic management, the shift from an oligopoly of political and military power to a greater number of effective centres of power, and the growing realization of the dangers released by the techno-economic model of industrialization and urbanization.[16] On the negative side was the proliferation of nuclear power, which would further perpetuate the asymmetry between world regions. One of the greatest threats came, however, from what Kothari called 'the long shadow of depoliticization'[17] and loss of faith in the role and capacity of the nation-state as the basic political organizational unit. There was a need for 'restoring the democratic and liberating role of the nation-state, returning to the issue of equity between and within nations, and re-emphasizing the North-South dimension of world order'.[18] At the same time, there was need also to 'gently but decisively intervene in the affairs of the states that were found to defy the norms of humane governance, decency and democracy, often in the name of upholding national autonomy and security'.[19]

The move towards a new world order 'required an intellectual understanding of available options on the one hand, and a political understanding of the issues involved in translating intellectual choices into concrete reality on the other'.[20] Kothari emphasized an alternative perspective that had two aspects. Firstly, there should be political autonomy for all states. Secondly, the WOMP values should be disseminated in the widest possible manner. The two aspects were related – one was to be conceived as a perspective for political action, the other as an intellectual effort.[21]

II

Kothari equated peace with absence of violence and contended that man's freedom and self-realization were threatened basically by violence. He observed, 'Violence is thus fast becoming a major consumer for human productivity and scientific advance in our time and has become the most dynamic element in the preservation of the name of world order. Central to the violence system is the arms race between nations.'[22] Associated with this was the increased sophistication of weapons of mass destruction and increased defence expenditure in the name of maintaining security and order.

He added, 'Vast transformations at the same time have been taking place in the relationship between human beings and their natural environment, in the stratification of societies under the impetus of a world sharply divided between the rich and the poor, and in the management of particular societies faced by internal discontent.'[23] As a result of these transformations, the scope of violence in human affairs had increased and threatened the very survival of man. The dangers inherent in the growing pressure of population on natural resources were made more serious by a techno-economic model whose increasing sophistication and speed threatened to reduce the importance of man in the civilization process. Many portents of the new technology had gradually diminished the importance of man and there had been a gradual redundancy of all men, except the highly skilled. Both modern population and modern technology would result in the obsolescence of human beings. The need was to put an end to the state of dependence that the existing structures of the world entailed, and to secure autonomy and self-reliance for national political communities.[24]

There were two broad dimensions along which violence was likely to increase: 'One of these is the degradation in the condition of man as a result of a declining subsistence function expressed in terms of a ratio between nature and man. The other is the accentuation in the degree of dominance that is the result of the deteriorating distribution function expressed in terms of a ratio of the power of the peripheries and the power of the centres.'[25] These two together threatened man's autonomy and possibly his very survival. Violence could be controlled only if men exercised a measure of self-control as an expression of their autonomy. The strategies for achieving autonomy and putting an end to dominance were resolving outstanding disputes; moving towards the structure of regional peace and integration; fighting against violation of justice and autonomy in international forums and institutions; and improving the position of these states as factors in world politics through internal consolidation, economic development and political legitimacy. Along with these, Kothari also advocated democratic decentralization, choice of an appropriate organizational technology and a decentralized state.[26]

Kothari described the present phase of world history. He equated the struggle for survival with the struggle for transformation of the present world into a just world. Peace could be achieved only when the process of transformation was accelerated. But this would be a difficult task because there were a number of paradoxes in such a process of transformation. The present world was a deeply divided world, marked by political divisions between states and sets of states, divisions between generations, and the fight for survival of the human species. Kothari emphasized the crisis and breakdown of the existing system. He provided a general picture of the fragmentation and disintegration of the old alliances, both domestic and international violence had increased heightened competition for scarce resources, the natural environment had disintegrated gradually, the protective cover of the biosphere had been eroded slowly, and the threat of a nuclear war loomed large.[27] A deep schism had developed between the world of knowledge and the world of reality.

Kothari conceptualized survival as the basic problematic of the human condition at the present juncture of world history.[28] He observed, 'At stake is the survival of the state as an instrument of change and liberation, identity and dignity; the survival of civilization; the survival of the species; the survival of the whole creation. The problematic is already affecting institutional structures, the behaviour of people, their psychic responses.'[29] He talked about the crises of human knowledge and crises in values, which had led to a struggle for survival in various forms – survival of life, survival of lifestyle, survival of states and the state system, and survival of power structures. 'Survival and transformation' or 'peace and development' were the two basic dimensions of human prospects, which were inextricably intertwined. In both these dimensions, the contemporary human condition had receded gradually and the prospects of the vision of an integral and unified human future based on bonds of solidarity and shared destiny seemed to be very bleak.[30]

Kothari tried to point out the changes in the international system, like the new phenomenon of interdependence, gradual disintegration of the nation-state system, and erosion of existing structures and cultures. These had gradually transformed the old order into a new order. The two essential components of the whole design of the prevailing world order model were the arms race and the global military-industrial culture. Demilitarization of the world regions required first the demilitarization of the mind. The movement for disarmament was being opposed by those used to the present world order model. Accordingly, a sense of threat had developed in the developed countries. The Third World countries voiced their protest against neo-colonialism and raised the demand for a New International Economic Order. Kothari found some similarities between the Third World movement and the growth of trade unionism in the West in the nineteenth century. The arms race dependence of the Third World on nuclear and conventional armaments had played a crucial role in maintaining the present pattern of domination and the overall culture of power politics. He said Third World countries should take initiatives to halt the arms race and to try to change the present structure of inequity and domination in global power relations.[31]

However, peace should be conceptualized beyond measures such as arms control, disarmament and demilitarization. Kothari observed, 'There are two large and basic caveats that they by themselves cannot deal with. One of them pertains to the instability of peace settlements. The second caveat concerns non-military threats to peace arising out of the socio-economic and political process.'[32] The present world is a world of deep dualism. He continued, 'It is a world characterized by accumulating insecurity and fear among the vast peripheries of the same interdependent world.'[33]

Kothari argued that a rapid polarization of the world had taken place – a polarization that was not predominantly ideological, but predominantly political. Therefore, the problematics of peace and development should be integrated. It was not possible to have peace under the present regime of development. The European Enlightenment and the theory of progress, the scientific and technological revolutions, the global impact of the Industrial Revolution and modern capitalism, and the concept of modernization of traditional societies had led to the prevailing paradigm of development. Recent manifestations of the prevailing paradigm of development were control over the environment, technological fixes and colonization of outer space for strategic and military ascendancy.[34]

Kothari believed that negative definitions of peace, which equated it merely with absence or elimination of war, were conceptually flawed. In order to be substantive and sustainable, peace must be characterized by positive features such as humanism, order, harmony, equity and justice. These dimensions must, therefore, be incorporated into the very conceptualization of peace itself. Negative definitions were also politically counterproductive, for they led policy makers to seek impractical and ill-guided solutions to the problems of conflict and war. Wars could not be eliminated by steps that merely sought arms control or even complete disarmament.

Therefore, unlike some of the early WOMP theorists, Kothari conceptualized peace as a process of transformation that was multi-dimensional in its nature. The task of building a peaceful world had to be addressed at several levels: military, ecological, economic, political and socio-cultural.[35] The traditional role of the state had to change, the ongoing conflicts over natural resources had to be contained and resolved, human rights had to be protected, the survival of cultures had to be ensured, tendencies towards global militarization had to be neutralized, and economic crises in various parts of the world had to be overcome.

One of Kothari's basic premises was that peace would be achieved only when all forms of dependence, characteristic of the existing world, came to an end and national political communities achieved autonomy and self-reliance. At the same time, these communities had to achieve internal consolidation, engage in democratic decentralization, provide equity and justice to the people, ensure economic development and gain political legitimacy.[36]

Kothari believed that peace had its own dialectic and a peaceful world order could be achieved only through a sustained dialogue between thinkers, activists and policy makers. He had great faith in the potential of the grass roots movements that had emerged in the recent past. He listed among these the peace movement, the environment movement, the women's movement, the movement for democracy and democratization, the movements waged by the young and the caring against violence, the human rights movement and the related struggles of tribes, minorities and ethnic groups.[37]

Kothari argued that the model appropriate for a peaceful world order was "a regional approach – a pooling of resources and economic and governmental systems. It is a model of a world composed of regional associations in the form of economic unions to begin with, and gradually moving towards federations of present-day nation-states, which will, in the course of time, become regional member-states of a world federation."[38] To start this process or to expedite it in regions where it had already been started, he emphasized the role of the educational process, of intellectuals, of a sustained dialogue between thinkers and men of action.

In providing for an alternative model, Third World countries should themselves take the initiative to improve both their own place and their place in the world. Third World countries should first undo the colonial system and the colonial psyche, which continued to persist. The most potent form of contemporary history should be creative nationalism and not internationalism or globalism.[39] Kothari continued, 'This requires a number of things: realization of real autonomy in these nations, solidarity among them, institutionalization of the autonomy process through regionalization and federalization, and the formation of intellectual and other movements in order to achieve all this. The real gap that is to be filled is of a political and psychological nature. Everything else, including economic development, will follow.'[40] Therefore, both the structure of present reality and its culture needed to be changed. It was only through these means that true integration could be achieved.

III

While discussing the WOMP value of economic well-being, Kothari was highly critical of the development theory that Western theorists offered to newly independent countries in the 1950s and 1960s as the panacea for their problems of poverty and economic backwardness. The theory promised brisk economic progress accompanied by 'movement from tradition to modernity, status to contract, and ascription to achievement'.[41] The premises and promises of this theory were embraced uncritically by policy makers in most Third World countries, since economic development and social progress were indeed their prime concerns.

Kothari argued that this model of development had failed miserably in delivering the promised progress. Instead, it had led to massive dislocations, unprecedented human suffering, serious ethnic and racial tensions, insecurity at all levels, the global arms race, increased gap between the rich and the poor, growing vulnerability of the states and growing pressures from the world power structure, amongst other things.[42]

Arguing that economies of scale were crucial to a country's economic development, the model advocated heavy industrialization achieved through massive induction of capital and technology. Since neither was available domestically in the Third World states, both had to be borrowed from the industrialist West, resulting in dependency rather than development and in exploitation rather than equity. The model also led to greater economic and social cleavages. There came to exist in these societies a major divide 'between a small, highly paid, capital intensive, "modern" sector and a large, subsistence level, labour intensive, "traditional" one'.[43] A small entrepreneurial segment and the urban middle classes reaped benefits at the cost of the poor, particularly the rural poor.

Even though Kothari's critique of the development theory was based essentially on his analysis of the Indian experience and his understanding of some other Asian countries, he shared a large common ground with the Latin American theorists of dependency and underdevelopment. These theorists provided a structural analysis of the relationship between metropolitan capital and peripheral economies and argued that development in the centre necessarily resulted in underdevelopment in the periphery. "Thus, development and underdevelopment could be described as two aspects of a single global process."[44]

The basic problem of all human development was the problem of freedom in human affairs and of democracy and the various institutions that sustained it.[45] Kothari saw hope in the secular assertion of Islamic power as manifested by the OPEC challenge of 1973 and the Iranian Revolution of 1979, which were successful in posing fundamental challenges to Western hegemony. The basic predicament of man was how he could achieve freedom while he was a member of civil society, a state. The state, along with its economy and technology, should promote human freedom. Therefore, the major task before all of us was that of humanizing the human enterprise called the state.[46]

Kothari conceptualized the problematic of development in the following words: "Development, deliverer of the people from poverty and injustice, or reason of state, providing structures of security, exploitation and exclusive lifestyles to the ruling elites of the world? The theory and 'paradigm' of development still keep repeating the former, the practice and politics of development keep moving towards the latter."[47] He was of the firm view that the modern developmental project had an intellectual (which, in turn, included philosophical and conceptual) role in resolving the crisis facing humanity.

But Kothari was not satisfied with merely providing a critique. He set out to reconceptualize the entire development problematic and provided an alternative concept of development because of the continuing underdevelopment and increased gap between the rich and poor nations (North versus South). The alternative had to be both analytical and political. As he put it, "The idea of alternatives, implying 'alternatives to what is', signifies a major dissatisfaction with ... the existing paradigms of both science and politics. It implies two considerations: that the world is becoming too uniform, too standardized, too dominated by a single conception of life and its meaning, with little scope for other available cultural and historical propensities and potentialities, and that such domination of a single conception has led to political and cultural domination by a single region of the world over all others."[48] The concept of alternatives not only entailed development policies, it also included visions of society and polity in the context of the evolution of the whole human community. The philosophical perspective underlining the concept of alternatives 'should affirm both the principle of autonomy of each entity (human as well as social) to seek out its own path to self-realization and the principle of integration of all such entities in a common framework of interrelationships based on agreed values'.[49]

Kothari drew the broad outlines of development strategies to be adopted by Third World countries. Removing unemployment must become their top priority. Establishment of heavy industries could not help substantially in this regard. Primary importance, therefore, had to be given to small scale industries and agricultural development. Once these were achieved, rural development should follow automatically. The gap in social and economic development between the city and the countryside would also be diminished. Kothari exhorted Third World states to devote substantial means to spread mass literacy, particularly among women and the economically weak and socially handicapped strata. He also laid stress on health, drinking water and public transportation for all. These were the elements of an alternative model of development.

While Kothari emphasized the obligation of development planners to provide the basic necessities of human life to all, he also argued that human beings must learn to limit their material wants and aspirations. Kothari characterized this dual transformation as the policy of minima and the policy of maxima.[50] Economic development that catered only to material aspirations produced consumerism; real development should affirm the autonomy to seek out the path of self-reliance.[51] Kothari articulated two principles of the preferred world: first, limitation of wants, and second, a highly decentralized and highly participatory democratic structure.[52]

Kothari emphasized the need and significance for alternative development, or the need to look beyond the Brandt Commission and North-South dialogues, beyond Cancun and mini summits. He argued that it was necessary to rethink the basis of self-reliance and the basic needs perspective, especially in the context of the rise of new actors and new social movements. The whole process of power and distribution should not be confined to relations between states, but should be seen as relations between peoples. He outlined the four signposts of his vision of alternatives: access to and control over natural resources; demilitarization and development; crisis in global economic relations; and human rights and survival of cultures were all equally necessary for the development process. There were five types of analysis within this conceptualization: the rise of new social classes, the rise of women, the position of the poor in the social structure, the role of the state in the process of development and liberation and the long shadow of consumerism. The role of communication had to be perceived against these changing perspectives, as part and parcel of the struggle for human liberation, freedom and justice; strengthening the struggles of communities, cultures and marginalized peoples; environmental preservation; and a basic commitment to values.[53]

Having noted all this, Kothari was not against international integration per se, but he was against forced integration. He supported the integration of regions and cultures into one common whole provided it was based on agreed values and democratic participation.[54] He articulated a new international development strategy that would give due regard to political and cultural factors as well as to alternative attitudes and values.[55] It emphasized four aspects: the political process, demilitarization, culture and sustainability (especially environmental or ecological). The new international development strategy had to be one that helped all members of the international community to 'promote genuine sustainable equity enhancing and people oriented development and remove and arrest the maldevelopment of both Third World and industrialized countries'.[56] Kothari also discussed the basic policy implications of such a strategy. These were collective global responsibility, accountability, removal of international stumbling blocks, confrontation or negotiation dialectic, approach to negotiations and timeframe. The key issues for the new international development strategy were self-reliance in the Third World, cultural roots to development, demilitarization as a development objective, access of the Third World countries to development resources, and Third World participation in the management of global commons. Kothari advocated collective assertiveness on the part of the Third World as well as consolidation through effective South-South negotiations.[57]

Thus, while the broad aim of economic development was raising the standard of living of the people, this entailed a number of steps, such as removal of poverty, the concept of minimum standards for all, and the concept of a maximum beyond which a person's economic welfare was not admissible. Kothari also emphasized specific policy issues such as a demographic policy, regional policy, territorial and federal policy, and ecological and educational policy in order to conceptualize the development problematic in the light of cherished values and preferred goals. He concluded by arguing that political economy was the science that joined these two perspectives of economic science and political science to achieve the goal of individual self-realization and community security.[58]

IV

Kothari first tried to diagnose the historical process that had brought about injustice and then proposed prescriptions for removing the objective sources of such injustice and the subjective sense of injustice. The colonial systems had made the developing countries dependent on the West for technology, aid and international trade. Kothari believed that social justice was inequitable with growth in gross national product (GNP). The history of the economic development of most of the countries in Latin America and South-East Asia exemplified this point aptly. He believed that the issues of social and political justice were directly linked to the developmental model chosen by a developing state. He underlined the need to draw proper lessons from the past experiences of state and nation-building. There were, he observed, two paths:

> There is, on the one hand, the modernization model, which seeks to integrate the new states into a global power structure and a world market and in the process undermine their autonomy and power to shape their own destinies. There is, on the other hand, what may be called the state building model, which seeks to conceive of the tasks of modernization, economic development and the rest as part of a general drive towards consolidating national autonomy and realizing the values of democracy, social justice and secularism.[59]

Whereas the Third World countries should have opted for the hard choice and adopted the state building model, unfortunately, most of them had adopted the Western model of development. They had lost their independence and autonomy and, as a result, were unable to ensure political justice to their citizens.[60] Caught in the vicious grip of poverty, backwardness and exploitation on the one hand, and proxy wars and militarization fuelled by superpower rivalry on the other, the Third World states lacked resources as well as the will and sense of responsibility to take up seriously the agenda of social and political justice for their poor populations.

There had developed a structural dualism – between the elite and the masses, between urban and rural areas, between the regions within countries, between the modern and traditional sectors, and between the minority and the vast majority in all the underdeveloped regions of the world, especially in the postcolonial states of Asia, Africa and Latin America. This was reflected in their income disparities, the living conditions of their lower income groups, their large regional disparities and their social pyramids.[61]

Kothari observed, 'In all these regions, the impact of modernization has resulted in growing disparities, a pervasive dualism in cultural and economic levels and expropriation of the benefits of modernization by a small upper middle class.'[62] He suggested the following preferred framework of policy perspectives and structural reform for the next quarter century of world development: focus on the individual, agricultural transformation, rural industrialization, social continuum, policy on education, ethic of consumption, nature of production and a social minima.[63] In order to realize justice in a world where there existed extremes of disparity and inequality both between and within nations, a precise policy perspective and the corresponding ethic of behaviour were necessary.

Kothari discussed the concept of management, which he referred to as managing the affairs of society. The management of social change or transformation necessitated an understanding of the nature of the social change taking place, such as scarcity of resources, slowing down of growth rates in both developing and socialist countries, the growing sense of insecurity both at the bottom and the top, the spectre of world militarization, the increasing deprivation of the deprived, decline of the traditional institutions of the modern state (especially in Europe), and decline of the autonomy and self-reliance of the Third World countries because of increased political, economic, strategic and technological pressures from the world power structure. After laying down the problems, Kothari discussed the tasks ahead for the managers and mediators of social transformation, with particular reference to developing societies. The fundamental task was to establish the identity, autonomy and self-reliance of the various entities in the struggle for justice.[64] However, he fragmented this fundamental task and identified three levels of tasks or forms of mediation for the management of social transformation. These were: one, the rebuilding, restructuring and restrengthening of states; two, rethinking the prevailing conception of economic development and increased awareness of a sense of their rights among the ordinary people in most Third World societies; and three, evolving a strategy whereby the present system could be replaced by aligning a new coalition of power.[65]

Globalization had not improved the capacities of the Third World countries, but it had nonetheless put them under greater pressure to conform to Western standards of human rights and other issues of social and political justice. Civil society formations had sprung up to advocate the cause of justice for women, Dalits, tribals and cultural minorities.[66] Kothari accorded greater importance to the non-party political process and non-governmental organizations in the promotion of social justice.

Kothari raised the issue of human rights and fundamental freedoms of citizens. The debate on human rights did not confine itself merely to the traditional distinction between civil and political rights on the one hand, and economic, social and cultural rights on the other. It also included within it the emerging redefinition of the development problematic as was reflected in the demand for the New International Economic Order and the new thinking and theories on alternative strategies of development and lifestyles. Thus, the issue of human rights was intertwined with the emerging debate on development. Development included not only economic factors, but also social, cultural and political factors. Kothari argued that the critique that had emerged throughout the 1960s and 1970s of the earlier patterns of development had been articulated in a variety of ways: 'the Dependencia School pioneered by some Latin American thinkers, the Limits to Growth and Ecological Schools, the Basic Needs School, the Self-Reliance School and, more strident than all these, the New International Economic Order School'.[67] On the other hand, those who supported the international status quo were trying to build new defences for the old order through the militarization of developing societies, the newly developed doctrine of containment, and threatening cultural identity and civilizational values in Asia, Africa and Latin America. Kothari discussed the different aspects of the relationship between human freedom and the nature of techno-economic development. He also discussed the issues of economic development, the issue of stability, the right to human dignity, removal of poverty and the whole question of lifestyle and living standards. The issue of equity and structural crisis in North-South relations was the central issue in the struggle for living standards as a basis for the achievement of human rights and fundamental freedoms.[68]

With the decline of the state or, more specifically, the erosion of 'institutional space', new forms of assertions of people's rights, 'exclusivist identities' and new social movements had emerged gradually to reflect the views of the grass roots workers and the deprived and marginalized sections of society. Over the years, there had taken place a phenomenal growth of new social movements, such as the women's movement, the environment movement, the human rights movement, tribal and ethnic minority assertions, the Dalit movement, and the growth of regional identities and nationalities, which were also broadening as movements. The social basis of the state had been transformed markedly. The early liberal defence of incremental diffusion of institutional spaces had given way to a more radical assertion of civil liberties and democratic rights.

Kothari, therefore, felt the need for a new democratic theory that would accept plurality, diversity, multi-ethnicity and multiculturalism, and would bind them through an active political process. New and creative spaces could be evolved within the framework of civil society and, along with that, the whole structure of the state could be restructured to realize the new goals, objectives and values. Kothari had dealt with 'this emerging series of issues in the relationship between the state and the democratic process in a period of growing social turmoil on the one hand, and a global managerial response to the same on the other'.[69] He wanted to civilize the state and make governance more humane.

Kothari argued that development, secularism and security were the objectives of the three dominant projects of the state. But, the states could not ensure social justice. The states were ruled by governments, which could not provide good governance primarily because of their takeover by 'corporate interests, the military-technocratic order, and by the ideology of national interest and national security'.[70] He emphasized the need for a transition from government of humans to humane governance. He observed, 'This movement involves making the dispensable indispensable – of bringing back human concerns to the centre of regulating both the state and civil society; of recovery of the basics and of first principles, thus creating an ethical order which is a source of values.'[71] So, he conceptualized the role and significance of grass roots movements or the new social movements as a source for humane governance. Within the framework of the macro-micro dialectic, he said our slogan as seen from a grass roots perspective should be, 'Think locally and transform globally', instead of the earlier 'Think globally and live locally'.[72] Kothari described the present crisis in the human condition as an 'intellectual crisis, a crisis of the knowledge system, a crisis of values and moral norms and also a crisis in the relationship between the intellectuals and the world which they live in'.[73] In dealing with these crises, he assigned primary responsibility to the intellectuals for building up a sustained democratic struggle.

Kothari talked about four interrelated processes – decline of the concept of state autonomy, increase in the coercive nature of the state, decline of governmental power, and attack on the secular power of the state. He related the failure of the state in social transformation within the global context. An unprecedented and accelerated arms race and the new international division of labour had led to a gigantic battle for survival all over the world. He pointed out that the failure of the system was embedded in a crisis of theory. It was in this context that he discussed the broad theme of people's movements and grass roots politics and, in general, the phenomenon of 'non-party political formations'.[74]

Kothari explored the relationship 'between an increasingly defensive status quo desperate to retain its power and forces of change and transformation that are getting increasingly restive and restless, conscious of the shackles that bind them and the need to move out of them, yet frustrated and disorganized and unable to cope with the growing repression and terror from the status quo'.[75] Since the middle of the nineteenth century, all social commentators had looked at this problem of the encounter between the forces of the status quo and those of change. But since the 1980s, the problem had assumed a new meaning because of 'the deep confusion and uncertainty about what really is under way on both sides of the equation – on the side of the global, regional local status quo and on the side of the agents of change and transformation from the very local and "micro" to the global and planetary macro'.[76]

Kothari discussed the changing nature of the state and its role in civil society, and its impact on the masses and people all over the world, especially the Third World. The contemporary confrontation between the classes and the masses had developed because 'the state had been captured by a convergence of class, ethnic, technological and military actors, by developmentalists, communicators and managers (including managers of votes)'.[77] The masses in the postcolonial world were disorganized because of the decline of the two conventional channels and modes of mobilization and struggle – political parties and trade unions. This had resulted in the emergence of a whole new class of people called activists. It was these groups of people that had initiated the new grass roots movements and new social movements. Kothari believed that all these movements could produce a macro challenge, a general transformation (whether one called it revolution or not), not through conventional channels, but through a non-party political process.[78] And, in order to create a just society, each state needed to move 'towards a pluralist, decentralized polity with a humane technology and relatively self-reliant economy, self-reliant for the people and not just for the state as has been the thinking on self-reliance till recently'.[79] All these would lead to the fulfilment of the desired values of freedom, social justice, political participation and the territorial basis of self-government.[80]

Kothari's views on the fourth WOMP value of ecology came in the form of his critique of Garrett Hardin's perspective on the subject. Kothari pointed out that there were two types of ecologists. The first was 'the eco-development school of ecologists who are concerned with making development both environmentally viable and socially equitable'.[81] He added, 'There is another school of ecology which believes in conservation pure and simple, with little or no regard either for the causes underlying today's runaway technology and its ravaging of the environment, or for the need for planning for the future which, while providing for the basic necessities of all, would ensure an ecologically sustainable strategy of growth.'[82]

Hardin's basic problem was that while he upheld the 'sanctity of the carrying capacity' of the planet, he was against structural changes in the global distribution of resources and power in improving the standards of living of the poor. Hardin's critique of the current development theory did nothing to promote justice and equity. He called for controlling the number of the poor because they would overtake and rob the richer parts of the world of their standards of living.[83] Kothari pointed out that Hardin was essentially a supporter of capitalism, 'privatism' and global dominance; his doctrine was essentially the doctrine of triage based on liquidation of the 'excess population' of the world. Hardin's analysis and prescriptions represented 'a combination of Malthusianism, militarism and both contempt for and fear of the world, masquerading under an echoate view of the human predicament', which was based on Kothari's 'sincere interest in the survival of civilization (read carrying capacity)'.[84] Kothari agreed with Hardin that the most pressing problem of social scientists was to create credible theory, which Hardin said was the 'Tragedy of Commons'.[85]

However, the Tragedy of Commons argument appeared inadequate because of a deepening of the environmental consciousness. Kothari agreed with Hardin in his critique of American foreign aid and, like him, considered it another form of foreign intervention. Kothari criticized foreign aid because it would further widen the gap between the rich and the poor and would become an instrument of imperial domination. Kothari agreed with Hardin that a new ecological theory was required, but this theory must endorse the idea of pooling of resources on a global scale. The ecological balance could be preserved only by using resources in equitable ways.

V

The transition to a preferred world was described by Kothari as 'Footsteps into the Future', which was also the title of one of his major books on WOMP. He said, 'One thinks in terms of footsteps into the future by operating at a number of levels, not catastrophic reversals of existing arrangements that may or may not produce the desired results.'[86] Contemporary society faced the basic problem of the increasing obsolescence of human beings and a correspondingly rising value of non-human artefacts and techniques, for which there was a rising demand in all countries, including the rich ones.

There had developed a growing dualism in the world – between the North and the South. The prevailing pattern of dominance had produced not simply a division of the world between dominant and dependent states, but also deep cleavages within the latter. It had produced a basic schism between the elite and the people, between the urban and the rural, between the educated and the uneducated, and it had led to the growth of a privileged class.

There were two other related facts. One was the continued increase in the expansion in the demand for, and hence the supply of, capital goods and research and development. The other was that the richer countries needed more and more capital resources. The critical sectors in the alternative model were employment, education and research. Employment and adequate income for all had to be ensured. A totally different approach to education should be adopted by emphasizing adult education, education had to be less bookish and more analytical, and technical skills should be related to the needs of the society. The Third World countries should define, develop and implement a series of alternative policies to carry out scientific research.[87] Kothari raised a very pertinent question: 'From where will these initiatives come, from which areas of the world, from which social strata, and through what combination of use of formal political power and movements of ideas and protest?'[88]

In the transition to the preferred world, Kothari contended that there was a need to resolve regional disputes regionally, moving towards comprehensive trade and cultural arrangements, towards economic unions, loose political confederations and, finally, towards a genuinely federal state incorporating the various regional units into a single juridical entity. Therefore, in order to move towards the preferred model, certain existing structures could be rebuilt, like redefining the role of ECOSOC, the United Nations General Assembly, the United Nations Security Council, specialized agencies of UN and disarmament. The Third World countries could achieve autonomy only when these guidelines were followed, when they strengthened their own countries and then struggled against external sources of hegemonic dominance and exploitation.

Kothari believed that the transition to the preferred world would operate 'at a number of levels, not catastrophic reversals of existing arrangements that may or may not produce the desired results'.[89] He argued that a federal structure that allowed greater autonomy and self-sufficiency at various levels of the system along with individual freedom of enterprise would form the key to a future world order model.

Kothari pointed out, 'A world political structure composed of autonomous nation states is accepted not only as a reality that cannot be simply wished away, but as a preferred reality that should be made more real than is the case in today's world of super, intermediate and marginal states.'[90] He added, 'The evolving world political pattern lends itself to some sort of a vertical multi-federal situation that appears to be the case if one looks at the secular trend in the development of both international cooperation and international conflict.'[91] The three tiers of authority in a federal system were local, regional and central. Federalism was a gradual development. It involved a gradual rise from local units to the region and from the region to the more inclusive nation. In order to move towards a federal and decentralized model of world order, a middle tier of world organization needed to be evolved. There were diverse factors such as history, tradition, language, culture and economic interdependence, which appeared relevant and helpful at the level of the nation-state. Kothari, therefore, advocated the importance of regional economic cooperation in order to enable greater federalization of the political process. The idea of regional economic cooperation had far reaching political implications, especially for the economically and politically weaker regions of the world, as compared, for instance, to the countries of the European Economic Community.[92]

Kothari concluded, 'It is this combination of, on the one hand, large federal structures able to fend for their autonomy and leading to a more equal distribution of political power in the world and, on the other hand, considerable scope for individual and local self-reliance that provides the key to our general model for the future.'[93]

VI

From the very beginning of WOMP, Rajni Kothari had consistently advocated a decentralized, Third World perspective of world order. There was no change in his views on WOMP even when he was no longer a part of it. Even today, he advocates a bottom-up perspective of world order so that the marginalized and deprived sections of society can get justice. According to Kothari, 'WOMP, which began as a Western liberal initiative, gradually became a global project on world order studies. Even though it was a liberal democratic initiative, some of the WOMP scholars (like Sakamoto from Japan) had their own radical views within their domestic countries. It was global in the sense that it had leading minds from different parts of the world, like the US, Europe, Asia, Africa, Japan and Latin America. But WOMP did not have its roots in the deep socio-cultural milieu.'[94] Kothari commented about WOMP:

> One is that the values they wanted to pursue. They operated through the intellectual arena – the university system, the pedagogic system, the knowledge system. They considered WOMP as part of the peace initiative. They believed that if the younger generation joined this peace initiative, we would succeed. I think that to that extent, they succeeded.
>
> One of the first institutional initiatives was taken by the World Law Fund, which is now called the Institute for World Order. From that point, it influenced curricula, degree of knowledge and students. WOMP brought in a large number of intellectuals – peace loving, foreign policy oriented and security oriented people. So, considering all these within the Western parameters, WOMP showed a degree of success despite the fact that the basic and dominant thinking in international relations considered it to be a rather romantic kind of thing. To some extent, it was romantic. Any new initiative should begin as a utopia. And that was what WOMP was. But later on, as it expanded, it got associated with other institutions, and it also got associated with the journal, *Alternatives*, which I actually started. It is now brought out by CSDS (Centre for the Study of Developing Societies) here and WOMP there.
>
> Basically, it was an intellectual effort within international relations, a radical thinking in international relations, of course. People like Richard Falk are today occupying very eminent positions in the

> field of international relations. WOMP was a partial success. It was not a complete success. It remained on the periphery of international relations. The fact is that WOMP has survived so far – it has an Institute for World Order and also a journal, *Alternatives*. All these show that though it was a limited success, it was a success as far as the West was concerned. WOMP was a partial success as it did not bring about fundamental changes in the world. It also did not bring about fundamental changes in realizing justice. It believed that through global effort, a better and just world could be created. To create a better and just world, you have to start from the bottom. While Saul H. Mendlovitz and the Westerners emphasize a top-down process, a global institutional model, I emphasize a process of decentralization, federalization, et cetera. That continued to be my basic difference with them.
>
> I wrote a major booklet called 'Towards a Just World' (which was also published in *Alternatives*) in which I have showed that justice cannot just be a global responsibility, the responsibility of the government, it requires the involvement of the people – elaborated in my whole thinking on grass roots initiatives, and also in the continued dialogue in WOMP. I don't think that the process of dialogue had been completely resolved.[95]

Kothari believed that it was now time to reinvigorate WOMP in order to arrive at some kind of a normative, benevolent world order. We reproduce here some of his views:

> My own feeling is that the time is ripe to reassert those values (the four world order values of peace, economic well-being, social and political justice, and ecological balance), the politics of those values. Because it is time when after the end of the Cold War, militarization is growing, authoritarian tendencies are growing, fascist tendencies are growing. Anything like WOMP, or a WOMP-like effort, should be started because of the seriousness of the situation today, at both the domestic level, and then at the international level. WOMP had slowed down. It is not moving. The key figures in it are keeping out. Ali Mazrui has his own Institute of Global Cultural Studies in Birmingham (in the United States). I myself, I said yesterday, that I have sent a resignation letter to Saul Mendlovitz. It required a lot of travel. I did not travel too much these days. Except for the Westerners, who can afford it? Even if WOMP itself provided the funds – Saul Mendlovitz was a good fund raiser, even then, it had become difficult.

> But I think it is a multicultural effort. In different parts of the world, WOMP-like efforts should be started for peace, justice and ecological balance. And as they develop, they can meet together at international conferences, et cetera. In fact, they should rebuild it in a federal way. This was what was lacking in the earlier WOMP. In fact, today, multiple cultural effort, multiple social effort, multiple political effort is needed where inequalities are growing, where injustice is growing, where violence is growing, and in those situations, a lot of effort is needed in Third World countries, Western countries. Fortunately, younger people in international relations, without joining WOMP, are highly idealistic thinkers, and are writing, not only in *Alternatives*, but in leading journals of international relations. The peculiarity of the situation is that WOMP-like efforts are needed more today. WOMP started as a Western liberal initiative, starting with the thesis of one world. What we need today is a second generation WOMP, in which new people and institutional structures are needed. New people can be recruited in leading organizations, which are recognized not only nationally, but also internationally. The fact that some of the individuals contribute to *Alternatives* is worthwhile. But they need a major window in international relations to WOMP-like thinking. They are fighting for justice, for democracy, for better human prospects, but not within the WOMP framework. We should move from WOMP I to WOMP II. We need to build a collective forum for peace, security, justice and an ecologically sound world.[96]

VII

If Kothari provided WOMP an Indian or, more broadly, an Asian perspective, Ali A. Mazrui enriched it further by lending it insights gained from his African experience of race and tribe relations. Mazrui analyzed WOMP values from the cultural perspectives of different regions and states. He posed the question: 'How can a shared culture be desirable on a world scale if it led to such convulsions in smaller societies?'[97] He believed that the ultimate solution to problems of world order was 'the promotion and consolidation of a shared culture' for the entire 'human race'.[98] For that, the dynamics of cultural change and social integration had to be understood in an interrelated manner.[99] Mazrui's approach was based on two major theories – 'the theory of normative convergence, intimately related to cultural integration, and the theory of dependency'.[100]

Since Mazrui emphasized the primacy of culture in all his writings, he sought solutions to all problems – domestic, international and global – in cultural modifications. The root cause of most world order problems was that cultures often promoted dualist and dichotomous ways of looking at the world. They postulated sharp divisions between 'us' and 'them' and assumed that a conflict necessarily existed between the native and the alien' the Orient and the Occident, the East and the West, the North and the South, and so on. This tendency towards dichotomization was as old as human civilization. It would be a mistake, therefore, to attribute it to the cold war divisions between capitalist and communist ideologies and states.[101]

Mazrui tried to exhibit 'the strong tendency toward the paradigm of bipolarity, which is manifested in monotheistic dualism' and explored 'its impact on contemporary world politics and international relations'.[102] He added, 'Our second concern is to try to demonstrate that at the international level, the class structure of the world is often defined in cultural rather than economic terms. The third thrust of our analysis is to illustrate how, in the absence of world government, the idea of community at the transnational level has come to be defined in terms of shared values and culture rather than shared political authority.'[103]

The dual paradigm in world order thinking had been shaped by two factors – by the culture of politics, which tended to dichotomize, and by the impact of monotheism on world culture.[104] The earlier versions of Judaism, Christianity and Islam were fused in the combination of these two ideas – the culture of politics and monotheism. Mazrui pointed out that while assessing the impact of these three monotheistic religions on the world order system, it was found that Christianity was the most fundamental force, followed by Islam and Judaism. Thus, monotheism continued to hold its dominance over international relations and world affairs, even though the cultural frontier of the world had moved forward.[105]

However, the old dualism had been replaced by a new dualism – the confrontation between the developed and the developing countries. The central dichotomy in the existing world had now become development and technology. Simultaneously, an increased secularization of the Western civilization was taking place. The two greatest challenges posed to Western civilization were, on the one hand, militant monotheism (Islam) and, on the other hand, self-conscious atheism (Marxism). But the world of Marxism, the world of Islam and Western civilization were all interrelated systems of values and ideas. In Marxism, the dialectic was dualistic; likewise, in both Christianity and Islam, there was constant tension between good and evil.

The existing world was divided among three cultural universes: Western, Islamic and Marxist. All of them betrayed a 'monotheistic' streak and 'its derivative patterns of cognition'.[106] Unfortunately, conventional world order thinking, too, had been coloured by this kind of dichotomization. There could be a consensus on a specific set of world reforms only when people across cultures shared a framework of social reasoning. Positive change, therefore, required a substantial measure of global cultural integration, built on consensus around new values. The creation of a preferred world order thus depended not merely on the principal values that WOMP itself postulated, it also needed consensus on several other supporting values.

Mazrui wrote, 'We see world reform as a problem of mobilizing consensus, we see consensus as a problem of building up supporting values, and we see this latter as an outgrowth of cultural convergence.'[107] He added, 'Values are inseparable from culture. Indeed, what is culture, but a system of interrelated values and social perspectives, active enough to condition the behaviour of its adherents?'[108]

The process of global integration emphasized normative convergence, which in this regard involved four stages of interrelationship between the diverse racial, national and cultural groups in the world. These were relationships of bare coexistence, contact, compromise and coalescence. The process of convergence started between the stage of compromise and the stage of coalescence. The mechanisms by which the process of integration moved from one stage to another stage were conflict and mobility.[109]

Mazrui also brought out the paradox of violence emerging precisely out of cultural integration. He substantiated his argument about the tension generating effects of cultural integration by illustrating some case studies drawn from the African political experience. The African societies of Rwanda, Zanzibar and Burundi have witnessed horrific brutalization despite their deep cultural integration. The violence occurred because the stratification systems in these regions were too unequal and, therefore, no longer viable.

The world culture which had evolved so far was definitely a Eurocentric world culture in that we continue to have cultural imperialism. Mazrui cited the example of Marxist communism as a branch of the Western intellectual tradition, which had been subsequently used by Third World scholars such as Samir Amin, Justinian Rweyemamu and Walter Rodney as a tool of analysis for interpreting social and international phenomena. It reflected the two dimensions of dependency – structural dependency and cultural dependency. Mazrui suggested regional autonomy as a way of removing the baggage of dependency and cultural imperialism. He emphasized 'regional autonomy with genuine participation in a world culture – by combining African problems and African perspectives with a continual reference to the world cultural picture'.[110]

Mazrui pointed out that purposeful world reform required transmission of ideas and their internationalization, rather than the establishment of formal institutions for external control. It was here that he proposed cultural engineering as the most promising approach toward world reform and he emphasized the objective of building a world culture. Cultural convergence demanded global dissemination of new ideas, but it did not necessarily require the establishment of new formal institutions. In many ways, the convergence was already beginning to occur. Global cultural convergence was being manifested both in the cruder forms of pop culture (or certain shared tastes in music, films, sports and magazines) as well as in the area of shared political emotions, prejudices and sensibilities.[111] To quote Mazrui:

> The spread of literacy, the role of technology in affecting lifestyles, the acceleration and facilitation of international travel, the international distribution of books and newspapers, the emergence of television programmes and films distributed on a world scale, the impact of the radio and the consolidation of external broadcasting services to other parts of the world as an aspect of foreign policy have all combined to introduce the beginnings of shared values, shared tastes and shared images.[112]

Mazrui suggested cultural ecumenicalism in the form of a World Federation of Cultures. The federation would not only work in coordination with the constituent cultures, but also borrow from regional and linguistic cultures. This would help correct imbalances produced by uneven creativity and dissemination in the federation.[113] Every schoolchild everywhere in the world should learn three languages – a world language (such as English or French), a regional language (such as German or Swahili) and either a national language (such as Swedish or Persian) or a sub-national language (such as Gujarati or Luganda).[114] Mazrui summed up his position by suggesting that the world order should be seen 'in terms of a federation of human cultural contributions, combining a global pool of shared achievement with local pools of distinctive innovation and tradition'.[115]

VIII

To Mazrui, peace entailed diminishing violence within, between and across states. However, he asserted that violence must not be understood in an undifferentiated and abstract manner. Historically, violence had played both a transformative and integrative role. It had been used for making revolutions as well as for nation building.[116] The most important revolutionary thinkers in the Third World were the late Frantz Fanon, Che Guevara in Latin America and Mao Tse Tung in Asia. The positive or negative role of violence depended on the form it took, and the form, in turn, often depended on the underlying causes.

The goal of peace, therefore, could not be achieved by merely devising legal-institutional mechanisms. A necessary prerequisite for addressing the issue of violence was an understanding of its real nature. All dimensions of culture – kinship, economic factors, the impact of ideas as well as the conditions exerted by political culture had to be taken into account in trying to understand violence.

Mazrui delineated three categories of violence: deviant violence, social violence and international violence. He also distinguished between civic violence and political violence. Collective violence was the most explicitly political form of social eruptions. Various factors related to kinship, economy, ideology and political culture exerted their influence in the eruption of violence.[117] Most important for our present purpose, Mazrui believed that

> the problem of world peace is in the initial stages a problem of domestic cultures and of relations between social groups in individual countries and of the values governing those groups. It could be said that all international wars have been so far externalized civil deficiencies, both cultural and social. To solve the

> problem of international conflict, therefore, necessitates an attempt to tackle the causes of domestic tensions and domestic pathologies.[118]

Mazrui concluded that the minimization of violence in world affairs had two necessary preconditions: the processes of state formation and nation-building.[119] While linking the revolution of identity in world affairs with the revolution of political consciousness, he pointed out that while social violence was regarded as a dependent variable, the denial of social justice and economic welfare were more basic social determinants. Culture and social stratification were the two domestic factors in the concept of domestic primacy in global issues. He added the concept of primordial cultural self-awareness to the Marxist idea of class struggle. He analyzed the link between local violence and international violence not merely in the causes, but also in the methods and strategies of conflict. He further discussed the crises in West Asia and Vietnam to focus on the varied issues that linked warfare to the inequalities of the technological age.[120]

Another foundational requirement for creating the preferred world order was economic restructuring. Economic relations had to be restructured in a manner that left no need for violent revolutions. The need was to ensure the economic well-being of the poor strata within weak states. The process of modernization, especially the modernization of economic culture, would be a key process in the transformation of the preferred world. Modernization involved 'first, the modernization of economic techniques and processes; second, the modernization of economic motivation; and third, the modernization of social stratification both domestically and internationally'.[121] Mazrui demonstrated that the world had to rely on a three dimensional process of modernization in order to have a comprehensive approach to economic reform.

Mazrui combined the problem of economic solutions to racial problems, with special reference to the attempts being made in East Africa and the United States to create an effective black entrepreneurial class. Both social justice and economic welfare, ominously beclouded by interethnic violence, was at stake here.[122] In other words, he discussed in relation to the American and East African experiments, the modernization of stratification and motivation. While in Kenya and Uganda, the United Kingdom had imposed a caste system based on racial gradation, in the United States, the

African Americans had gradually moved, or were in the process of being promoted, from the status of a lower caste to the status of a lower class. When capitalism and the caste system interacted in the racially mixed situations in Africa and the United States, the cultural heritage of India and the cultural heritage of the Anglo-Saxon powers merged for a while.[123]

The question of economic mobility remained critical for both social justice and economic welfare in the international sphere, even though there existed vital differences between an international class system and an international caste system. There were differences between horizontal and hierarchical divisions of labour. The formation of an effective local entrepreneurial class in every developing country was of crucial importance. Since it was impossible to have complete equality, the pursuit of social justice and increased economic welfare should seek to maximize mobility among domestic classes and among different economic gradations of state, rather than altogether abolishing classes. Mazrui also distinguished between achievement motives and extension motives on the question of modernizing motivational patterns. The extension motive, which referred to 'the capability of one nation to empathize economically with another, needed to be nourished to greater efficacy in the international sphere'.[124]

Mazrui's ultimate dream was a global village based on egalitarian interdependence. He observed, "A mature interdependence would entail a better relationship, based in part on effective mutual vulnerability, between the technologically superior Northern Hemisphere and the sources of primary products to the South."[125] He also observed that

> The two processes of rising expectations in the Southern Hemisphere and diminishing complacency in the Northern, promoted in part by the impact of global communications, should result in a more balanced villagization of human perspectives. When man succeeds in recapturing selectively the ethos of kinship obligations and applies the ethos not to small scale societies, but to human relations at the global level, the process of retribalizing the world in the direction of egalitarian interdependence will indeed be well under way. The preferred world of the 1990s should be, in the ultimate analysis, a world under the influence of such a vision.[126]

Mazrui dealt essentially with kinship culture and problems of identity. He elaborated on 'monogamy and descent in black-white relations', where he demonstrated the relevance of kinship culture to world order problems. He examined two things – first, the relationship between monogamy and racism, and, second, the impact of differential miscegenation on systems of descent.[127] In other words, he examined the political sociology of patterns of matrimony and descent across racial boundaries. In exploring this domain of human experience, Afro-Arab relations were used as a foil to Afro-European relations. He demonstrated that strict monogamous attitudes correlated with other forms of intolerance. Strict monogamous Puritanism tended to correlate with racial intolerance, including a disapproval of racial mixture at large. For example, as compared to Islam, Christianity in Africa was more culturally arrogant in its attitude to native customs. However, from the sociological point of view, it was in the ranking of children, rather than in the sexual divide, that the real importance of interracial meeting could be seen. Keeping that in mind, Mazrui categorized miscegenation as descending (the North American model), ambivalent (Latin America), divergent (South Africa) and ascending (the Afro-Arab polygamous culture – Sudan and Zanzibar). He pointed out that among the various types of miscegenation, it was the ascending miscegenation, signifying a hierarchy of relationships, which could solve the problems of racial cleavage, even though it would not ensure equality and parity of esteem between races. Therefore, in the years ahead, in order to ensure equality between races and parity between sexes, the quest should be for symmetry in biocultural assimilation.[128]

Mazrui also traced the historical background of the Asian presence in East Africa. He addressed aspects of kinship culture insofar as they conditioned the dynamics of Indo-African relations in that particular East African society.[129] In this regard, he discussed in detail the practice of sati (the cremation of the wife on her husband's funeral pyre) in India and the custom of *devirattee* (in which the wife was inherited by her husband's brother upon the death of her husband) in Africa, as well as the wider cultural and spiritual ramifications of these two systems. His correlation of the ideas of kinship to nationhood was only an extension of the principles of tribal cohesion. He also examined economic culture and differences in performance between Africans and Asians.[130]

Mazrui examined 'distance and demonstration in black-yellow relations', too. Adopting the strategy of moving from the general to the particular, he discussed the broad lines of the history of Japan and China in a racial perspective to the specifics of Mao's policy for Eastern Africa. He demonstrated that China's relations with Africa had moved in three circles of affinity: first, solidarity based on shared racial and colonial humiliation (pan-pigmentationalism); second, solidarity based on shared underdevelopment and indigence (pan-proletarianism); and finally, solidarity based on socialism itself (pan-socialism).[131] In discussing Sino-African relations, Mazrui focused specially on Kenya and Tanzania. He pointed out that in the history of race relations in the world, two concepts, both of which had emanated from the West, had been critically important. The first one, the concept of the 'yellow peril', was designed as a warning to the white races to beware of the potential conquering power of China and Japan. The other was the concept of the 'white man's burden', inspired by a desire to conquer others.[132] Mazrui emphasized that even though the two yellow giants had played a significant role in reducing the distance between Africans themselves, the biocultural distance between Africa and both Japan and China persisted. The world would witness transformation of the yellow peril into the yellow paradigm, as the Third World would now imbibe Japan and China as their relevant pair of role models rather than the United States and the former USSR. This kind of strategy would reduce the Eurocentrism of the world and would help in the evolution of a more symmetrical world culture.[133]

Thus, Mazrui focused essentially on the interplay between kinship culture and racial identification, and between sex and group dynamics. Later on, he examined how the struggle for the three world order values as postulated by WOMP, peace, social justice and economic well-being, were affected by kinship culture. It was with this objective in mind that he looked at the transition from the rights of kinship to those of citizenship as a movement towards expanding empathy.[134] The cultural determinants of group behaviour range from the clash between kinship loyalty and global perspectives in Africa to the interplay between violence and masculinity in the history of human cultures. While the sexual division of labour was related to the tensions between war and peace, systems of descent were affected by questions of social justice and economic welfare. Therefore, a slow transition from kinship to citizenship was taking place. In the United States, while the white Americans were witnessing expanding empathy, the African Americans were witnessing receding empathy. There were evidences of receding empathy in South Africa among both the black and white populations. The cause of family planning and population control lacked adequate credibility in Africa. The issue of population would link the two principles of the maximization of social justice and the minimization of violence – if the blacks and the whites came into a confrontation with each other, either in active combat or in terms of hostile attitudes. The need was to expand the concept of kinship beyond kith, towards man.[135]

The two major crises in the quest for a just world order were the crises of 'dissensus' and stratification. Social justice as an ideal was more relativistic, more culture bound than either economic welfare or the question of what constituted a minimization of violence. However, the concept of social justice within each culture could change from generation to generation.

Mazrui also elaborated on political justice. There was a need to address the violence that sometimes accompanied the process of cultural convergence, while examining the relationship between violence and culture, which might take place in situations of asymmetry between cultural donors and cultural recipients. The stronger country might dominate the weaker country and force the weaker country to adapt itself to the new culture, rather than its own indigenous culture. He examined these postcolonial tensions of political and cultural adjustment, especially as illustrated in Africa.[136] Two trends clearly discernible in Africa were political unrest and increasing cultural revitalization.

At the same time, Mazrui pointed out that a new kind of global apartheid had emerged after the end of the Cold War. The two world wars had been fought basically by the white races themselves. Initially, the Cold War, too, was an extension of intra-white rivalries, but it gradually engulfed the whole world. With the end of the Cold War, the confrontations within the white world had largely come to an end (even though micro-level conflicts continued as between the Serbs and the Croats, the Irish and the English, the Ukrainians and the Russians). What was more important to note about the end of the Cold War, however, was the fact that the United States, in its role as the only hegemonic power, had succeeded in imposing its market ideology all over the world in a historically unprecedented way. This had led to the increased marginalization of Africa. It had also put into question the nation-state as a political entity. Since the state could no longer play an integrative role, the world was getting divided on the basis of race and skin colour.[137]

Mazrui said, 'The triumph of those market ideologies is polarizing the globe along racial lines more deeply than ever, with black people almost everywhere at the bottom, white people in control of global wealth, and Asian people in intermediate levels of stratification.'[138] Noting the distinction between structural and overt forms of racism, he added, 'While structural racism is dividing the world between rich white guardians and poor black wards, overt racism in the Northern Hemisphere is having almost equally devastating consequences.'[139]

Mazrui argued that the problems of fragile institutions and of fragmented identity were responsible for much of the political upheaval in Africa. He, therefore, advocated a pendulum model of social change. It was not merely as support for a particular leader or party, which might fluctuate between elections, but in terms of swings between the whole political systems, that the pendulum effect became effective.[140]

IX

Making a conceptual distinction between the three kinds as well as stages of interdependence, Mazrui argued that the history of the nineteenth and twentieth centuries had seen a transition from 'primitive interdependence' to 'feudo-imperial' interdependence. The latter was deeper and more pervasive than the former, but it was also more one sided and exploitative. The need was to move to the third, 'mature' kind of interdependence, which would be based on the mutual vulnerability of the Northern and Southern Hemispheres. Mazrui suggested that mature interdependence would require the one sided penetration of the feudo-imperial era to be balanced by Third World counter-penetration of the First World.[141] Mazrui's definition of a cultural federation is reproduced here:

> A cultural federation in our sense is not a neatly institutionalized arrangement, but a pattern of cultural relationships based ultimately on three principles. These principles are, first, an acceptance of cultural interdependence among the constituent parts; second, an acceptance of the principle of parity of esteem among the constituent cultural units, 'coordinate in their powers, so that none of them is able to dominate the others'; and

> third, a promotion at a federal level of 'cultural fusion', which is the equivalent of sharing the central power of sovereignty in a political federation. In a cultural federation, we might call the federal level the shared culture or joint culture, and call the lower units simply constituent cultures.[142]

Mazrui followed his discussion by examining the conditions hospitable to cultural federalism. He pointed out that the predisposing conditions for cultural federalism were imperialism, a geographical neighbourhood (leading to a cultural neighbourhood) and similarity of political institutions (leading to an atmosphere of potential political empathy). The World Federation of Cultures sought to combine the two principles – the principle of cultural pluralism and the principle of a shared civilization. Mazrui also elaborated and discussed in detail the four dimensions or constituent elements of culture – kinship culture, intellectual culture, economic culture and political culture. He summed up by saying that while kinship culture tended always to be parochial, political, economic and other intellectual ideas could be rapidly disseminated, transferred and assimilated in spite of other cultural differences. Kinship culture not only had a significant impact on race relations and the whole problem of colour prejudice and tensions, but also had significant underlying implications for certain problems of world order.[143]

Mazrui visualized changes at three levels for cultural federalism. First, greater mobility, both physical and intellectual, would lead to greater cultural linkages and harmonization. Second, he emphasized 'the importance of language as a medium of cultural convergence and as a major factor in intellectual mobility itself'.[144] Movement had to occur from reliance on communal, national and regional languages towards a global language. The English language could play that role after it had been suitably ridden of its colonial and Anglo-American biases.[145] While Mazrui advocated 'a global language policy for a global cultural heritage',[146] he also emphasized the need to reduce the dominance of Western culture in the global pool of human civilization. Finally, what was needed was a more egalitarian and creative educational policy, which would help broaden intellectual horizons and create a new international morality, making the rich and the strong recognize their obligations towards the poor and the weak, and thus lay down the basis of a 'Pax Humana and a man centred system of values'.[147]

Mazrui also elaborated on the relationship between 'education and world culture'. He discussed the role of modern education in the evolution of global cultural convergence in the intellectual sphere. The impact of education was often closely related to the impact of Christianity in black Africa. In the United States, the most dramatic eruptions among African Americans were either in the form of anomie, which could take the form of despair and total withdrawal, as values disintegrated totally, or in the form of aggressive counter-dependency, which would take a militant stand against the domination from which it had not fully escaped. He also referred to the two interrelated processes of socialization and acculturation in Africa. Moreover, the three values of tolerance, toil and teamwork (referred to as the three Ts of nationhood and global responsiveness) needed to be promoted in order to form and increase the capability for tolerating differences, commitment to social application and endeavour, and readiness to cooperate and collaborate with others to achieve shared goals.[148] He also discussed 'cultural schizophrenia and the acute phenomenon of dependency within Africa, which is still more submissive than aggressive, especially in Francophone Africa'.[149]

Mazrui suggested two policy recommendations. Firstly, African secondary schools should have African headmasters, especially where there were a number of white teachers. Secondly, there should not be any white expatriates in black primary schools. In other words, the African schools should Africanize their entire teaching staff and also introduced the principle of cultural parity in the educational curriculum. Thus, Mazrui concluded that adequate world reform would need some degree of homogenized intellectual culture.[150]

In trying to work out shared images, Mazrui contended that the most important image for any human being was the self-image. He argued that human judgements could be reduced to three areas – legal judgements, moral judgements and judgements of taste or aesthetics. He discussed the place of images in the global world and also the role of changing tastes in the process of changing images. He substantiated his argument by illustrating the relationship between the image of innocence and the image of violence. He pointed out that arts and sports could act as central agents of cultural diffusion, after religion and imperialism. In his discussion about aesthetic homogenization, he emphasized that the link between the aesthetic and the sensual, the spiritual and the physical, was a link between art and life. The contact in African history between art and life, and aesthetics and sensuality, opened up a domain of reciprocal feedback in the quest for cultural symmetry as between donors and recipients. The domain of mutual images also underwent a positive transformation with such reciprocity in tastes.[151]

Mazrui dealt with the impact of all kinds of human judgements on world order and social change. In world affairs in the twentieth century, a new Pax Humana had emerged due to the rise of new internationalist ideologies, the rise of the United States as a superpower and the emergence of the Third World, which consisted of the postcolonial states of Asia, Africa and Latin America. He also pointed out the two paradoxical trends in human relations relevant for the phenomenon of empathy and for the role of culture. While, on the one hand, judgements on human behaviour moved from aesthetics in relations among individuals and among groups domestically, on the other hand, the trend in relations between states had moved from the diplomacy of propriety to the diplomacy of principles.[152]

Mazrui contended:

> The world of the 1990s ought, therefore, to aim for the maturation of these two trends – increased social and welfare legislation, diminishing moral self-righteousness with regard to the private behaviour of others, and widening horizons of personal choice and personal taste. In the international system, on the other hand, the world of the 1990s should aim to consolidate the trend toward a new international morality, susceptible to the obligations of the strong toward the weak, the rich toward the poor, and of each toward a concept of Pax Humana and a man centred system of values. Behind both trends remains the impact of culture on emotive responses. Our concept of human culture remains profoundly cultural in its roots, and our evaluation of world trends springs from an interpretation of changing cultural patterns behind both individual and national behaviour. To a certain extent, the problems of world order are concerned with the interplay between the sacred and the secular in man's emotions and judgements, and these, in turn, find their origins in the world of values and cultural perspectives.[153]

How can we move towards a 'shared humanity'? How can we overcome or transcend the structural and economic dependency on the Northern Hemisphere in order to have a World Federation of Cultures? This was the central issue before Mazrui. He looked on the October War in West Asia in 1973 as a particular episode in international politics on the structural and economic front and examined its global implications. He advocated that the Third World must systematically employ two complementary strategies – the strategy of counter-penetration and the strategy of interpenetration. The October War in 1973 was significant not only for Afro-Arab relations, but also in its striving to create a new and just economic order. Mazrui also discussed the phenomenon of normative convergence and cultural diffusion and future ideological trends. He believed that while the metropolis needed to be socialized, the periphery should be nationalized. He concluded that the world needed to change to achieve the World Federation of Cultures and that it should promote the values of reduced violence, social justice and economic well-being, as outlined by WOMP.[154]

Mazrui outlined 'a model world federation of cultures' because he believed that several different structural arrangements were valid for a World Federation of Cultures. This whole idea of a World Federation of Cultures, rather than being a blueprint for a particular set of new institutions, was primarily a perspective on human arrangements. In this model, Mazrui emphasized the principle of triple representation – by nationality, by region and by language – in order to achieve cultural integration. It was only when, through cultural integration, a World Federation of Cultures would emerge, that the world could be reformed in the direction of the values outlined by WOMP – peace, social justice and economic well-being.[155]

Notes

1. Rajni Kothari, 'Under Globalisation: Will Nation-State Hold?', in *Economic and Political Weekly* (1 July 1995), 1604.
2. Rajni Kothari's interview on WOMP to Sujit Lahiry on 1 June 2002.
3. Rajni Kothari, 'Under Globalisation: Will Nation-State Hold?', in *Economic and Political Weekly* (1 July 1995), 1603.
4. Rajni Kothari, *Memoirs: Uneasy is the Life of the Mind* (New Delhi: Rupa, 2002), 33.
5. Ibid.
6. Rajni Kothari, 'Globalisation and 'New World Order': What Future for the United Nations?', in *Economic and Political Weekly* (7 October 1995), 2516–17.
7. Rajni Kothari, *Footsteps into the Future: Diagnosis of the Present World and a Design for an Alternative* (New Delhi: Orient Longman, 1974), 12.

8. Interview with Rajni Kothari by Sujit Lahiry on 1 and 2 June 2002 (see Appendices).
9. Rajni Kothari, *Footsteps into the Future: Diagnosis of the Present World and a Design for an Alternative*, op. cit., 113.
10. Ibid., 149.
11. Ibid., 6.
12. Ibid., 17–18.
13. Ibid., 11.
14. Ibid., xx.
15. Ibid., 16–17.
16. Ibid., 2.
17. Rajni Kothari, 'Globalisation and 'New World Order': What Future for the United Nations?', in *Economic and Political Weekly* (7 October 1995): 2516–17.
18. Ibid.
19. Ibid.
20. Rajni Kothari, *Footsteps into the Future*, 21.
21. Ibid., 34–45.
22. Ibid., 80–81.
23. Ibid., 85.
24. Ibid., 85–96.
25. Ibid., 99.
26. Ibid., 106–13.
27. Rajni Kothari, 'Peace in an Age of Transformation', in *Culture, Ideology and World Order: Studies on a Just World Order,* No.5, R.B.J. Walker, ed. (Boulder: Westview Press, 1984), 329–31.
28. Rajni Kothari, 'Peace in an Age of Transformation', 323–27.
29. Ibid., 327.
30. Ibid., 332–41.
31. Rajni Kothari, *Rethinking Development: In Search of Human Alternatives* (London: Aspects Publications, 1990), 83–94.
32. Ibid., 9.
33. Ibid., 9–21.
34. Ibid., 65.
35. Rajni Kothari, 'Peace in an Age of Transformation', 359–60.
36. Rajni Kothari, *Footsteps into the Future: Diagnosis of the Present World and a Design for an Alternative*, 107 and 110–13.
37. Rajni Kothari, *Transformation and Survival: In Search of a Humane World Order* (London: Aspects Publications, 1990), 50.

38. Rajni Kothari, *Rethinking Development: In Search of Human Alternatives*, 66–67.
39. Ibid., 68–74.
40. Ibid., 83.
41. Ibid., 121.
42. Ibid., 179–84.
43. Ibid., 123.
44. Ronald H. Chilcote, *Theories of Comparative Politics: The Search for a Paradigm Reconsidered* (Boulder: Westview Press, 1994), 217.
45. Rajni Kothari, 'Towards a Just World', in *Towards a Just World Order*: Studies on a Just World Order, Vol. I, Richard Falk, Samuel S. Kim and Saul H. Mendlovitz, eds (Boulder: Westview Press, 1982), 601.
46. Ibid., 579–601.
47. Ibid., 146–50.
48. Ibid., 570–601.
49. Rajni Kothari, *Transformation and Survival: In Search of a Humane World Order* (London: Aspects Publications, 1990), 144.
50. Rajni Kothari, *Rethinking Development: In Search of Humane Alternatives*, 18–19.
51. Ibid.
52. Rajni Kothari, *Transformation and Survival: In Search of a Humane World Order*, 146–50.
53. Rajni Kothari, *State against Democracy: In Search of Humane Governance* (Delhi: Ajanta Publications, 1988), 2.
54. Rajni Kothari, *Rethinking Development: In Search of Humane Alternatives*, 9, 143–44.
55. Ibid., 147–53.
56. Ibid., 154.
57. Ibid., 158–60.
58. Rajni Kothari, *State against Democracy: In Search of Humane Governance*, 37–54.
59. Ibid., 117.
60. Ibid., 111–17.
61. Rajni Kothari, *Transformation and Survival: In Search of a Humane World Order*, 43.
62. Ibid., 44.
63. Ibid., 45–50.
64. Rajni Kothari, *State against Democracy: In Search of Humane Governance*, 55.

65. Ibid., 55.
66. Ibid., iii-v, 1–2, and 69–70.
67. Ibid., 56–58.
68. Ibid., 60–68.
69. Ibid., 70.
70. Ibid., 117.
71. Ibid., 111–17.
72. Ibid., 118–31.
73. Ibid., 131–32.
74. Ibid., 132.
75. Rajni Kothari, *Rethinking Development: In Search of Humane Alternatives*, 107–8.
76. Ibid., 108–10.
77. Ibid., 112.
78. Ibid.
79. Ibid., 112–17.
80. Rajni Kothari, *Transformation and Survival: In Search of a Humane World Order*, 183.
81. Rajni Kothari, *Rethinking Development: In Search of Humane Alternatives*, 107.
82. Ibid., 108.
83. Ibid., 108–10.
84. Rajni Kothari, *Footsteps into the Future: Diagnosis of the Present World and a Design for an Alternative*, 149.
85. Ibid., 150.
86. Rajni Kothari, *Rethinking Development: In Search of Humane Alternatives*, 144–45.
87. Ibid., 163–77.
88. Ibid., 147–54.
89. Rajni Kothari, *Footsteps into the Future: Diagnosis of the Present World and a Design for an Alternative*, 119.
90. Ibid., 185.
91. Ibid., 184–88.
92. Ibid., i.
93. Ibid., 5.
94. Rajni Kothari's interview on WOMP to Sujit Lahiry on 2 June 2002.
95. Ibid.
96. Ibid.

97. Ali A. Mazrui, 'World Culture and the Search for Human Consensus', in *On the Creation of a Just World Order – Preferred Worlds for the 1990s*, Saul H. Mendlovitz, ed. (New Delhi: Orient Longman, 1975), 1–12.
98. Ibid., 12.
99. Ibid., 3–12.
100. Ibid., 3.
101. Ali A. Mazrui, 'The Moving Cultural Frontier of World Order: From Monotheism to North-South Relations', in *Culture, Ideology and World Order: Studies on a Just World Order,* No.5, R.B.J. Walker, ed. (Boulder: Westview Press, 1984), 24–42.
102. Ibid., 25.
103. Ibid.
104. Ibid.
105. Ibid., 25–42.
106. Ibid., 41–43.
107. Ali A. Mazrui, 'World Culture and the Search for Human Consensus', op. cit., 4.
108. Ibid., 4.
109. Ibid., 7–10.
110. Ibid., 16–23.
111. Ibid., 5.
112. Ibid.
113. Ibid., 36–37.
114. Ibid.
115. Ibid., 37.
116. Ali A. Mazrui, *A World Federation of Cultures: An African Perspective* (New York: The Free Press, 1978), 211–12 and 227–29.
117. Ibid., 231–43.
118. Ibid., 245.
119. Ibid., 243.
120. Ibid., 246–47.
121. Ibid., 271.
122. Ibid., 274–83.
123. Ibid., 284–85.
124. Ibid., 303.
125. Ibid., 328.
126. Ibid., 303–4.
127. Ibid., 81.

128. Ibid., 81–113.
129. Ibid., 118.
130. Ibid., 118–34.
131. Ibid., 137–46.
132. Ibid., 137.
133. Ibid., 146–63.
134. Ibid., 165.
135. Ibid., 165–85.
136. Ibid., 191.
137. Ali A. Mazrui, 'Global Apartheid: Structural and Overt', in *Alternatives* 19 (1994), 185–86.
138. Ibid., 186.
139. Ibid.
140. Ali A. Mazrui, *A World Federation of Cultures: An African Perspective*, 191–210.
141. Ibid., 307–8 and 325–28.
142. Ibid., 70.
143. Ibid., 71–77.
144. Ibid., 334.
145. Ibid., 353.
146. Ibid.
147. Ibid., 435.
148. Ibid., 355–79.
149. Ibid., 379.
150. Ibid., 377–80.
151. Ibid.
152. Ibid., 419–33.
153. Ibid., 435.
154. Ibid., 437–71.
155. Ibid., 473–97.

6 A Critical Analysis of the Ideas of Saul H. Mendlovitz and Samuel S. Kim

We will visit briefly in this chapter the ideas of Saul H. Mendlovitz and Samuel S. Kim – two important Western WOMP theorists. While they shared with their colleagues the common commitment to the values of peace, economic well-being, social justice and ecological balance, they were particularly concerned that these values should not remain abstract and generalized statements of ideals. Applying as much to the means as to the ends,[1] these values were expected to shape also the politics of transition. It was for this reason that the two theorists favoured 'operational definitions of values', which provided an 'insight into the social costs and benefits' and thereby made it possible to 'assess trade-offs between values and to tell whether there has been any progress in a given period of international history with respect to the realization of world order values'.[2] They stated: 'Our search here, then, is for a more detached or objective appreciation of values as goals.'[3]

This chapter is divided into seven sections. The first section deals with Mendlovitz's ideas on the origin, genesis and development of WOMP. The second section, which deals with Mendlovitz's ideas on peace and socio-political justice, is rather brief for two reasons. One, we find that his views on these two values closely resemble those of Richard Falk, which have been discussed already in a previous chapter. Two, Mendlovitz did not pay any notable attention to the two other values of economic well-being and ecological balance. The third section takes up Mendlovitz's ideas on the transition to a preferred world. The fourth section deals with Kim's WOMP methodology. The fifth section takes up Kim's discussion of war and peace. The sixth section deals with Kim's analysis of economic well-being, while the seventh section deals with his views on socio-political justice, ecological balance and the question of the transition to a preferred world.

I

Mendlovitz deservedly occupied a special place in the evolution of WOMP. He was not only the founder-director of the project, but also the main inspiration behind its becoming globally representative. Though himself a Western scholar, he worked hard to bring in non-Western scholars and their perspectives. Mendlovitz was interested in providing a more realistic and practical approach to the search for a just world order. He firmly believed that human intervention could move the world in a desired direction only when the nature of the major challenges and problems was adequately understood. The most significant problems of international relations included the arms race, the risks of general war, transnational terrorism, economic stagnation, scarcity of natural resources, environmental pollution and, in the case of the Third World countries, consolidation of the state.

Mendlovitz elaborated on the genesis, development and future of WOMP. We reproduce here what he said with regard to the genesis of WOMP:

> WOMP was initially conceived in response to pedagogical needs not related to the study of the problem of elimination of war as a human social institution. It was originated in the early 1960s by a small number of United States citizens who wished to introduce the subject matter of war prevention within formal academic environments. The individuals involved at the outset of this programme brought to it a seriousness one associates with those individuals and groups who, between the eighteenth and nineteenth centuries, advocated and participated in the global movement to abolish slavery, or with those persons in this century who have been participating in the dismemberment of colonialism and imperialism.[4]

Mendlovitz believed that a global identity would be produced by the conception of world order as enunciated by WOMP. Since the world was integrated materially, ecologically and spiritually, a global society would emerge. Despite the divisiveness, strife and different perceptions of the world, a global identity was adopted in order to overcome these differences. The development of a global community was essentially an exercise of the imagination. Moreover, the just world order approach emphasized the need to bring about fundamental changes in the nature of international relations. System change was a mixture of aspirations and trends and included both normative and empirical dimensions. Mendlovitz argued, 'System change does not necessarily mean political integration or centralization at the supranational level, much less "world government". It means a fundamental rearrangement of structure so that a different configuration of actors with different orientations toward power, security, well-being and governance will emerge.'[5]

Mendlovitz depicted images of the preferred world and elaborated on the transition tactics and pathways necessary to move towards such a world. He focused primarily on and elaborated in detail the three distinct stages in the development of WOMP. The first stage (1961–68) emphasized the image of an orderly world system generally constituted by a core of strengthened international institutions. Rather than each state having a decentralized and laissez-faire management of power, it was believed that the governments of all the states, in consonance with their distinct national interests, would bring about some kind of institutional centralization in order to create a world police force at the global level. However, in this arrangement and restructuring of power, the states would not lose their autonomy and the possibilities of the emergence of some form of world government were remote. It were Granville Clark and Louis B. Sohn who actually formulated and enunciated this approach in *World Peace through World Law*, which was initially published in 1958 and subsequently revised twice. The United Nations Charter was amended and some functions, capabilities and resources from national governments were transferred to a tightly knit body of global institutions in the Clark-Sohn proposals. The prospects of transition were based on the peace system.[6]

Mendlovitz's writings were often marked by bold optimism and self-assurance. He believed that the world was integrating materially, ecologically as well as spiritually, and that a global society was emerging. A global identity would overcome the differences that currently divide the world. Writing in 1975, for example, he could declare with aplomb that there was 'no longer a question of whether or not there will be world government by the year 2000'.[7] The questions really are: 'how it will come into being – by cataclysm, drift, or more or less rational design'.[8]

II

Though Mendlovitz gave due regard to the other values of WOMP, he believed that peace had to be accorded primacy in theory and priority in practice. His writings until 1982 focused almost exclusively on the value of peace. However, at least initially, his definition of peace was rather restricted – he considered it almost synonymous with prevention of war. His approach to peace could be characterized as legal-institutional. His conviction was that war could be prevented with the help of appropriately enacted international laws.

Mendlovitz discussed the contribution of law to the study of war prevention. He argued, 'It is sufficient to think of law as the empirical processes of legal institutions that an intelligent and moderately informed person would characterize as law. On this basis, it is then reasonable to assert that within most modern states, law interacts with the significant social process of the society, and that this is true whether law is viewed as a product of social forces or as an active agent within the social system. This constant interaction of law and social processes provides an initial rationale for the adoption of a legal perspective whenever a major social problem is being investigated, especially if one remains sensitive to the unsolved problems of casualty in the interaction.'[9]

Mendlovitz continued, 'In all modern states, of course, legal institutions are used as the principal means for the control and regulation of violence. Although the international legal system exhibits a rather primitive formal structure at present, and regulates violence, to the extent that it does so, differently than does law in domestic societies, the legal perspective is nonetheless applicable to international problems.'[10]

Mendlovitz held that international law provided a realistic general framework. He was not deterred by the common criticism that solutions suggested from a legal-institutional perspective were too idealistic and utopian to be put into practice. As he pointed out,

'One should not minimize the fact that the experience of living under law is almost universal and that law can be appealed to in all societies as a rational method for achieving order and even justice in human affairs.'[11] Turning around the position taken by the critics, he added:

> Aside from a very few philosophical anarchists, most reasonable people – and this would include, for example, even revolutionaries and victims of oppression – envision a world in which law is properly used to control violence, resolve conflicts, redress harms and promote social justice. In short, law as a method and goal for a world peace movement makes sense to the people of the world and to their governments. It is on the basis of this reasoning that it seems possible to conclude that law does provide a realistic and logical point of departure for a serious study of war prevention. Using *World Peace through World Law*, the student is asked to evaluate whether the existing provisions of the United Nations Charter, the suggested Clark-Sohn revisions, or alternatives offered by other writers are necessary, feasible and fair.[12]

In order to make implementation of international law effective, it was imperative that a transnational police force be created and assigned the task. Mendlovitz discussed the nature of the proposed transnational force, taking into account size, recruitment and training, location, financing, control and operations. He further discussed the impact of such a transnational police force – on the operations of enforcement agencies and on attitudes and behaviour. The transition process was then elaborated. The issues of general constituency mobilization, UN enforcement operations, control procedures and the relevant norms of enforcement were considered in the strategy for establishing a transnational police force. Under this, he discussed the roles of three different sets of people and organizations, and these three groups, he said, could be viewed as a system or subsystem operating within the overall context of world politics.[13] He contended, 'A transnational enforcement agency can be established only if it enjoys at least limited support among all three systems. The strategy proposed here is to increase the leverage of the people in the third system by institutions within the second system to encourage powerful actors in the first system to give greater weight in decision making to long range self-interest.'[14]

Mendlovitz discussed the United Nations enforcement operations, third party intervention and the role of the transnational police in the future. He made a sketch of hypothetical developments in order to show how an effectively functioning police force could be developed. The transnational police force would help in creating a more humane 1990s and would enhance justice and peace, provide rewards and punishments, and reduce the use of military power.[15] The transnational police force would work as an integral part of international organization. Such an arrangement would have a dual advantage: More directly, 'the goal is to increase the governing ability of global organizations',[16] and at a deeper level, it would help in transforming the very nature of politics. The sharp demarcation presently maintained between national and international politics is based on strictly defined principles of sovereignty, nationalism and territoriality. The division not only generates conflicts that could have been easily avoided, it also makes their resolution difficult by robbing international law of the authority so easily granted to municipal law. The transnational police could help in reversing the logic of such injurious distinctions. By operating at levels that are at once national and transnational, the police 'domesticates international politics and transnationalizes national politics'.[17]

Mendlovitz suggested that a course on war prevention be taught in social science departments in colleges and universities.[18] Such a course would create the intellectual environment conducive to world peace.

In his later writings, Mendlovitz seemed to be intertwining the values of peace and social justice when he started upholding the ideal of 'just world peace'. He (along with R.B.J. Walker) explained how peace and justice could be intertwined. They argued, "Peace must be understood as more than just the absence of war. Hence, the juxtaposition of peace with justice. They all take it for granted that peace is threatened by processes that are global in scope. Hence, the phrase 'just world peace' in which each of these three words is taken equally seriously."[19] At the same time, Mendlovitz began to identify social movements as the most important source of global transformation. Social movements 'raise crucial questions about the nature of political life in a world of rapid change, both in terms of where political action ought to take place and in what form it ought to occur'.[20]

Mendlovitz (along with Walker) tried to link the concepts of peace and politics and looked at and analyzed them from the perspective of social movements. Mendlovitz discussed the different traditional meanings of peace and how the concept of peace underwent a fundamental transformation with the development of nuclear weapons and because of the complex nature of the forces giving rise to modern political conflicts. He argued, 'Thus, not only is it necessary to treat peace as more than just the absence of war, and to refuse to separate peace from justice, it is also necessary to understand the pursuit of peace as part of a widespread, if often inchoate, attempt to generate new forms of political practice in the face of fundamental historical change.'[21]

Mendlovitz pointed out, 'Whatever else is going on in the modern world, the most pressing problems on the political agenda arise from or are intensified by the increasingly global scale of the processes that now shape human activity everywhere. They all also agree that whatever else is going on at the level of the state or even among international institutions, some of the most interesting and hopeful political processes are to be found among the numerous recently formed social movements.'[22] Mendlovitz added:

> While states and the states system may still dominate political life, the most significant sources of historical change are now to be found in both large scale structural transformations and small scale social movements that occur both 'above' and 'below' the level of the state. They do not suggest that the state is on its way out as a political force. Rather, they explore the connections that seem to be occurring between large scale global processes and local social movements, which remain more or less invisible to those who examine political life even at the level of the state, and will be significantly transformed as a consequence of these processes and struggles. They argue that new understandings of what peace might mean and how it might be pursued have to arise out of an assessment of these process and struggles.[23]

Mendlovitz thus juxtaposed the themes of peace and social justice. The emergence of social movements was itself not new. They could be traced back to the 1860s. Their emergence could be traced back to three major historical processes that took place after the Age of Discovery.[24] 'The ideological revolution of egalitarianism, the technological and scientific revolution and the closely allied industrial cybernetic revolution'[25] had led to the evolution of a global community. They had also converged problems such as war, poverty, social injustice, ecological instability, identity crisis and alienation into global issues. At the same time, the gradual failure of the United

Nations and its related agencies in finding solutions to these problems convinced the concerned activists across the world that traditional international institutions could not provide appropriate or adequate forums to resolve these problems. What was needed instead was direct involvement in what could be called global politics.[26]

The difference, therefore, was that whereas the older movements[27] were 'concerned primarily with changing the relationship between employers and workers' or 'with the assertion of identity between competing ethno-national groups', the more contemporary movements had developed broader perspectives and scope. They promoted causes such as peace, human rights, environment protection, rights of indigenous peoples and alternate forms of economic life. Mendlovitz was not entirely happy, however, with the anti-statist stance often taken by such groups. The basic challenge before these social movements, he thought, was 'to generate creative connections with other progressive actors, whether they were people working within state structures, international organizations, or even states themselves'.[28] The positive impact of social movements was described by Mendlovitz in the following manner:

> Nevertheless, historical experience suggests that some of the most creative energies for social change do come from social movements. They present a sober assessment of specific challenges that have to be met. They offer some idea of how the grand visions and aspirations of the past need to be reworked to respond more coherently to the conditions of the present. They raise crucial questions about the nature of political life in a world of rapid change, both in terms of where political action ought to take place and in what form it ought to occur.[29]

III

Mendlovitz envisaged the preferred world order system as an alternative to the present world order system, and as one that would more likely be able to realize world order values. The preferred world would be based on what might be called 'system change' or 'system transformation' and various active social forces in this world would ultimately help in the transition to the preferred world. He also considered and depicted transition tactics and pathways. Mendlovitz pointed out, 'Part of imaging of the future is to consider transition tactics and pathways. These should not be thought of as predictions, but rather as indications of how system change could come about and as recommendations for actions that would embody world order values. The depiction of a transition process cannot be a substitute for a theory of social change, but it is an essential element in a world order approach.'[30]

We will now look at the various research strategies advocated by Mendlovitz as early as in 1975 for moving from the contemporary world to the preferred world. Firstly, there should be appropriate criteria for evaluating workability and feasibility as well as appropriate testing procedures for each strategy. Secondly, notions of time and time horizons were very critical with regard to both feasibility and workability. Thirdly, the dynamics of the relevant environment within which one's desired changes must take place should be adequately defined. The environment was usually described as the nation-state system itself and very little destabilizing or fundamental dynamics was ascribed to it. However, this could jeopardize our conceptualization of alternative futures and transition processes. Fourthly, the conceptualization and presentation of a preferred world was usually very difficult.[31] Mendlovitz raised a number of fundamental questions about the nature of the preferred world: For example, 'How much and what kind of behavioural detail should be used to describe the workings of the preferred world? What are the differences between revolutionary and reformist rhetoric and, more importantly, what bearing does this answer have on concrete strategies and programmes? How much attention is paid to immediate public issues and how are they made to relate to the preferred future, to explicate the method and perspective of the author?'[32]

As director of WOMP, Mendlovitz also elaborated on the various 'possible alternatives' for the transition to the preferred world put forward by different WOMP participants from different regions. In this context, some of the issues that Mendlovitz had argued and that had surfaced during WOMP discussions were:

- The extent to which an institutional or single actor oriented conception of the world political system was useful either for understanding how the system operated, how it might be made to change, or how it could or should operate. Such conceptions seemed to some to stultify imaginative thinking about alternatives and to mask important change potentials in the current system.
- In thinking about transition, some argued for the 'primacy of the domestic factor', that is, fundamental reform in national

societies, particularly within the major countries, preceding global social change. Others argued for the primacy of the global agenda and the critical role of the transnational functional and political movements and institutions. This debate identified two further issues needing more attention:

- Which problems required policy making and review at what level of social organization from the individual to the global? How much centralization and decentralization were appropriate in the various substantive arenas? What were the relevant criteria for deciding the appropriate level or mix of levels?
- What were and what might be the linkages between these levels for purposes of analysis, policy making and practical implementation?[33]

Mendlovitz believed that world government was inevitable by 2000. As he himself put it, 'It is my considered judgement that there is no longer any question of whether or not there will be world government by the year 2000. As I see it, the question we should be addressing to ourselves are: How it will come into being – by cataclysm, drift, or more or less national design – and whether it will be totalitarian, benignly elitist, or participatory (the probabilities being in that order).'[34]

Mendlovitz concluded with the following remarks: 'In short, I believe that the global community has emerged and global governance is not far behind. To my mind, this book and the other volumes in the *Preferred Worlds for the 1990s* series are a contribution to the serious dialogue about what will be the normative basis and the constitutive structure of the global community. Hopefully, this set of essays will contribute to the creation of the social processes necessary for a more just and peaceful world order.'[35]

IV

Samuel S. Kim emphasized a cross-cultural, transnational search for a just and humane world order. Kim's approach may be summarized as 'transnational and cross-cultural in value preferences, systematic in scope and interdisciplinary in methodology, giving special attention to attitudinal, normative, behavioural and structural problems involved in the politics of system transformation. The issues, patterns and trends of world politics are described, evaluated and projected, and strategies for bringing about an alternative world order system are suggested – all within this explicitly normative framework of world order studies.'[36]

Kim was equally critical of realism, neo-realism and Marxism, the dominant approaches in the study of international relations, and sought to provide an alternative dimension to world order studies.[37] He believed that the world was constituted of contradictory, contending and counter-pulling forces. 'The challenging task of world order studies,' he said, 'was to become familiar with the contradictory forces of creativity and destruction that affect the struggle for human emancipation.'[38] The search for a just world order 'necessarily centres upon the mastery of these contending forces'.[39] A dialectical framework of challenge and response must, therefore, become the basis of macro-level structural studies of the world system. This approach involves a diagnostic or prognostic task of describing present world order conditions and trends; a modelling task of designing preferred futures; and a prescriptive task of mapping a transition process, including concrete steps and an overall strategy.[40]

One of the most central and elusive tasks in world order studies was the development of a sound theory and praxis of system transformation. Kim defined system transformation as 'the art of the possible or the art of the impossible, depending on how realism is defined'.[41] He attempted to 'define and elaborate the underlying assumptions, operational values and principles, images of preferred world futures, and transition strategies of a just world order approach to system transformation'.[42]

The general methodology and orientation applied by Kim was that of an alternative, non-Machiavellian, non-Marxist, non-violent, non-deterministic and non-apocalyptic approach to system transformation. He argued, 'System transformation does not ipso facto mean political integration or centralization at the global level, much less world government. Rather, it means a fundamental change in the existing values, norms and structure in such a way, and to such an extent, that a different configuration of actors with different orientations toward power, security, well-being and governance emerge. This is what is meant by the quest for a just world order.'[43]

Kim provided a bird's eye view of the transformation of international politics. He took a system transforming approach to world order. He re-examined and reformulated various meanings of the term to establish an integrated conception of world order transformation. He described transformation variously as a 'transcultural concept, transdisciplinary concept, revolutionary concept and as a diachronic concept'. He defined world order transformation as 'a series of long term and largely irreversible changes and trends in the established values, norms and structure of international society, resulting in a new pattern of relationship between its constituent units (actors)'.[44] He added, 'In short, I conceptualize world order transformation as a dialectical and discontinuous process entailing broad and fundamental changes in the defining characteristics of the international system (that is, the values, norms and structure).'[45]

The system could be said to have been transformed if there were some basic changes in the key variables, such as change in the composition of the system actors, change in the power structure, change in the norms of statecraft, and change in the pattern of the system process. Kim defined and elaborated the basic terms – values, norms and structure – used in his concept of diachronic analysis.[46]

Kim examined the degree of continuity and change in the historical international systems. He focused on international norms and structure as casually dominant variables in shaping the behaviour of the actors and in maintaining, reforming or transforming international society, as part of his diachronic analysis. The critical turning point in the transition from the medieval to the modern system of international relations was the Treaty of Westphalia. Kim, therefore, accepted 'Westphalia as a starting point against which subsequent changes can be broadly described and evaluated for their overall impact on the evolution of international systems through four historical periods: the Classical period (1648–1789); the Concert period (1814–1914); the League period (1919–39) and the post-war period (1945–present)'.[47]

During the Classical period, the principle of state sovereignty, or its corollary, the principle of state equality, was the dominant principle. It shifted to the emergence of the concept of state-nation or nation-state during the Concert period. This period also witnessed the rise of the international governmental organizations (IGOs) and non-governmental organizations (NGOs) with their own norms and rules. The League period saw the first organized attempt to restructure the normative foundations of world order through the establishment of the League of Nations in the wake of World War I. Another step forward in the progressive delegitimization of war was the Kellogg-Briand Pact of 1928 (also known as the Pact of Paris) of

1928. During the 1930s, the interaction between the nation-states was dominated by fragmentation, autarky and unilateralism.[48]

The post-war period saw the demise of the Eurocentric and multipolar international system and the emergence of a new global system. The new global system was comprised of two superpowers, half a dozen exhausted middle powers (former great powers), small powers (ex-colonies) and mini powers (ex-mini colonies) along with an increasing number of non-state actors (such as IGOs, NGOs and transnational corporations) and international regimes. There had been a shift in the post-war system from a state-centric to a mixed actor structure. Kim pointed out that though the post-war system began with a bipolar structure, yet, there had been a more dramatic decline of bipolarization. The 1960 Declaration on the Granting of Independence to Colonial Territories and Peoples, the 1970 Declaration of the Common Heritage of Mankind, the Declaration on the Establishment of a New International Economic Order (NIEO), the Programme of Action on the Establishment of an NIEO, and the Charter of Economic Rights and Duties of States posed major challenges to all the post-war economic regimes moulded in the image of Pax Americana.[49]

Thereafter, Kim discussed the change and continuity in world politics. The predominant concern of actors since the inception of the modern states system at Westphalia had remained 'security'. Kim pointed out that 'every "world order planning" since Westphalia has been to avert the last great war ... Every world order system has been maintained or changed by the interactions of a few dominant actors, and has been designed more to manage inter-state relations than to satisfy global human needs. Excepting the League period as somewhat anomic and abnormal, the longevity (and viability) of every world order system has become progressively shorter.'[50]

There should be a fundamental change in the status and function of the state in the global system for system transformation, argued Kim. With the rapid rise and proliferation of non-state actors, nuclear weapons of global range, and transnational transactions, the nation-state would die out gradually. And with that, the new sense of transformation politics, Kim pointed out, was translated into 'clarion calls for a new international economic order, a new world information order, a new international technological order, a new world food order, a new global ocean regime, and so on. The interchangeable use of the terms, "international" and "world" (or global), also suggest a dialectical tension between the forces of a new "world" order and of a new "international" order. The transformative forces for a struggle of this magnitude, once leashed, can be halted or detracted, but cannot be banned for good."[51]

Kim concluded that the crucial question was: 'Will this world historical transformation come about through another cataclysmic global war as of yore, or can we intervene in time to shift it into a non-violent and non-apocalyptical direction?'[52]

Kim attempted to explore the relevance of a world order theory for the pursuit of a more just and humane world. He examined the contending conceptions of international relations theory and then suggested the general contours of a world order theory in its own and comparative terms. Kim defined theory as 'a logically interrelated set of propositions and hypotheses that specify a causal relationship between one or more antecedent (independent) variables and a consequent (dependent) variable capable of explaining and predicting specified classes of phenomena'.[53] He adopted the instrumental view of theory to world order studies (because it could help in knowing where we are and where we are going or ought to be going).

At the heart of Kim's approach was the belief that the politics of centralism and the conventional agendas of governance and global reform would not work. Substantial restructuring needed to be carried out at the state and sub-state levels.[54] The WOMP approach had focused primarily on the realization of values as solutions to world problems. It had identified itself with the voices and the struggles of the oppressed, in order to provide an alternative dimension to world order studies.[55] Kim concluded with the following observation:

> World order studies has two ambitions: to establish an enduring academic presence and to provide a basis for a movement for social change that encompasses issues of global scale. Only time will tell whether its reading of contemporary history as disaster prone and as favourable to the struggle of oppressed peoples is correct, and whether, if correct, these struggles can be carried to completion without provoking catastrophe. As it is, the world order approach provides an alternative to both Machiavellianism and Marxism for students concerned about the shape of things to come in international life.[56]

V

Quite like Mendlovitz, Samuel S. Kim, too, conceptualized peace essentially in terms of prevention of war. Pointing to the 'pervasiveness of war through time and across space', Kim[57] argued that it continued to act 'as the main motivating force of change in relations among sovereign states'. He lamented the fact that 'there are no effective mechanisms of peaceful change in international society'.[58]

Kim observed that there had been three distinct stages in the study of war, each with a different approach: 'the mono-disciplinary approach of traditional international relations, the interdisciplinary approach of peace research, and the transdisciplinary approach of world order studies'.[59] Discussing the conceptual and methodological assumptions and value preferences of these approaches, Kim rejected as inadequate all the variants found in traditional international relations theory, be it the 'pessimistic inevitability school', the 'utopian blueprint school', or the 'mono-causal school'.[60]

Kim agreed with Falk that war had to be understood as a 'social system'. Defining the 'war system', both of them argued that it was 'an all-embracing structure of mutually interlocking organizational and behavioural variables, in which violence or force is accepted and legitimized as the ultimate arbiter of social conflicts at all levels of human society'.[61]

Therefore, in order to move decisively from the war system to a peace system, war should be understood in all its dimensions: "It is not easy to disentangle 'war' from its economic, social, psychological, cultural and normative complex of interactions that has shaped human struggle over the course of centuries."[62]

While trying to establish the causes of war, Kim and Falk emphasized the need for an 'interdisciplinary etiological approach, drawing upon insights and findings of relevant disciplines involved in the study of human behaviour in general and human conflict behaviour in particular'.[63] Kim borrowed concepts from different disciplines such as law, philosophy, ethics and theology. Both Falk and he found a definite relationship between war and knowledge, war and ideology, war and survival, war and history, war and security and, lastly, war and world order.[64]

Kim pointed out that the concept of security had been nationalized, militarized and globalized ever since the end of World War II. The concept of 'international regimes' could be employed gainfully in assessing these trends. He divided international security regimes into three categories – 'the international arms trade regime; the international arms control regime; and the international disarmament regime'.[65] The working of these regimes revealed the structural problems in the existing international hierarchy. As long as the militarized conception of security and the present structure of global dominance did not change, the arms race would persist.[66]

Kim was equally concerned about forms of violence other than wars. He defined violence as 'a pathological force that destroys or diminishes life sustaining and life enhancing processes'.[67] Violence needed to be minimized 'in both a narrow (direct/physical) and broad (indirect/structural) sense'.[68]

Kim believed that international law had to play a crucial role in reducing the frequency and intensity of war and violence. It could help in peaceful resolution of differences before they escalated into violent conflicts and wars. At a deeper level, international law could promote world order values. This was so because

> lawmaking is a value shaping and value realizing process. A world order approach requires a teleological appraisal of the role of contemporary international law and law making in terms of widely affirmed human aspirations and needs for peace, economic well-being, social justice and environmental protection.[69]

In this context, Kim analyzed the changing perceptions of international law, as a result of which classical notions of international law were giving way. He argued,

> The nature of international law, or at least the general perception of it, has changed considerably since the Peace of Westphalia. As the normative foundation of the Westphalian international order (1648–1945), classical international law has long been perceived as a juridical expression of the ideological cultural hegemony of the politically dominant Western societies during the heyday of colonial expansionism. The Third World was able to challenge it only collectively, as a global actor in the United Nations lawmaking process. The resulting 'new' or 'contemporary' international law, spawned by the United Nations' legislative process, has gradually come to be directed for the protection of the weak against the interventionary pressures of the strong.[70]

While this was a definite sign of progress, much more was needed to be done. Kim added, "The basic challenge ahead is to seek a better interface between United Nations lawmaking and the voices of the unheard and unrepresented by opening up more and more channels of communication and contact with the non-state social actors and forces struggling at periphery of the present world order system".[71]

VI

Kim pointed out that global inequities, which continued to persist everywhere, had two dimensions – human and national. The human dimension consisted of the fact that the poor of the world did not have access to basic human needs such as food, shelter, safe drinking water, primary health care, literacy and remunerative employment. Hunger persisted not because global food stocks were inadequate, but because global distribution of income was such that the poor had no purchasing capacity. The population explosion in the poorest developing countries, too, could be traced back to poverty, illiteracy and lack of primary health care, leading to high mortality rates. Lack of safe drinking water led to widespread waterborne diseases, such as diarrhoea, malaria and schistosomiasis.[72] The national dimension of global inequities was reflected in the patterns of overdevelopment-underdevelopment, dominance-dependence and centre-periphery relations among states, perpetuated by the post-war economic order established under the Bretton Woods agreements. The demand for a New International Economic Order made in the 1970s addressed this dimension of global inequities and sought equitable access to capital, markets, resources and technology.[73] The demand did not succeed because the capitalist world economy had sufficient payoffs and penalties at its command to divide the poor nations. Moreover, there existed a 'capitalist global knowledge industry which sells modernization theory as the only path to the promised land'.[74]

Kim examined the defining characteristics of the two normative principles of distributive justice arising from these dimensions of inequities: the NIEO principle and the Basic Human Needs principle. The elusive role of the state for human well-being was the central normative dilemma. Since the state continued to exist despite ideological, geopolitical and developmental divisions, it was the only organization which could promote general economic well-being and fulfil the Basic Human Needs principle. However, sometimes, the state would promote only urban centred class interests, and acts as an instrument of status drive in international politics.[75]

The two principles of distributive justice could not be realized unless the poorest countries and the worst-off groups participated in the decision making process at the national and global levels.[76] He stressed the need to reconcile the two and suggested possible ways of doing so in world order studies.[77]

VII

On the question of social justice, Kim confined himself largely to the discussion of human rights. Human rights are those claims and demands that are essential to the protection of human life and the enhancement of human dignity.[78] Human rights, according to Kim, have passed through three successive stages: 'the first generation of civil and political rights; the second generation of social, economic and cultural rights; and the third generation of solidarity rights'.[79]

The struggle for human rights was part of the age old struggle for human emancipation, which originated initially in the West in the wake of the Enlightenment, and had now spread all over the world. But human rights still remained a major issue even in the First World. A normative inquiry into global human rights politics was, therefore, extremely important.[80] Since there was widespread human rights abuse, an interface between the human rights and world order agendas, according to Kim, should be based on the following premises:

- Every human life, regardless of its location in social, territorial and ethnic space, is of equal value and, therefore, entitled to equal protection;
- Each human life is an end itself and, as such, it cannot be devalued as a means to the rights of others;
- Each human person or group is entitled to democratic participation in the shaping and reshaping of human rights values;
- Each human person is entitled to equal benefit in the sharing of human rights values;
- Human rights are mutually interdependent and indivisible, but some rights are more basic and essential than others in human development; and
- The affirmation of the supreme value of human life and dignity is the only way to reconcile the conflicts between cultural relativism and universal human rights norms.[81]

The world order-human rights interface would, therefore, require active pursuit of the following tasks: 'clarifying of core assumptions and principles; redefining human rights; formulating the human rights – human needs nexus; and establishing a world order hierarchy of human rights'.[82]

Kim was influenced by the works of Barry Commoner[83] and Harold and Margaret Sprout[84] on environmental issues. He used the notion of the 'ecological problematic' to encompass 'the whole indivisible complex of conceptual, psychological, normative and structural processes and problems that set the parameters of system transformation'.[85]

Kim argued that the ecological crisis was historically a product of the worldwide pursuance of what he called 'centre model core industrial capitalism'.[86] This form of capitalism produced exploitative and unjust social structures, and distorted domestic as well as international development. He believed that ecological stability and human well-being were interrelated. A healthy model of economic development, therefore, had to take care of 'eco-development' as well. According to him, 'a just and humane eco-order should satisfy the following value requirements: socio-economic justice; basic human rights; humane governance; and ecological safety'.[87] This called for a transformation of both intra-national and inter-national structures. It also called for changes in the basic social values reflected in individual behaviour and lifestyles.[88]

Kim divided the global environment into a complex set of distinct, but closely intertwined and interacting, sub-systems. On the one hand, there was the natural environment, consisting of atmospheric, marine and terrestrial environments. On the other hand, there was the social environment, constituted by such human activities as population growth, resource use and militarization.[89]

In order to know the extent to which the present international system was capable of realizing the world order value of ecological balance, Kim examined three types of activities: expansion of knowledge, shaping of values, and implementation processes. With regard to the knowledge expansion process, Kim emphasized research, information exchange and monitoring because these were delineated in the United Nations Environmental Programme (UNEP). The value shaping process was concerned essentially with the preparation and adoption of multilateral declarations, conventions and treaties. Kim undertook a detailed discussion of the two

United Nations Conferences on Human Environment held at Stockholm in 1972 and at Nairobi in 1982. He brought out the notable features of the Stockholm Declaration and examined its limitations. He reviewed the progress made in environmental law in the post-Stockholm period and the role of UNEP therein. He drew attention to the problems in UNEP's implementation process and tried to redefine its implementation role.[90] Kim concluded:

> Ultimately, the quest for a decent environment is but one part of the quest for a more just and humane world order. The quest to bring the social environment into harmony with the natural environment does not seem too promising without normative, structural and behavioural transformations in both domestic and international societies. The transformations envisaged in this alternative eco-developmental path depend on the extent to which non-state actors – dedicated private citizens, local and national groups and transnational NGOs, all currently crying out for recognition at the edges of the power structure – can mobilize their renewable normative energies and political resources to form a broadbased, sustainable movement.[91]

Kim's attitude is best described as 'concerned optimism', a combination of pessimism about the present human condition, but necessary self-mobilizing optimism about human capacity, the principle of indeterminacy as well as the possibility of continuity of the present amongst others. The preferred future world required, according to Kim, a transformation from the domain of 'facts' to the domain of 'values'.[92]

Kim thought of transition as 'a series of normatively purposive and politically planned processes designed to change the course of human development; we mean the process of building relevant and reliable bridges and pathways to connect us to the preferred futures'.[93]

This involved 'the designing of possible alternative scenarios of preferred world futures' and laying down 'broad orientational guides for the transition process'.[94] A constant balance would have to be maintained between the desirable normative goals and feasible transition strategies in the search for a relevant utopia. 'How' and 'where' we look were the two determining factors for the prospect of a relevant utopia.[95] Kim added, 'The quest for a just world order is a collective, transnational struggle in which individuals and groups at different systemic levels join hands, actively participating in ongoing social, political, economic and cultural processes that embrace all of humanity.'[96]

Notes

1. Richard Falk, Samuel S. Kim and Saul H. Mendlovitz, 'Introduction – Voices of the Oppressed', in *Toward a Just World Order: Studies on a Just World Order,* Vol. I, Richard Falk, Samuel S. Kim and Saul H. Mendlovitz, eds (Boulder: Westview Press, 1982a), 14.
2. Richard Falk, Samuel S. Kim and Saul H. Mendlovitz, 'General Introduction', in *Toward a Just World Order,* 2–3.
3. Ibid., 3.
4. Saul H. Mendlovitz, ed., *On the Creation of a Just World Order: Preferred Worlds for the 1990s* (New Delhi: Orient Longman, 1975), ix.
5. Richard Falk, Samuel S. Kim and Saul H. Mendlovitz, 'General Introduction', in *Toward a Just World Order: Studies on a Just World Order,* Vol. 1, Richard Falk, Samuel S. Kim and Saul H. Mendlovitz, eds (Boulder: Westview Press, 1982a), 3.
6. Richard Falk, Samuel S. Kim and Saul H. Mendlovitz, 'General Introduction', 5.
7. Saul H. Mendlovitz, 'Introduction', in *On the Creation of a Just World Order,* Saul H. Mendlovitz, ed. (New Delhi: Orient Longman, 1975), xvi.
8. Ibid.
9. Saul H. Mendlovitz, 'The Study of War Prevention: Toward a Disciplined View', in *Toward a Theory of War Prevention: The Strategy of World Order,* Vol. I, Richard Falk and Saul H. Mendlovitz, eds (New York: World Law Fund, 1966a), 387.
10. Ibid., 387–88.
11. Ibid., 388.
12. Ibid.
13. Robert C. Johansen and Saul H. Mendlovitz, 'The Role of Enforcement of Just Law in the Establishment of a New International Order: A Proposal for a Transnational Police Force', in *International Law: A Contemporary Perspective: Studies on a Just World Order,* Vol. 2, Richard Falk, Friedrich Kratochwil and Saul H. Mendlovitz, eds (Boulder: Westview Press, 1982b), 355–60.
14. Ibid., 1982b, 360.
15. Ibid., 1982b, 360–63.
16. Ibid., 347.
17. Ibid.
18. Saul H. Mendlovitz, 'The Study of War Prevention: Toward a Disciplined View', in *Toward a Theory of War Prevention,* Richard Falk and Saul H.

Mendlovitz, eds, 385. The major source of war prevention came from a book, *World Peace through World Law,* by Granville Clark and Louis B. Sohn. For details, see Granville Clark and Louis B. Sohn, *World Peace through World Law,* 3rd Edition (Cambridge, Mass.: Harvard University Press, 1966).

19. R.B.J. Walker and Saul H. Mendlovitz, 'Peace, Politics and Contemporary Social Movements', in *Towards a Just World Peace: Perspective from Social Movements,* Saul H. Mendlovitz and R.B.J. Walker, eds (London: Butterworths, 1987), 11.
20. Ibid.
21. Ibid., 5.
22. Ibid.
23. Ibid., 5–6.
24. Saul H. Mendlovitz, 'Introduction', in Saul H. Mendlovitz, ed., *On the Creation of a Just World Order,* xvi.
25. Ibid., xvi.
26. Ibid., xvi-xvii.
27. Ibid., 9.
28. Ibid., 10.
29. Ibid., 10–11.
30. Richard Falk, Samuel S. Kim and Saul H. Mendlovitz, 'General Introduction', in *Toward a Just World Order: Studies on a Just World Order, Vol.1,* Richard Falk, Samuel S. Kim and Saul H. Mendlovitz, eds (Boulder: Westview Press, 1982a), 4.
31. Saul H. Mendlovitz, 'Introduction', in *On the Creation of a Just World Order,* Saul H. Mendlovitz, ed. (New Delhi: Orient Longman, 1975), xiv.
32. Ibid., xiv.
33. Ibid., xv-xvi.
34. Ibid., xvi.
35. Ibid., xvii.
36. Samuel S. Kim, *The Quest for a Just World Order* (Boulder: Westview Press, 1984), 2.
37. Richard Falk and Samuel S. Kim, 'World Order Studies and the World System', in *Contending Approaches to World System Analysis,* William R. Thompson, ed. (London: Sage Publications, 1993), 203–04.
38. Samuel S. Kim, *The Quest for a Just World Order,* 2.
39. Ibid.
40. Richard Falk and Samuel S. Kim, 'World Order Studies and the World System', 211.
41. Samuel S. Kim, *The Quest For a Just World Order,* 9.

42. Ibid., 12.
43. Ibid.
44. Ibid., 17.
45. Ibid., 21.
46. Ibid.
47. Ibid., 27.
48. Ibid., 27–42.
49. Ibid., 44–46.
50. Ibid., 52.
51. Ibid., 55.
52. Ibid.
53. Ibid., 58.
54. Richard Falk and Samuel S. Kim, 'World Order Studies and the World System', in *Contending Approaches to World System Analysis*, 203–04.
55. Ibid., 203–04.
56. Ibid., 233.
57. Richard Falk and Samuel S. Kim, 'General Introduction', in *The War System: An Interdisciplinary Approach,* Richard Falk and Samuel S. Kim, eds (Boulder: Westview Press, 1980), 1.
58. Ibid., 1.
59. Ibid., 6.
60. Ibid., 3–4.
61. Ibid., 2.
62. Ibid., 1–6.
63. Ibid., 5.
64. Ibid., 7–12.
65. Samuel S. Kim, *The Quest for a Just World Order,* op. cit., 116.
66. Ibid., 132–3.
67. Ibid., 95.
68. Ibid.
69. Samuel S. Kim, 'The United Nations, Law Making and World Order', *Alternatives* (1983), 656.
70. Ibid., 644.
71. Ibid., 670.
72. Samuel S. Kim, *The Quest for a Just World Order,* 137–50.
73. Ibid., 150.
74. Ibid., 191.
75. Ibid., 162–70 and 192–93.
76. Ibid., 193.

77. Ibid., 194.
78. Ibid., 209.
79. Ibid., 197.
80. Ibid., 196.
81. Ibid., 208.
82. Ibid., 207.
83. Barry Commoner, *The Closing Circle: Nature, Man and Technology*, (New York: Alfred A. Knopf, 1971).
84. Samuel S. Kim, *The Quest for a Just World Order*, 245.
85. Ibid., 293.
86. Ibid., 246.
87. Ibid., 250.
88. Ibid.
89. Ibid., 251–70.
90. Ibid., 274–92.
91. Ibid., 297.
92. Ibid., 322.
93. Ibid., 333–34.
94. Ibid., 302.
95. Ibid., 341.
96. Ibid., 301.

7 Assessing WOMP

Towards a Critique

I

It is easy to dismiss WOMP as a dismal failure. Critics would not be wrong in pointing out that none of the core values of WOMP have been realized even remotely. The world is still ridden with both domestic and international conflicts; large segments of populations across the globe continue to suffer from poverty, unemployment, backwardness, poor health, low life expectancy and illiteracy; democracy is non-existent or precarious in several countries; human rights are routinely violated; inequality of all kinds persist; and ecological crises have only deepened. We are no closer to what the preferred world ought to be even in the middle of the 2000s, let alone the 1990s. In retrospect, WOMP appears to have woven nothing but naïve and empty dreams.

What seems to make such criticism legitimate is the nature of WOMP's claims. After all, its proponents had striven hard to give their work a 'scientific' character. They were not interested in abstract or contra-factual philosophical engagement with normative questions. They were, in their own assessment, doing 'policy research'. They set values as goals to be achieved, they looked for 'operational definitions' of these values, they worked out 'strategies' and timeframes for making the transition from the actual to the desirable and even designed quantitative indices for measuring progress. They claimed their work was not only analytical and practical, but also predictive. They wished to be taken seriously as futurologists. The founder director of the project had claimed that there could be 'no question' that world government would not be achieved by 2000.[1] He and his colleagues were proved utterly wrong. Could they not now hide behind the common excuse that large scale, unanticipated developments do occur sometimes, as they did in the late 1980s and early 1990s? They might be better off admitting that their 'science' was unsound, if not altogether bogus.

There is no defending the WOMP theorists on these counts. First of all, they must admit that their 'science' had indeed let them down. They could then claim that they were not the only ones so let down. Realists of a 'scientific' temperament did not come out any less scathed by the unanticipated developments. Social 'scientists' of all descriptions have often met the same fate in the last five decades. One might argue, therefore, that there was something bogus about the whole project of building social and behavioural sciences, so fashionable and so dominant in the 1960s, particularly in the United States. WOMP was formally launched in the late 1960s in the United States. It simply got ensnared. We must remember that WOMP did not start that way. In its formative years, it was more 'traditional' in its espousal of peace.

There has been a long tradition of social inquiry associated with the spirit of the Enlightenment – a combination of faith in rationalism, progress and science. Many idealists and visionaries were drawn to it. Marx was one of them. He too made predictions that went terribly wrong. His communist vision was never realized. But has his analysis and critique of capitalism been proved wrong by that failure? In all such cases, a more balanced approach would be to separate the analytical from the predictive and the prescriptive. WOMP should be no exception.

II

If, in methodological terms, the limitations of WOMP were actually the limitations of 'scientific' enterprise in social 'sciences', in philosophical terms, its limitations were the limitations of liberalism. WOMP was out and out a liberal project in its assumptions, aspirations, predilections and prejudices. Its complete aversion to the very idea of revolutionary politics, not as a virtue but even as a necessary evil, remained undiminished even when its preferred politics of intellectual and pedagogic engagement bore no fruit. WOMP started off as a project of Western – in fact, American – liberals. However, even when its narrow base was sought to be expanded by including non-Western theorists, those thus included were all liberals, whether they came from Asia or Africa. The 1960s was the decade of ideological juxtapositions, but WOMP never thought of including in its ranks a Soviet, East European or independent Marxist, or even a non-Marxist socialist. WOMP sought to build a world order model after dropping half the ideological world of that time from its considerations. Thus, WOMP opened itself to the charge that it was doing nothing but packing in suitably subtle idealist disguise a form of Pax Americana.

This charge could not have been more unfair. WOMP was liberal, no doubt, but it was the most comprehensive liberal critique of the dominant liberal assumptions, arrangements and institutions that characterized the post-war 'free world'. Falk was vociferous about the 'invisible oppression' that marked First World democracies. If Third World intellectuals found Soviet style socialism attractive despite its authoritarianism, the reason was that the most brutish forms of capitalism in the Third World were tolerated, even encouraged and sponsored, by the First World liberal regimes. Kim located the roots of most existing problems in the inequities of the liberal capitalist international order. All WOMP theorists were critical of the Bretton Woods institutions, they highlighted the structures of dependence these institutions had created and perpetuated, and the peripheralization and pauperization they had caused in the Third World. WOMP theorists supported the demand for a New International Economic Order.

WOMP theorists argued that metropolitan capitalism controlled the production and distribution worldwide, not merely of material goods, but also ideas and knowledge. Its hold over global academia and popular media was so complete that it could reproduce endlessly replicas of its own image in the Third World. The modernization theory was a prime example of such concealed manipulation. Propagated by the American social theorists of the 1950s and 1960s, the theory promised a painless passage to progress and prosperity to the Third World policy planners, alluring them into giving it preference over its alternatives, be these the Soviet style planning and regulation of the economy or the more indigenous and locally specific paths of development.

WOMP theorists, particularly Rajni Kothari, built a trenchant critique of this model of development, showing that it had not merely failed miserably in delivering the goods, but had also increased the gap between the rich and the poor and led to massive dislocations and unprecedented human suffering, unemployment, serious ethnic and racial tensions, dependence on massive external borrowings and vulnerability to external pressures. A small, capital intensive modern sector had been created at the expense of large, labour intensive, subsistence based sectors of the economy.[2]

Global capitalism thrived not merely by creating dependency in investments and manufacturing, but also by promoting consumerist aspirations. Fights against it, therefore, involved not merely creating autonomous and self-reliant alternative models of production, but also creating artificial needs. WOMP theorists were in favour of not only an alternative path of development, but an alternative notion of development itself, based on the notion of meeting the minima of 'basic human needs'. They gave a call for 'ethics of consumption'. Overconsumption led as much to social distortions and destruction as did forced underconsumption in backward economies.

Not all liberals, however, were equally vehement in their criticism of world capitalist economy. The WOMP critique is a product not of liberalism per se, but of a particular kind of liberalism. This later kind of liberalism is not a champion of unbridled freedom of the market or of international trade; it has no stomach for the instability, inequities and injustice that laissez-faire can often produce. WOMP's liberalism reflects a clear preference for political liberalism heavily infused with a welfarist spirit over the economic liberalism represented by libertarians.

III

WOMP is much better known for its critique of realist and neo-realist interpretations of international relations as well as world order. Its critique challenges the core assumptions made by these interpretations in fundamental ways.

The most fundamental assumption of realism relates to the centrality, sanctity and irreplaceability of states as the basic constituent actors of world politics. WOMP has a more pluralist view and believes that non-state actors such as transnational organizations, sub-national groups and people's movements play an increasingly important role in the contemporary world. More crucially, non-state actors change the very nature of world politics because they are neither prisoners of the national security paradigm, nor do they engage in the conflict producing competitive struggle for power. In such a world, there is no room for taking lightly what was earlier dismissed as the legal-institutional approach. What is needed instead is transforming the nature and functioning of both international law and international organizations. If need be, the United Nations Charter should be changed to allow for an effective interface with non-state actors. International law, too, should be reoriented to reflect the needs, not merely of states, but also of communities. WOMP rejected the realist description of world politics as 'anarchical' and refused to see the division between domestic and international domains as watertight. Rather, it wished to blur the distinction by 'domesticating international politics' and 'externalizing domestic politics'. It even suggested the creation of a 'transnational police force' that would operate simultaneously in both domains.[3]

At another level, WOMP postulated the notion of human security and thereby threw a fundamental challenge to the realist notion of security, which was narrow, militaristic and territorial. Such notions of security bred militarism, a self-perpetuating syndrome that served narrow elite interests and endangered human survival by creating a 'war system', inducing wars and arms race. Human security, on the other hand, protected and promoted people's livelihood, dignity, social and political justice, and a healthy environment.

Closely related to the realist notion of security was the realist notion of peace. Desire for peace was subordinated in realism to the need for security and was, therefore, sought as a secondary value. WOMP very quickly outgrew the negative definition of peace as absence of war and postulated a positive notion of 'just peace', which denoted harmonization of interests. WOMP also broadened the scope of peace efforts by viewing violence as pathology and addressing all forms of collective violence, rather than just war.

IV

In the light of the comments made in the foregoing sections, it should be easy to see that the relevance of WOMP has increased, even though the movement itself might have declined. Globalization, as we witness it today, has a neo-liberal agenda, which undermines self-reliance by forcing the removal of all protectionist policies. At the same time, it is based on the hegemony of the United States, which reflects the changed structure of power hierarchy in the post-Soviet world. Yet, globalization comes packaged as a panacea for all global ills, thanks to American and Western domination in academia and mass media. So overwhelming is this dominance that conventional vocabularies of resistance – emanating in nationalist, regionalist and radical socialist discourses – have been eroded considerably. There is a dire need for reconstructing an effective vocabulary to combat globalization.

Globalism as visualized by the WOMP theorists continues to offer us such a vocabulary. Falk's conceptualization of 'humane governance' based on globalization from below is particularly relevant in the age of globalization from above.[4]

WOMP's contemporary relevance is best described as a counter-hegemonic project the way it was outlined by Antonio Gramsci. Gramsci showed how the materially dominant class used its own normative and conceptual vocabulary in such a manner that it could be uncritically internalized by the dominated classes. He called this the process of hegemonization. He argued that socio-political emancipation was virtually impossible if such internalized beliefs were not systematically destroyed by counter-posing alternative ideas. Gramsci pointed out that this was a slow process that often experienced setbacks.[5] Considering this, WOMP's setback must be seen with what Kim called 'concerned optimism', rather than abject pessimism.[6]

Notes

1. Richard Falk, Samuel S. Kim and Saul H. Mendlovitz, 'General Introduction', in *Toward a Just World Order: Studies on a Just World Order,* Vol. I, Richard Falk, Samuel S. Kim and Saul H. Mendlovitz, eds (Boulder: Westview Press, 1982), 3.
2. Rajni Kothari, *Rethinking Development: In Search of Humane Alternatives* (London: Aspect Publications, 1990), 123 and 179–84.
3. Robert C. Johansen and Saul H. Mendlovitz, 'The Role of Enforcement of Just Law in the Establishment of a New International Order: A Proposal for a Transnational Police Force', in *International Law: A Contemporary Perspective – Studies on a Just World Order, No. 2,* Richard Falk, Friedrich Kratochwil and Saul H. Mendlovitz, eds (Boulder: Westview Press, 1982), 347.
4. Richard Falk, 'The Making of Global Citizenship', in *Global Visions: Beyond the New World Order,* Jeremy Brecher, John Brown Childs and Jill Cutler, eds (Boston: South End Press, 1993), ix and 39–40. See Chapter

4, Reference 41, for detailed discussion on Falk's conceptualization of globalization from above and globalization from below.

5. Stephen Hobden and Richard Wyn Jones, 'Marxist Theories of International Relations', in *The Globalization of World Politics: An Introduction to International Relations*, John Baylis and Steve Smith, eds (New York: OUP, 2001), 205–08. For details, see Antonio Gramsci, *Selections from the Prison Notebooks*, edited and translated by Quinton Hoare and Geoffrey Nowell Smith (New Delhi: Orient Longman, 1996).
6. Samuel S. Kim, *The Quest For a Just World Order* (Boulder: Westview Press, 1984), 322.

8 Revisiting WOMP in the Contemporary World Order

A Futuristic View

In the preceding chapters, we analyzed what is meant by 'order' and, more specifically, 'world order'. We have also looked at the alternative perspectives on world order – the realist and neo-realist, liberal and neo-liberal, Marxist and neo-Marxist. However, the thrust of our work has been essentially a critical analysis of a major transnational research enterprise, the World Order Models Project (WOMP), which was established in the late 1960s. We have tried to examine the major and specific ideas of the WOMP ideologues and scholars in the form of a thematic study. However, as we have discussed in the last chapter, at the end, WOMP appears to have woven nothing, but naïve and empty dreams. Even at the beginning of the 2010s, the conceptualization of a preferred world, as visualized by the WOMP theorists, seems no closer to reality. However, that does not make WOMP irrelevant, for all social and political philosophies, especially normative political philosophy, since time immemorial, have ended in a utopia. Therefore, rather than take up any preoccupied notions of order and world order, we will try to demystify the existing paradigms and look for alternatives – the notion that supposedly formed the basic argument and crux of the WOMP theorists.

Our aim in this chapter is to unravel the different images of the emerging world order and to examine how we can rejuvenate and restructure the WOMP spirit in the contemporary world order. Is it really possible to have such a world order as visualized by the WOMP theorists, or is it a farfetched 'midnight dream' or a 'distant projected utopia', given the fact that the contemporary world order reflects the dominance of neo-realist and neo-liberal theories and assumptions? We start with the basic assumption that it is indeed possible to have a more humane, benign and just world order, as visualized by the WOMP theorists, but what would have to be taken into account is the contemporary nature of the social world as well as world order, essentially encompassing the geopolitical and geo-economic dimension. The nature of the preferred world ought to be devised in such a manner that it is all inclusive. Exclusion of individuals, communities, marginalized groups, states and social movements needs to be addressed adequately. An equally important question that needs to be addressed is that of transformative politics in order to bring about the desired changes. There is a dire need, therefore, to re-conceptualize the preferred world in such a manner that individuals and communities can realize their best 'self' and the voices of dissent emanating from below at the grass roots level within the broader liberal as well as socialist paradigms are addressed adequately.

Accordingly, this chapter is divided into nine sections. The first seven sections analyze the positivist perspectives on world order. The first four sections look at the dominant realist perspectives on world order, as outlined by Robert E. Harkavy.[1] We have already explained and analyzed the different varieties of realism in a comprehensive manner in Chapter 2. These are the three bloc neo-mercantilist thesis, or geo-economics; the multipolar balance of power model; the unipolar dominance model and the bipolar redux model. The next three sections take up the other alternative perspectives on world order – the global village model, the clash of civilizations model and the zones of peace versus zones of turmoil model. All three models, which are essentially positivist in their approach, try to create an international society based on compatibility between the religious, cultural and civilizational norms of the actors participating in the system. The eighth section delves into the post-positivist perspectives on world order. It also provides a critique of Harkavy's sevenfold typology of world order, all of which are essentially positivist in their approach. The concluding section raises the question whether the contemporary world order is indeed a neo-liberal or a neo-realist world order, or whether it is a synchronization of the various positivist and post-positivist perspectives on world order? It also tries to evaluate whether and how the WOMP spirit, based on the four world order values, can be best accommodated and fine-tuned in the contemporary world order. In doing so, we will explore the extent to which the WOMP spirit can be restructured, reoriented and rejuvenated in the contemporary world order, so that the world order becomes more benign and humane, and the world becomes a better place for mankind to live in.

I

Three-Bloc Neo-Mercantilist Thesis, or Geo-Economics

The traditional realist theory emphasizes military conflict and war among sovereign states in the international arena in order to not just protect and preserve their security, but annex territories and thus enhance their status. However, the disintegration of the Soviet Union has ushered in a new kind of post-Cold War world, in which military conflicts between the great powers is gradually becoming obscure and obsolete, as a result of the looming threat of a nuclear war, the development of nuclear weapons and the associated factor of nuclear deterrence. Moreover, sound economic strength is required for initiating a war and that is lacking in most places. Consequently, geo-politics is being replaced gradually by geo-economics. This raises the question whether realism can still be regarded as a useful theory to explain contemporary world politics.

The geo-economic realists believe that though military conflict is becoming increasingly remote and redundant now, military competition and conflict among the great powers is gradually, but discernibly, paving the way for economic rivalries among nation-states in contemporary world politics. Therefore, in stark contrast to the traditional realists, who 'trace relative gain concerns to the ever present threat of war', the geo-economic realists relate 'those concerns to the threat of war, but also to the desire for foreign policy autonomy or the pursuit of economic prosperity'.[2] Michael Mastanduno explains this point quite vividly:

> Nation-states remain the principal actors and their competition for markets, raw materials, high value added employment and mastery of advanced technology becomes a surrogate for traditional military competition. Success in geo-economic competition brings the nation-state economic prosperity and discretion in its foreign

> policy. It also enables the state to remain at the cutting edge of military research and development. Geo-economic realists believe that economic and technological competition will remain at the centre of great power relations until traditional security competition reasserts itself. Military security may once again become a scarce commodity if military technology changes radically or if and when revisionist states assert themselves as great powers seeking to change the international status quo.[3]

In the same vein, Kenneth Waltz, a major neo-realist scholar, while analyzing the contours of the emerging international order, points out, 'Economic competition is often as keen as military competition, and since nuclear weapons limit the use of force among great powers at the strategic level, we may expect economic and technological competition among them to become more intense.'[4] Quite similarly, Richard Samuels and Eric Heginbotham developed the concept of 'mercantile realism' and pointed out that 'security threats were as much economic as military, that powerful states will engage in economic balancing and that geo-economic interests may be pursued at the expense of traditional political and security interests'.[5]

Apart from Waltz, Samuels and Heginbotham, Walter Russell Mead (1990), Jeffrey Garten (1992), Lester Thurow (1992), Laura Tyson (1992) and Edward Luttwak (1993) all have further developed the three bloc geo-economic model in contemporary times. The assumption of these geo-economic theorists is that there are three competitive economic blocs in the contemporary world. These are:

- A Japan-led Pacific Rim region, including Korea, Southeast Asia and China;
- A United States-led Western Hemisphere bloc centred on the North American Free Trade Agreement (NAFTA) and potentially encompassing Latin America; and
- A Germany-centred European bloc, assumed to include Russia and other ex-Soviet states and, perhaps, also North Africa.[6]

However, Mead, Garten, Luttwak and Thurow did not share this monolithic view of the likely possibilities of which bloc would ultimately evolve as the dominant one in the contemporary world. While Mead and Thurow predicted that the European bloc would ultimately evolve as the dominant bloc and the United States-led bloc would be the weakest in a fierce competitive struggle between these three geo-economic blocs,[7] others held widely different views and perceptions. Let us go over these geo-economic theorists' varied perceptions on world order.

Mead's fundamental assumption was that Europe would by all means try to perpetuate bloc politics, rather than move towards a free market, 'open global economy'. In strengthening its hold on bloc politics, Europe would use its decisive power and leverage over the former Soviet bloc countries, which would essentially serve as sources of low wage industries for Europe. Mead forecast the possibility of Europe importing oil from Africa and Russia and raw materials from the United States and Japan. Further, as the former Soviet bloc countries built up a well developed agricultural system, the European bloc would begin to enjoy large agricultural surpluses. In addition to this, Europe would be able to develop high technology industries, rather than import goods and services from the United States and Asia.[8]

Mead saw the possibility of the Asian bloc led by Japan as a rising power, which would not possess the capacity to curtail United States' technological exports, but would be able to exploit the United States as a source of raw materials and as a market for industrial goods, as well as import raw materials and low end manufactured products from China and Southeast Asia. Moreover, Japan would be able 'to export capital goods and high technology products to all these markets plus NAFTA and Oceania in an (asymmetric) exchange for food, minerals and entertainment products'.[9]

Thurow also predicted the possibility of a rising Japan. He argued that Japan's propensity to rise was essentially because of 'its status as the world's largest net creditor, its world record trade surplus, and its propensity to invest in plant and equipment (per employee) at a rate triple that of the United States and twice that of Europe', along with 'Japan's educational levels, particularly its ability to educate the bottom half of its high school classes'.[10]

Mead argued that while the European bloc would emerge as the strongest frontrunner in global geo-economic competition, followed by the Asian bloc led by Japan, the third position would be taken by the United States-led NAFTA. This would essentially be the result of three factors: firstly, the economy of Latin America being in doldrums; secondly, the United States-led bloc relying heavily on West Asian oil; and thirdly, the precarious position of the United States' external economy. Mead further argued that so fluid was the

United States' external economy that eventually, the Japanese yen and the European euro would outpace the US dollar in the international financial economy.[11]

Thurow contradicted Mead's argument by arguing that in the next century, the United States would continue to be the military superpower, 'thanks to America's stock of real economic assets, its superior per capita income and average productivity, its universities, and a domestic market' as well as its 'cultural strengths'.[12] However, he added a note of caution: "To be a double superpower, (the United States) will have to be willing to invest in being an economic superpower, and on top of that, make whatever investments are necessary to remain a military superpower."[13] While remaining optimistic about the United States' superpower status, Thurow enumerated the negative and flip side of United States' policies, especially 'America's atrophied educational system, international debts, low levels of civilian research and development, and decaying infrastructure'.[14] The desired policy changes that Thurow, therefore, insisted the United States should make is to move from 'consumption to investment and solve the educational problems associated with its non-college workforce'.[15]

Michael Mastanduno, while summing up the diverse perspectives of the geo-economic realists, pointed to its three basic tenets. Firstly, the geo-economic realists 'expect great powers to mobilize for international economic competition'.[16] Accordingly, they expect the states to readjust their national economic systems in a manner that is advantageous for their national firms. While the competitive position of the nation-states may vary, some of the plausible strategies suggested by the geo-economic realists are 'partnerships between government and industry in research and development, export promotion, industrial policies, selective protectionism, and the shedding of costly military commitments'.[17]

Secondly, geo-economic realists argue that states will try to augment their relative gains in their foreign economic policies, whether there is a possibility of military warfare or not. Accordingly, states need to readjust their national economic policies to maximize their own relative gains.[18]

Thirdly, geo-economic realists argue that in global geo-economic competition, powerful states need to formulate their relations with their weaker neighbours in such a manner that their positions are enhanced. In this regard, Thurow points to a three structured world in the post-Cold War period. These are essentially an Asian bloc led by Japan, a European bloc led by Germany, and NAFTA led by the United States. The dominant power in each region will ensure that more economic advantages accrue to them rather than to their economic competitors. Consequently, the geo-economic realists foresee the possibility of globalization being undermined by regionalization.[19]

II

The Multipolar Balance of Power Model

In not so sharp a contrast to the three bloc geo-economics model, the multipolar balance of power model was also based on the traditional realist or neo-realist school of thought in international relations. This thesis advocated the emergence of a multipolar world after the collapse of bipolarity in 1991. The period between 1648 (beginning with the Treaty of Westphalia) and 1945 was characterized by multipolarity, when multiple great powers and multiple alliances were the dominant 'trajectories' around which world politics revolved. Moreover, these great powers focused on economic and diplomatic cooperation among themselves. However, the post-1945 period in international politics was marked by bipolarity, where the two superpowers – the United States and the former USSR – continued to exert and show their own economic, political, military and ideological domination over each other. Two apt visible manifestations of this Cold War conflict were in the domain of the weapons of mass destruction (WMDs), especially nuclear weapons (along with chemical and biological weapons) as well as their respective military alliances. Bitter conflict eschewed between the United States-led military alliances (NATO, SEATO and CENTO) and the former USSR-led military alliance (the Warsaw Pact countries). Theorists who advanced the multipolar balance of power model argued that the post-1945 bipolar model was a historical fallacy. Under the banner of the Third World and the Non-Aligned Movement (NAM), most of the postcolonial states of Asia, Africa and Latin America exerted a moderating influence in the international conflicts of the day. The spirit of Third Worldism helped in averting a Third World War.

However, the collapse of bipolarity in 1991 raised speculative debates about whether the emerging world order was unipolar or multipolar. Realists and neo-realists of all persuasions rejected outright the formation of a unipolar world order dominated by the United States as a historical anomaly. This was voiced in a more pertinent manner in one of the fundamental presumptions of Kenneth Waltz, a major neo-realist thinker, who argued that 'states balance power, and thus the accumulation of preponderant capabilities in the hands of any single state will stimulate the rise of new great powers, or coalition of powers, determined to balance the dominant state'.[20] Moreover, since security and the matrix of power relationships determine the most important outcomes in international relations as viewed by the realist and neo-realist theorists, the Cold War would eventually and quite inevitably lead to a multipolar world order and not a unipolar one.

Neo-realists particularly argued that the demise of bipolarity would eventually usher in multipolarity. The transition from a bipolar system to a unipolar one, as some scholars predicted after the disintegration of the Soviet Union, was a false anomaly, according to the neo-realists. They argued particularly that the bipolar system would eventually transform itself into a multipolar system, wherein there would be several great powers, with the United States, perhaps, the preponderant and most dominant power. This argument of 'incipient multipolarity' is most commonly found in the writings of the major neo-realist thinkers of the post-Cold War period. Moreover, small and weak states would always try to align themselves with the great powers. This would be so, Waltz believed, because 'states are power seeking and security conscious, not because of human nature, but rather because the structure of the international system compels them to be that way'.[21]

The question of states retaining their autonomy was paramount in neo-realist theory. This becomes amply clear from some of the historical events of the Cold War period during the 1980s, when there was intensification of the arms race between the two superpowers, following United States President Ronald Reagan's reference to the Soviet Union as an 'evil empire'. It was also during this period that there were trade wars and other disputes between the United States and Japan, as also the United States and Europe. It essentially reflected 'state competition' and was primarily concerned with their respective power positions.

However, Waltz said that bipolar systems would eventually move to a multipolar system, though he also argued that much more stability, peace and security was to be found in bipolarity than in multipolarity. This analysis, therefore, contained the logical argument that the period of the Cold War reflected a period of international peace and stability. This argument of a stable bipolarity was further extended by John Mearsheimer, who essentially advocated a neo-realist stability theory.

In a widely discussed and perceptive article, John Mearsheimer argued that 'bipolarity will disappear with the passing of the Cold War and multipolarity will emerge in the new international order'.[22] Quite like Waltz, Mearsheimer argued that bipolar systems enhance the chances of peace and stability because of three factors. Firstly, the existence of two superpowers minimizes the chances of war between several great powers; secondly, there was almost a rough super equality between the United States and the former USSR; and lastly, both superpowers possessed an equal nuclear weapons arsenal, which ensured nuclear deterrence. As Mearsheimer himself pointed out, the Cold War between the United States and the former USSR 'was principally responsible for transforming a historically violent region into a very peaceful place'.[23]

Mearsheimer argued that the defining feature of international politics in the post-Cold War period would be increasing military or security competition among the great powers, which would result in conflict and instability at both the regional and global levels, rather than usher in peace, stability and harmony. Nuclear deterrence, as it prevailed during the Cold War period, would cease to exist, as several great powers, such as Japan and Germany, as well as less powerful states tried to acquire nuclear weapons. This would possibly enhance the looming threat of a nuclear war. As Mearsheimer argued:

> the prospects for major crises and war in Europe are likely to increase markedly if ... this scenario unfolds. The next decades in a Europe without the superpowers would probably not be as violent as the first forty-five years of this century, but would probably be substantially more prone to violence than the past forty-five years.[24]

However, such emerging multipolar systems would be much more unstable. As Mearsheimer explained, 'The departure of the superpowers would also remove the large nuclear arsenals they now maintain in Central Europe. This would remove the pacifying effect that these weapons had on European politics.'[25] Waltz projected the emergence of five great powers in a multipolar world – 'Japan, Germany, China, the European Union and a revived Russia'.[26] But Mearsheimer forecast the emergence of five major players – Germany, France, Britain, Russia and, perhaps, Italy – plus a number of minor powers.

Similar arguments were advanced by Christopher Layne, who argued that Japan and Germany would become independent great powers, rather than remain 'trading states' and they would not be subordinate partners to the United States. As Layne put it, 'A policy of attempting to smother Germany's and Japan's great power emergence would be unavailing because structural pressure will impel them to become great powers regardless of what the United States does or does not do.'[27] Further, security alignments would become more fluid and fuzzy and depend eventually on the national interests of the states, a familiar realist presumption.

Jackson and Sorenson pointed out that Mearsheimer's 'hypothesis seems to be confirmed by the outbreak of conflict and war in the former Yugoslavia (Croatia, Bosnia Herzegovina and Kosovo in Serbia) and in the former Soviet Union (Azerbaijan, Armenia, Georgia, Moldova and Russia itself – in Chechnya)'.[28] However, Jackson and Sorenson were also to quick point out the false assumptions of the multipolar hypothesis on world order at a different level. They elucidated:

> It is worth pointing out, however, that these places are outside the Central European heartland, where the neo-realist thesis about the instability of the post-Cold War era is meant to apply most. In that part of Europe, since the late 1950s, something entirely different had been happening that Mearsheimer's neo-realist hypothesis seems to ignore: the integration of the European nation-states into the European Union, the core of which consists of Germany and France, who have created a very close partnership over the past several decades. The end of the Cold War has not put an end to that relationship; if anything, it has made it even more important. In other words, the European Union and particularly the Franco-German core of that emerging political community discloses a new international relationship between the major and minor powers of Europe that neo-realism's thesis about bipolarism versus multipolarism seems unable to comprehend. This historical transformation may be better understood by liberal approaches to international relations.[29]

III

The Clash of Civilizations Thesis

In sharp contrast to the three bloc geo-economics model and the multipolar balance of power model, both of which fall within the broader rubric of the realist and neo-realist tradition in international relations, Samuel P. Huntington posited the clash of civilizations thesis as the possible image of the future world order. Accepting culture and civilization as the decisive basis for explaining world order realities, Huntington foresaw cultural and civilizational conflicts in the emerging world order in the coming decades. He said:

> It is my hypothesis that the fundamental source of conflict in this new world will not be primarily ideological or primarily economic. The great divisions among humankind and the dominating source of conflict will be cultural. Nation-states will remain the most powerful actors in world affairs, but the principal conflicts of global politics will occur between nations and groups of different civilizations. The clash of civilizations will dominate global politics. The fault lines between civilizations will be the battle lines of the future.[30]

Tracing the genealogy of the various types and patterns of international conflicts since the Treaty of Westphalia (1648), Huntington divided them into three different phases. The first phase witnessed 'primary conflicts in the Western world' by and large 'among princes – emperors, absolute monarchs and constitutional monarchs attempting to expand their bureaucracies, their armies, their mercantilist strength and, most important, the territory they ruled'.[31] The second period spanned the period between the French Revolution of 1789 and World War I (1914–18) and witnessed increasing and sporadic conflicts between nation-states. However, the second phase was different from the first phase insofar as the nature of the conflicts marked a shift from conflicts between princes to conflicts between nation-states. The third phase symbolized a paradigm shift from the first two phases, with the nature of conflicts descending to ideological conflicts and rivalry between capitalism and communism, and the conflicts proliferating essentially from the Bolshevik Revolution in Russia in 1917 and its subsequent reactions and ramifications. This ideological rivalry between capitalism and communism led, as Huntington pointed out, to 'a struggle between the two superpowers, neither of which was a nation-state in the classical European sense and each of which defined its identity in terms of its own ideology'.[32] Common to all these conflicts in the three distinct phases was that all these conflicts took place within the Western civilization. However, what is distinctive and new is that henceforth, 'the great conflicts may occur between, not within, civilizations'.[33]

Huntington's core proposition was that 'culture and cultural identities are shaping the patterns of cohesion, disintegration and conflict in the post-Cold War period'.[34] Juxtaposing culture and civilization together, Huntington defined civilization as 'the highest cultural grouping and the broadest level of cultural identity people have short of that which distinguishes humans from other species'.[35] He supported his core proposition with five supporting corollaries. These are:

- For the first time in history, global politics is multipolar and multicivilizational; modernization is distinct from Westernization and produces neither a universal civilization in any meaningful sense nor the Westernization of non-Western societies.
- The balance of power among civilizations is shifting: The West is declining in relative influence; Asian civilizations are expanding their economic, military and political strength; Islam is exploding demographically with destabilizing consequences for Muslim countries and their neighbours; and non-Western civilizations are generally reaffirming the value of their own civilizations.
- A civilization based world order is emerging: Societies sharing cultural affinities cooperate with each other; efforts to shift societies from one civilization to another are unsuccessful; and countries group themselves around the lead or core states of their civilization.
- The West's universalist pretensions increasingly bring it into conflict with other civilizations, most seriously with Islam and China, at the local fault line wars level, largely between Muslims and non-Muslims, they generate 'kin country rallying', the threat of broader escalation, and hence efforts by core states to halt these wars.
- The survival of the West depends on Americans reaffirming their Western identity and Westerners accepting their civilization as unique, not universal, and uniting to renew and

> preserve it against challenges from non-Western societies. Avoidance of a global war of civilizations depends on world leaders accepting and cooperating to maintain the multicivilizational character of world politics.[36]

Huntington identified eight major civilizations that would determine the future of international politics. These are 'Western, Confucian (Sinic), Japanese, Islamic, Hindu, Slavic-Orthodox, Latin American and possibly African'.[37] He espoused that 'fault lines between civilizations are replacing the political and ideological boundaries of the Cold War as the flashpoints for crisis and bloodshed'.[38] He prophesied clashes between the West and militant Islam as well as between the West and Christianity as the flashpoints of 'bloody crisis' in the evolving world order. In this regard, he essentially focused 'on the cultural lines of demarcation between Western Christianity and Orthodox Christianity in Europe, and between the latter and Islam'.[39]

The conflict between the West and a militant Islam would be the most severe threat to the survival of mankind. How this conflict would endanger world peace is something we will discuss a little later, but let us now turn our attention to the other fault lines within the clash of civilizations that Huntington postulated. This has been well documented by Harkavy:

> Other fault lines that contain potential for large scale future conflict include that between the Arab Islamic civilization and the animist or Christian Africa to the South, and that between the Muslim and Hindu civilizations in South Asia. One might also interpret potential conflict between the United States and either Japan or China as a clash between Western and Confucian civilizations.[40]

Huntington disputed the emergence of a unified world under one universal civilization; rather, he emphasized the fragments and fragmentary nature of the world under the invariable existence of different civilizations. In the post-Cold War period, he speculated on the end of the Western phase of international politics, with the tide now turning to 'the interaction between the West and non-Western civilizations and among non-Western civilizations'.[41] Further, 'in the politics of civilizations', Huntington argued, 'the peoples and governments of non-Western civilizations no longer remain the objects of history as targets of Western colonialism, but join the West as movers and shapers of history'.[42]

Huntington offered six basic causes for the clash of and between civilizations. These have been well summarized by Stephanie Lawson:

> Differences among civilizations are not only real; they are basic. Civilizations are differentiated by history, language, culture, tradition and, most importantly, religion. Since these differences are the products of history, they are not going to disappear soon. Moreover, they are far more fundamental than differences between political ideologies, being less susceptible to change. Although differences do not inevitably lead to conflict, the evidence over the centuries shows that civilizational differences have in effect generated the most prolonged and violent conflicts.
>
> Since the world is becoming an increasingly smaller place, the interactions between people of different civilizations are increasing. Such increasing interactions have the effect of intensifying civilizational consciousness as well as differences between and similarities within civilizations. This tends to invigorate differences and historical animosities, whether these are real or imagined.
>
> Economic modernization and social change throughout the world are weakening longstanding local identities as well as the nation-state as a source of identity. In many places, religion has moved in to fill the vacuum, often taking the form of fundamentalist movements.
>
> The West has a dual role in enhancing civilizational consciousness. Since the West appears at the peak of its power, this has prompted a return to the roots phenomenon among non-Western civilizations.
>
> Cultural differences are less mutable and hence less easily compromised and resolved than political and economic ones. In the former Soviet Union, for example, Communists can become democrats, but Russians cannot become Estonians. But even more than ethnicity, religion discriminates sharply and exclusively among people. Someone can be simultaneously half-French and half-Arab, but it is more difficult to be half-Muslim and half-Catholic.
>
> Increasing economic regionalism is reinforcing civilizational consciousness. Moreover, successful regionalization may succeed only when it is rooted in a common civilization. For example, the European Community is founded on a shared European culture and Western Christianity, and the success of the North American Free Trade Agreement depends on the continuing convergence of

Mexican, Canadian and American cultures. Japan presents a contrasting case. It faces many difficulties in creating a comparable economic activity in East Asia because it is a unique civilization in itself. The expansion of economic relations among Japan's East Asian neighbours, however, is proceeding apace because of their shared culture.[43]

Huntington assumed that the next conflict would be a war between civilizations, taking into account conflicts such as the Afghan War, the Gulf War and the wars in Bosnia, the Persian Gulf and the Caucasus.[44] In other words, what he sought to argue was that the Cold War ideological clash would pave the way for a clash between civilizations, where the defining parameters of the new set of conflicts and antagonisms would be culture, civilizations and identity. Further, while the earlier conflicts took place within the broader rubric of Western civilization, the new conflicts would be between the West (Western Europe) and the Rest, essentially encompassing West Asia, China, Asia and even post-communist Russia. And in the conflict between the West and the Rest, one can foresee a conflict between the West and Islam. Here, Huntington cited the ongoing and ensuing conflict between liberal democracies and Islam, especially as reflected in the Afghan War, the Gulf War and, more precisely, during the post-Cold War period in the events of 11 September 2001 and its inevitable ramifications, as exhibited by the United States' interventions in Iraq and Afghanistan. These events testify to the conflict between Western and Islamic civilizations, and especially the more orthodox and conservative traditions in Islam. This civilizational difference essentially springs from the differences in value systems between the West and Islam or, to put it in a much broader and wider sense, the entire Rest, where there are much more deep rooted traditional and ascriptive notions of values and value systems, resulting in bloody conflicts. The reason for this conflict is essentially because the majority of the countries that constitute the Rest, especially West Asia, China, Asia and post-communist Russia, do not adhere to the liberal democratic values of individualism, pluralism, democracy and human rights.[45]

Huntington, therefore, hypothesized the formation of a new international order following the collapse of the Soviet Union, the end of the Cold War and the ushering in of an era of globalization. As a result of globalization, the world is gradually becoming a global village, resulting in the weakening of state and local loyalties. But at the same time, it has heightened the increased cultural differences between communities, as a result of which communities have tried to create their own identities in terms of the cultures rooted in their past. This has led to a kind of cultural revivalism. Most of these communities have deep-rooted civilizational differences. As Simon Murden explained it, 'In reality, the differences between civilizations ran deep: they were about man and God, man and woman, the individual and the state, and notions of rights, authority, obligation and justice. Culture was about the basic perceptions of life that had been constructed over centuries.'[46]

Since Huntington accepted culture as the defining element of the emerging world order, in effect, he argued that 'though states remained key actors, civilizational politics became real when states and peoples identified with each other's cultural concerns or rallied around the "core state" of a civilization'.[47] While the powerful unitary states in the West, including the United States, the United Kingdom, Germany and France, had a closely linked core, and while the Orthodox, Hindu, Japanese and Sinic civilizations were concentrated in certain regions, Islam did not have a clear core state. Even though a pan-Islamic consciousness existed, there was widespread intra-civilizational conflict within Islam, as a number of Islamic states such as Iran, Iraq, Egypt, Turkey, Saudi Arabia, Indonesia and Pakistan wanted to spread their own spheres of influence, control and domination. However, none of these Islamic states had the decisive power and authority to mediate between conflicts within Islam as well as between Muslim and non-Muslim groups. Huntington identified Islamic militancy, 'indigestibility', population and demographic expansion, economic weakness and underdevelopment of Muslims as the possible sources of conflict between the West and Islam.[48] He raised the question 'as to why, as the twentieth century ends, Muslims are involved in far more intergroup violence than people of other civilizations'.[49] Some of the causes he identified are enumerated below:

1. First, the argument is made that Islam has from the start been a religion of the sword and that it glorifies military virtues. Islam originated among 'warring Bedouin nomadic tribes' and this 'violent origin is stamped in the foundation of Islam. Muhammad himself is remembered as a hard fighter and a skilful military commander'. (No one would say this about Christ or the Buddha.) The doctrines of Islam, it is argued,

dictate war against unbelievers and unbelievers, and when the initial expansion of Islam tapered off, Muslim groups, quite contrary to doctrine, fought among themselves. The ratio of *fitna* (internal conflicts) to jihad shifted drastically in favour of the former. The Koran and other statements of Muslim beliefs contain few prohibitions on violence and the concept of non-violence is absent from Muslim doctrine and practice.

2. Another possible source of Muslim-non-Muslim conflict is what has been referred to as the 'indigestibility' of Muslims. Indigestibility, however, works both ways: Muslim countries have problems with non-Muslim minorities comparable to those which non-Muslim countries have with Muslim minorities. Even more than Christianity, Islam is an absolutist faith. It merges religion and politics and draws a sharp line between those in the Dar al Islam and those in the Dar al Harb. As a result, Confucians, Buddhists, Hindus, Western Christians and Orthodox Christians have less difficulty adapting to and living with each other than any one of them has in adapting to and living with Muslims. Ethnic Chinese, for instance, are an economically dominant minority in most Southeast Asian countries. They have been successfully assimilated into the societies of Buddhist Thailand and the Catholic Philippines; there are virtually no significant instances of anti-Chinese violence by the majority groups in those countries. In contrast, anti-Chinese riots and/or violence have occurred in Muslim Indonesia and Muslim Malaysia, and the role of the Chinese in those societies remains a sensitive and potentially explosive issue in a way in which it is not in Thailand and the Philippines.[50]

Huntington hypothesized cultural conflict to be operating at two levels – micro and macro. Micro-level conflicts could be witnessed across 'local fault lines', where diverse groups belonging to different civilizations were at cross-purposes with each other. And of all the fault lines within his widely popular clash of civilizations thesis, Islam had more 'bloody borders', which would continue to proliferate unless there was a steady decline in the Muslim population in the second and third decades of the twenty-first century. Huntington hypothesized broader macro-level cultural conflicts to precipitate between the West and the Rest or the non-West. And within the Rest, this conflict was likely to head in the direction of conflicts between the West versus Islam and the West versus Sinic. The conflict between the West on the one hand, and the Islamic and Sinic civilizations on the other hand, would therefore not be fought over territorial issues, but invariably over broader inter-civilizational issues such as arms control, control of oil, Islamic terrorism and fundamentalism, as well as the West's attempts to promote the liberal values of democracy, individualism and pluralism, which are widely contested by the 'theocratic', 'authoritarian' and hegemonic Islamic and Sinic civilizations.

Huntington said that there would be no universal civilization of the kind envisaged by 'idealists' in the relevant future, instead, there would be a world of different civilizations, each of which would have to learn to coexist with the others if world peace were to prevail.[51] As he himself concluded, 'In the emerging era, clashes of civilizations are the greatest threat to world peace, and an international order based on civilizations is the surest safeguard against a world war.'[52]

Looking at the evolving contemporary global politics, one finds that Huntington's clash of civilizations thesis, especially his prediction of a civilizational war between the West and Islam, is indeed becoming a reality. The rise of Islamic fundamentalism, extremism and terrorism and its constant conflicts with the West testify to this. While the evolution of Islamic fundamentalism has a long history, its immediate rise is traced to the Afghan War, which saw the rise of the Taliban and the al-Qaeda as two notorious Islamic fundamentalist groups, and the defeat of the Soviet forces in Afghanistan. This was followed by the Gulf War, in which Western intervention in the conflict between the two Islamic states of Iraq and Kuwait over control of oil mobilized the Muslims to resist Western dominance together. This further catapulted the rise and revival of the al-Qaeda and the Taliban as well as several Islamic fundamentalist and terrorist groups operating in Islamic states such as Pakistan, Egypt, Saudi Arabia, Indonesia, Iraq and Iran. These Islamic fundamentalist groups practised and spread the message of the politics of jihad, whereby they quite brutally and treacherously committed heinous crimes on innocent civilians and armies. The former United States President, George Bush, referred to this threat from Islamic fundamentalism and terrorism as 'Islamofascism'. As Bush elucidated, 'They try to spread their jihadist message – a message I call, it's totalitarian in nature – Islamic radicalism, Islamic fascism, they try to spread it as well as by taking the attack to those of us who love freedom.'[53]

The rise of Islamic fundamentalism and terrorism was reflected in the events of 11 September 2001 and the ensuing bloody conflict between the West and Islam. The United States' intervention in Iraq and Afghanistan was essentially to curb this rise of Islamic fundamentalism and spread the message of peace and democracy. While the United States has succeeded partially in bringing about democracy in these two Islamic states, it has not succeeded in curbing the wings of the al-Qaeda, which have grown phenomenally like a 'wild horse'. The United States needs to evolve more effective counter-terrorism measures to control this menace of Islamic fundamentalism and terrorism. The conflict between the West and Islam is essentially a conflict between the superiority of Western civilizations over the orthodox and conservative Islamic civilizations. One can, therefore, say that a civilizational war between the West and Islam has already started, which can become more severe in the years to come. Certainly, then, Huntington's thesis is coming to fruition. But can civilization be defined only in terms of religion? We will evaluate Huntington's hypothesis in the eighth section of this chapter.

IV

The Unipolar World Order: The US-Centric System

Charles Krauthammer contradicted the first three models of world order discussed above and predicted a model of world order that was pivoted around the dominance of the United States, inevitably suggesting the United States' unipolarity. Krauthammer's argument stemmed from his belief that the end of the Cold War and the decline and disintegration of the Soviet Union had paved the way for a dominant American role in the contemporary world. The emerging post-Cold War world order was, therefore, neither bipolar nor multipolar – it was unipolar. As Krauthammer pointed out:

> The most striking feature of the post-Cold War world is its unipolarity. No doubt, multipolarity will come in time. In perhaps another generation or so, there will be great powers coequal with the United States, and the world will, in structure, resemble the pre-World War I era. But we are not there yet, nor will we be for decades. Now is the unipolar moment.[54]

Quite similarly, Krauthammer argued that the post-Cold War world was precisely unipolar. As he elaborated eloquently:

> International stability is never a given. It is never the norm. When achieved, it is the product of self-conscious action by the great powers, and most particularly of the greatest power, which now and for the foreseeable future is the United States. If America wants stability, it will have to create it. Communism is indeed finished; the last of the messianic creeds that have haunted this century is quite dead.[55]

The United States' military, economic, political and diplomatic assets and power makes it the most pre-eminent and dominant power in the contemporary world. It enables it to intervene in different countries and situations that threaten its national security. The United States' interventions in the Gulf War, Iraq and Afghanistan were primarily to protect and preserve its national security interests. The Gulf War first showed 'the true geopolitical structure of the post-Cold War world', which was 'brought sharply into focus by the Gulf crisis: a single pole of world power that consists of the United States at the apex of the industrial West'.[56]

In sustaining its unipolar status, Krauthammer suggested the revival of the American 'isolationist' policy because of its popular and natural appeal. The isolationist policy will probably help the United States to defend its vital national security interests in a much more comprehensive manner. This was well exhibited by the Gulf War, wherein the United States intervened essentially to protect its vital national security interests. Krauthammer summed up this point quite lucidly:

> Iraq's invasion of Kuwait and hegemonic designs on Arabia posed as clear a threat to American interests as one can imagine – a threat to America's oil based economy, to its close allies in the region and, ultimately, to American security itself. The rise of a hostile power, fuelled by endless oil income, building weapons of mass destruction and the means to deliver them regionally and eventually inter-continentally (Saddam has already tested a three stage rocket) can hardly be a matter of indifference to the United States.[57]

A major threat to the United States' national security in the post-Cold War world was the proliferation of weapons of mass destruction (WMDs). The United States was gravely threatened by the fact that a number of states were trying to acquire (some states were already in possession of WMDs) nuclear, chemical and biological weapons as well as their means of delivery. These weapons seriously jeopardized not only regional security, but also world security. The United States tried to deter the states, among them Iraq, Iran, Libya and North Korea, that were trying to acquire the WMDs. The United States had already declared some of these states 'rogue states' that could threaten international peace and security. The United States had also adopted the policy of pre-emptive action and it was trying hard to ensure that world peace and security were not disturbed by these rogue states. Krauthammer observed: "With the rise of the weapons state, there is no alternative to confronting, deterring and, if necessary, disarming states that brandish and use weapons of mass destruction. And there is no one to do that, but the United States, backed by as many allies as will join the endeavour."[58]

Krauthammer actually evolved a threefold strategy to put a moratorium on the development of WMDs by these states. Any effective strategy, he pointed out, should include three elements – 'denying, disarming and defending'. He elaborated on these three elements:

> First, we will have to develop a new regime, similar to COCOM to deny yet more high technology to such states. Second, those states that acquire such weapons anyway will have to submit to strict outside control or risk being physically disarmed. A final element must be the development of antiballistic missile and air defence systems to defend against those weapons that do escape Western control or pre-emption.[59]

The idea of a unipolar dominance model also echoes and finds resonance in Francis Fukuyama's end of history thesis, in which he pointed out that with the disintegration of the Soviet Union, there was a universal triumph of liberal democracy and the end of the Communist ideology. It essentially reflected the superiority of Western liberal ideas and democratic values over Communist ideology. It also symbolized the end of the era of Marx and Marxism. History has proved that all the assumptions of Marx lie belied and any possibility of their revival seems remote. The future lies in adopting and synchronizing with Western democratic values and assumptions. Huntington, while revoking the idea of a superior United States-led economic bloc, observed:

> In contrast to other countries, the United States ranks extraordinarily high in almost all the major sources of national power, population size and education, natural resources, economic development, social cohesion, political stability, military strength, ideological appeal, diplomatic alliances, and technological achievement. It is, consequently, able to sustain reverses in any one area, while maintaining its influence stemming from other sources.[60]

The United States, thus, invariably represents the dominant power in every field, whether it is a strong economic and technological foundation, military power or a strong export base, and it has also benefited substantially from the processes intertwined with globalization – free market, free labour and free capital. It has very low unemployment rates, low inflation and it spends substantially on education, research and development and on development activities. The United States has the best higher education industry – this is borne out by the fact that higher education quality has been abysmally poor in both China and India, which forces students from the top institutions in India to migrate to the United States.[61]

The American unipolar dominance model also finds resonance in George Modelski's long cycles theory. Modelski perceived of five long cycles of about a century each, while trying to evaluate the global patterns of leadership since the advent of the Renaissance. These are elaborated below:[62]

> 1494–1580: Portugal is the leading power.
> 1580–1688: The Netherlands is the leading power.
> 1688–1792: Britain is the leading power.
> 1792–1914: Britain is the leading power.
> 1914–73 (and beyond): The United States is the leading power.

Each of these five phases or periods, Modelski argued, 'passed through four phases – global war, emergence of the world power, delegitimization of that power, and deconcentration of power'. It is important to note that Modelski believed that each of the previous world powers had dominant navies and 'acted as the world's commercial hub'.[63]

Modelski argued that the global dominance of the United States had been challenged since 1973, following the Organization of the Petroleum Exporting Countries (OPEC) crises (when the OPEC countries raised the price of oil substantially, but remained underdeveloped), the gradual evolution of rival economic powers in Asia, and the Soviet hegemonic onslaught with its expansion of naval power and near nuclear parity with the United States, thanks to the ratification of Strategic Arms Limitations Talks I (SALT-I) in 1972.[64]

But Modelski's analysis was confined to the period of the Cold War. In the post-Cold War and post-Soviet world, the United States remained the burgeoning and undisputed leader, not only in world politics, but also in world economy.

A number of scholars, such as Eliot Cohen, Andrew Krepenvich, William J. Perry and William Owens, have observed that 'the quantum leap made by the United States in the "systems of systems" approach – integrating space technology, smart weapons, computers and communications is beyond the reach of any competitor today. In sum, the unipolar moment may last, but only so long as Russia, Europe, Japan and China are unable or unwilling to replicate the sinews of high technology warfare pioneered by the United States.[65]

In a 2008 article in *Foreign Affairs*,[66] Richard N. Haas said that the emerging world order was not unipolar, bipolar or multipolar; it was essentially a non-polar world order. He elaborated on his central argument with two corollaries. While, on the one hand, the United States remains unsurpassable and unbeatable even with the rise of an ascendant Rest, at the same time, its own position, which now seems to be in a somewhat precarious position, needs to be strengthened on many fronts. However, one can still argue that no other rival power or powers have emerged to counter the United States' dominant position, so well entrenched is it in the contemporary world. Haas elaborated:

> In this world, the United States is and will long remain the largest single aggregation of power. It spends more than $500 billion annually on its military – and more than $700 billion, if the operations in Afghanistan and Iraq are included – and boasts land, air and naval forces that are the world's most capable. Its economy with a GDP (gross domestic product) of some $14 trillion is the world's largest. The United States is also a major source of culture (through films and television), information and innovation.[67]

At the same time, Haas sounded a note of caution as well as a sense of pessimism about the United States' supremacy. He argued that while, on the one hand, the United States' share of global imports has been reduced drastically to 15 per cent, the West Asian countries as well as countries such as China and Russia are growing at a phenomenal rate of some $3 trillion, mainly as a result of their oil and gas exports. And with the European Union's euro all set to surpass the American dollar, the United States' economy is bound to be affected. Haas pointed out, "The United States' fiscal position has decreased from a surplus of over $100 billion in 2001 to an estimated deficit of approximately $250 billion in 2007. Perhaps more relevant is the ballooning current account deficit, which is now more than 6 per cent of its GDP."[68] However, though the United States' economy might have dwindled somewhat, no great power rivals have emerged to challenge its supremacy. In other words, Haas emphasized the pivotal role of the United States in an essentially non-polar world, even though he argued that unipolarity has almost ceased to exist. In a similar vein, while evaluating the West versus the Rest dichotomy in the contemporary world order, Fareed Zakaria argued:

> The world is changing, but it is going the United States way. The rest that are rising are embracing markets, democratic government (of some form or another), and greater openness and transparency. It might be a world in which the United States takes up less space, but is one in which American ideas and ideals are overwhelmingly dominant.[69]

While China is believed likely to have the same GDP as the United States in the near future, China's uneven economic growth (unemployment is growing at an alarming rate in that country), political instability and population explosion have doomed its chances to ever challenge the United States. Russia is plagued by a shrinking population, internal political instability and is largely trying to rebuild its economy, which is now a cash crop economy. However, Russia has been able to build its economy also because of its oil and gas reserves, which makes it an energy rich country. Like Russia, Japan, too, is saddled with a diminishing and shrinking population and, worse, an unviable political culture that will hold it back from ever playing the role of a great power. India, though an emerging power, is bottlenecked by demographic challenges, poor infrastructure, bureaucratic red tapism and rampant corruption. The only region that has a GDP growth greater than that of the United States is the European Union (EU), but the EU is neither a nation-state (in the classical sense of the meaning of the nation-state), nor can it act collectively and in unison as a great power.[70]

A cursory glance of the power position of some of the emerging dominant states thus reveals the inherent dominant and superior position of the United States in the contemporary world. The Rest is likely to rise, but it will be unable to challenge the United States' supremacy anytime soon. However, the United States needs to set its own house in order in many sectors if it wishes to retain its supremacy. Haas pointed out:

> The United States can and should take steps to reduce the chances that a non-polar world will become a cauldron of instability. This is not a call for unilateralism; it is a call for the United States to get its own house in order. Unipolarity is a thing of the past, but the United States still retains more capacity than any other actor to improve the quality of the international system.[71]

What then can be the plausible strategies for the United States to retain its unparalleled supremacy? To begin with, it needs to re-examine its energy policy, so that power does not fall in the hands of rogue states. The OPEC crisis in 1973 gave the West Asian countries enormous wealth and they emerged as oil rich, energy surplus countries, causing much annoyance to the United States' military-industrial complex. The West Asian countries, because of their oil and gas reserves (the economy of most of these countries is fully dependent on oil) and because they are part of global cartels like OPEC, can artificially cause global oil prices to spiral upwards, resulting in countrywide inflation across the globe, as has happened recently.

The United States also needs to refocus and strengthen its homeland security system as well as its policy of pre-emptive strikes and institute more effective counter-terrorism measures to control and combat the menace of Islamic fundamentalism. The United States' Global War on Terror needs to be pro-activated to curb the wings of the al-Qaeda and the Taliban, which have now spread their wings far and wide, even setting up safe bases in many Southeast Asian countries, in addition to Islamic countries. Bruce Hoffman pointed out:

> The United States and its allies must refocus their attention on Afghanistan and Pakistan, where al-Qaeda began to collapse after 9/11, but has now regrouped. And they must recognize that al-Qaeda cannot be defeated by military means alone. Success will require a dual strategy of systematically destroying and weakening enemy capabilities – that is, continuing to kill or capture senior

> al-Qaeda leaders – and breaking the cycle of terrorist recruitment... Only by destroying the organization's leadership and disrupting the continued resonance of its radical message can the United States and its allies defeat al-Qaeda.[72]

Along with effective counter-terrorism measures to combat Islamic fundamentalist and terrorist groups, the United States' policy of promoting the democratization wave worldwide also needs to be sharpened. On these and other issues such as global warming, climate change (the more recent summits were the Bali meeting on climate change held in December 2007 and the Copenhagen Summit held in December 2009) and environmental stability, the United States needs to adopt a policy of cooperative multilateralism, rather than unilateralism. The Global War on Terror is a prime manifestation of this cooperative multilateral approach that the United States needs to initiate.

At the same time, on a different plane, the United States has given the globalization process further momentum. Its policy makers assume that increasing trade, investment, flow of capital and goods between countries and across borders will not only rejuvenate the United States' economy, but also ensure greater harmony, stability and an economic boom as well as development in the contemporary world. As Thomas L. Friedman, in a widely debated book, *The World is Flat*, argued, the United States needs to promote and boost policies such as a global free trade system and also open up those restricted sectors and markets (like agriculture) that have been state dominated till now, 'thereby bringing more countries into the global free trade system, which will increase demands for goods and services, spur innovation, and reduce both unemployment and job migration across the globe'.[73] All these plausible strategies will quite effectively transform a 'resilient' United States into a 'thriving' United States, the superiority and primacy of which in global leadership, world politics, and in ushering in new industrial and technological communications will remain unparalleled and undisputed.

V

The Zones of Peace versus Zones of Turmoil Model

In the aftermath of the Cold War and the disintegration of the Soviet Union and Eastern Europe, Max Singer and Aaron Wildavsky put forward the Zones of Peace versus Zones of Turmoil thesis, which essentially pushes into the background the core ideas of the nation-state, national interest and national power. Singer and Wildavsky pointed out that adequate comprehension of the real world order required the United States to separate it into two parts. The first part was the 'zones of peace, wealth and democracy', which included the countries of 'Western Europe, the United States and Canada, Japan and the Antipodes, which together have about 15 per cent of the world's population'. The second part was the 'zones of turmoil, war and development', which was comprised of the countries of 'Eastern and Southeastern Europe, the territory of the former Soviet Union, and most of Africa, Asia and Latin America'.[74] The core argument of Singer and Wildavsky's thesis is stated below:

The political relations among the countries in the zones of peace and democracy will not be influenced by relative military power. Nor will these nations be divided into competing military blocs seeking to balance each other's power. There probably will be plenty of national and other conflict, but the decisive special characteristic of this conflict is that no one will believe that it can lead to war. Moreover, the countries in the zones of peace and democracy will have most of the power in the world, so they will not face a serious threat to their national survival or freedom, regardless of their outcomes in the other zones.[75]

To explain why the zones of peace, wealth and democracy would be more peaceful, Singer and Wildavsky put forward the following reasons:

> The reason the zones of peace and democracy can be expected to have internal peace – even if there are ample conflicts – is that all the countries in these zones are democracies. A central pillar of the next world order is that modern democracies do not go to war with one another, do not even seriously imagine the possibility of being at war with one another.[76]

Singer and Wildavsky argued that democracy itself would be a potent instrument to achieve peace in the first part of the world because democracy would eliminate the inherent fear of being conquered or destroyed. Both scholars believed firmly that democracy would push to the background issues of national security concerns, which would be reduced in the near future in the zones of peace. As they pointed out eloquently: 'A happy by-product of the disappearance of the Soviet Union is that the world is relieved from having to pretend to believe in the moral equivalence of superpowers; we can again understand that democracies are morally better and militarily less threatening.'[77]

This theory of peace and democracy prevailing in the zones of peace, wealth and democracy was first echoed by liberals such as Kant, Woodrow Wilson and Norman Angell around the time of World War I. It was based on the presumption that liberal democracies were inherently peaceful because liberal democratic governments were usually 'pacific' and would not wage war against each other. The prospect of peace and stability in these states was, therefore, a logical corollary. Wilson's primary emphasis was on peace, democracy and self-determination as well as the creation of an international order to be managed by an international organization, leading to the foundation of the League of Nations and, later on, the United Nations. Angell's core emphasis was on modernization (inexplicably referring to Western modernization) and 'interdependence, which will reduce the likelihood of war and simultaneously enhance the possibilities of peace and stability in the liberal democracies'.[78]

Immanuel Kant's theory of perpetual peace (1795) advanced the idea that perpetual peace was sought to be achieved through 'constitutional' and 'mutually respectful states', also referred to as 'republics', which would eventually establish perpetual peace in the world. Tim Dunne has summarized Kant's ideas nicely:

> For Kant, the imperative to achieve perpetual peace required the transformation of individual consciousness, republican constitutionalism and a federal contract between states to abolish war (rather than to regulate it as liberal realists such as Hugo Grotius had argued). This federation can be likened to a permanent peace treaty, rather than a 'super-state' actor or 'world government'.[79]

In recent times, this line of thinking of enhancing peace, wealth and democracy in liberal democracies was well articulated by Michael Doyle (1983) and Bruce Russett (1983), who advanced the democratic peace theory. The democratic peace theory was based upon three basic assumptions. The first assumption was that conflict resolution among democratic states was usually peaceful. The second was that there were certain common values that prevailed in liberal democratic states. The third was that democratic states had much more economic cooperation among themselves. Republican liberals, therefore, assumed that the zones of peace among liberal democracies would be optimum.[80] Moreover, liberal democratic states were much more peaceful and wealthy because there was much less possibility of war between liberal democratic states (such as the United States and Canada) than between authoritarian states.

Bruce Russett, while further contributing to this debate, pointed out that it was primarily due to the 'norms and strategies characteristic of democracy to democracy relationships' that we were able to understand the prevalence of peace and absence of war in the liberal democracies and thereby steadily expand the zones of peace.[81] Russett explained the democratic peace theory in the following manner:

> The end of ideological hostility matters doubly because it represents a surrender to the force of Western values of economic and especially political freedom. To the degree that countries once ruled by autocratic systems become democratic, a striking fact about the world comes to bear on any discussion of the future of international relations: In the modern international system, democracies have almost never fought each other. This statement represents a complex phenomenon: (a) democracies rarely fight each other (an empirical statement) because (b) they have other means of resolving conflicts between them and, therefore, do not need to fight each other (a prudential statement), and (c) they perceive that democracies should not fight each other (a normative statement about principles of right behaviour), which reinforces the empirical statement. By this reasoning, the more democracies there are in the world, the fewer potential adversaries ... democracies will have and the wider the zones of peace.[82]

On the other hand, zones of turmoil are usually unstable, ungovernable, overpopulated and exhibit rampant and large scale systematic violence, 'mass murders, famines and epidemics committed by governments or wars' (all showing a tendency towards disaster), and a democratic deficit as fragile democracies tend to subvert to authoritarian regimes.[83] However, there is a possibility of the expansion of democracy even in the erstwhile Soviet Union and the East European countries. The liberal-idealist tradition received a major boost with the collapse of the Soviet Union and the East European countries and also the simultaneous resurgence of a neo-conservative and neo-liberal world (popularly referred to as neo-cons) in explaining the contours of the contemporary world order. In supporting the case for peace and democracy, Singer and Wildavsky pointed out:

> The exclusive legitimacy of democracy comes partly from the failure of communism and fascism, partly from the fact that there is no existing ideology that challenges democracy – with the partial exception of Islam – and partly from the example of the zones of peace. The fact that the rich and powerful countries are all democracies is potent support for theoretical argument in favour of democracy and for democracy's inherent appeal to human beings.[84]

Justifying the democratic argument, Singer and Wildavsky further argued, 'Democracies will continue to have the power to intervene decisively through most of the zones of turmoil – except parts of Asia – even if the United States and other NATO armies are substantially reduced.'[85] They continued:

> There will almost certainly be wars in the Middle East and Africa during the next century. They may be as long lasting and bloody as the stalemated war between Iraq and Iran, which took over a million lives. But it is important to understand that the forces fighting in those wars will not be forces capable of serious sustained fighting against the forces of greater democracies.[86]

Singer and Wildavsky stressed on 'real peace' and they defined it as 'not only the absence of war, but also freedom from fear of war – (which) is what makes the international order in the zones occupied by modern mass wealth democracies something new in this world'.[87] Singer and Wildavsky pointed out that the zones of peace were essentially 'modern mass high wealth democracies', with high living standards and boasting of a 'productive citizenry' and a 'complex information intensive economy', or what they termed 'quality economies'.[88] They also identified a direct correlation between democracy and wealth and democracy and peace, arguing that countries that were democratic were usually wealthy and peaceful. And 'modern' essentially connoted that these states were also technologically advanced, thanks to their high productivity and the benefits they accrued from the information and communication revolution, a by-product of the process of globalization. The term, 'productivity', primarily denoted people's productive behaviour.

Singer and Wildavsky argued that democracies do not go to war against each other because of four reasons. Firstly, democracies take most major national decisions keeping their peoples' aspirations in mind. Secondly, most of the leaders in successful democratic political systems deploy non-violence as a strategy to solve political conflicts. Thirdly, democracies take the concept of community as a whole – both majority and minority opinion. Lastly, there is a strong semblance and element of kinship between people living in democracies than exists between those living in authoritarian or dictatorial regimes.[89]

The fact that democracies usually abjure violent methods both in their domestic relations as well as foreign policy has been best explained by R.J. Rummel, who made a comparative study of the possibilities of waging war in both democratic as well as non-democratic countries. It will be apt to quote here the main argument of Rummel, who has been quoted by Singer and Wildavsky. Rummel pointed out, 'In this large body of historical experience, democracies had a much lower chance of going to war with other forms of government – with equal opportunities. And the more democratic a country was, the less likely it was to get into substantial wars.'[90] The conclusions, therefore, are quite in consonance with the liberal-idealist tradition, the Kantian tradition of perpetual peace as well as the more recent democratic peace theory posited by Michael Doyle and Bruce Russett.

The zones of peace will bring about peace, democracy and wealth because 'democracies' ability to help others depends on their having a strong belief in and understanding of what they have been doing: democracy, market economies and ethical and social values'.[91] They would no longer be governed by the classical balance of power concept, even though these nations would continue to be governed and guided by those traditional norms of diplomacy and politics. Singer and Wildavsky argued: 'In the new order, however, one of the most potent sources of conflict will be gone – nations will not have to manoeuvre to maintain a military balance of power. None of the countries in the zones of peace will be in military blocs, worrying about becoming weaker than another military bloc.'[92]

Singer and Wildavsky argued that some fragments of geo-economic conflict were a possibility in the zones of peace, especially between the United States, Japan and the European Union. Such conflicts would be related primarily to issues such as competitive subsidies, trade restrictions and monetary policies. But these conflicts would never come in the way of their core national interests. And, because of globalization and increasing regionalization, these geo-economic conflicts were likely to be minimized.

The zones of turmoil, on the other hand, would witness the rise and dominance of authoritarian governments and very weak and fragile democracy, and they would be plagued by violence, hatred, bloodshed and overpopulation – in one phrase, virtually 'ungovernable nations', which would force people to migrate to democratic regimes. In a similar vein to this argument posited by Singer and Wildavsky, Robert D. Kaplan pointed out 'how scarcity, crime, overpopulation, tribalism and disease are rapidly destroying the social fabric of our planet'.[93] Kaplan substantiated this argument with the example of West Asia. He argued that criminal anarchy posed the real 'strategic' threat to the world community, where there was wide prevalence of 'demographic, environmental and societal stress'.[94]

Kaplan's main work pointed to two kinds of simultaneous developments. The first was that there had taken place a gradual erosion of the national and international borders, and the second, 'that private armies, transnational terrorist groups and drug cartels are rising to challenge the authority of traditional states and international law'.[95] Kaplan elucidated a 'thesis of a more disaggregated world steeped in tribal and civilizational conflict'.[96] The geopolitical divisions that divide nation-states is, therefore, an 'epoch of themeless juxtapositions, in which the classificatory grid of nation-states is going to be replaced by a jagged glass pattern of city-states, shanty-states, and nebulous and anarchic regionalisms'.[97]

Singer and Wildavsky also underlined the importance of cultural factors in the zones of turmoil. They argued, "Much of the history of the zones of turmoil can be written in terms of the different ways cultures respond to the 'onslaught' of modernity – some of which will be violent and irrational. Certainly, this is one way to see the current behaviour of Iran."[98]

But, perhaps, in a very futuristic sense, Singer and Wildavsky said that there might be a possible reversal of this authoritarian trend to move towards democracy, even though the idea of implanting democracy seemed to be bleak currently, especially taking into account the potent threat posed to the United States by the Islamic powers. Singer and Wildavsky pointed out:

> Democracy will lose some ground in the next few years because the shallow or questionable democracies that initially took the place of

> communist governments do not have strong roots and face tremendous economic and ethnic problems. Also, most of the other democracies in the zones of turmoil have not yet built the basis for stable democracy ... By the law of averages, some of these shallow democracies will fail at least once before finally achieving stable democracy. But very gradually, the number of people living in stable democracy will become a larger and larger share of the world's population.[99]

What then can be the plausible strategies for the countries in the zones of turmoil to move towards stable democracy? To begin with, these countries have to take into account the struggle for democracy (which is, for example, at a very nascent stage in the former Soviet Union and East European countries, plagued as they are by 'democratic deficit') as well as the processes of economic development in consonance with the processes of the global economy. Secondly, most of these non-democratic regimes lack political legitimacy. 'The two causes of this illegitimacy,' said Singer and Wildavsky, 'are the lack of any systematic challenge to democracy after the failure of communism and the development of a professional military ethic of supremacy.'[100]

Singer and Wildavsky argued that after the disintegration of the Soviet Union, communism had ceased to be an ideology, except in China, Vietnam, North Korea and Cuba. It was Islam that now epitomized authoritarian theocratic rule and government. Democracy was almost non-existent in Islamic countries, essentially because democracy has an antithetical relationship with Islam, where there is a fierce battle between Islam and the West. One can obviously refer to the rising menace of Islamic fundamentalism and terrorism in the form of the al-Qaeda and the Taliban, the 11 September 2001 incident and the consequent Global War on Terror.

What Singer and Wildavsky and Kaplan thus envisaged was not a conflict between the North and the South. Harkavy pointed out:

> That thesis seems to have become passé in the light of the political collapse of the Marxist-Leninist regimes in the Third World and the intellectual collapse of dependency theorists who predicted North-South conflicts over resources, terms of trade or immigration. The burden of the chaos theory, rather, is that the wealthy, peaceful nations will increasingly become gilded ghettos – or armed camps – in the midst of a sea of violent, suffering humanity, unable to help the 'zones of turmoil' and ultimately

> unable to remain unaffected by it. Compared to such a vision of demographic and ecological collapse, the vanities of great power competition would seem beside the point.[101]

Foreseeing how nuclear weapons would alter the relationship between countries in the zones of peace and the zones of turmoil, Singer and Wildavsky pointed out that countries in the zones of peace and democracy would be hesitant to take offensive action against a nuclear armed country in the zones of turmoil, who, despite possessing nuclear weapons, would not wage any offensive action against the peaceful, democratic countries in the zones of peace. They speculated on the possibility of an armed nuclear world in the zones of turmoil, especially in the Asian countries (India, China, Pakistan, Korea) as well as many Islamic countries (most of the countries in West Asia, Pakistan and Afghanistan are plagued by Islamic fundamentalism and terrorism), Russia and many former East European countries.

The United States' consistent policy in the post-Cold War period, therefore, has been to promote stable democracy (including rule of law), economic growth, peace, justice and individual freedom in the zones of turmoil, so that war, violence, government murder, poverty and disease are reduced. However, the basic objective of the United States as a major country in the zones of peace, wealth and democracy is to 'help others to find their own right course' and thus lay the foundation for greater individual freedom, and thereby also consolidate peace and democracy.

VI

The Global Village Model

The global village model stands in sharp contrast to the earlier discussed models. While most of the earlier models were based on realist and neo-realist theories, others were based on the cultural and civilizational norms of actors participating in the system. For example, the clash of civilizations thesis predicted civilizational clashes between the eight major civilizations. It also predicted 'bloody' wars between Islam and the West. The rise of Islamic fundamentalism, extremism and terrorism, not only in West Asia, Pakistan and Afghanistan, but also in most of the countries of

Southeast Asia, especially since 11 September 2001, testifies aptly to the accuracy of Huntington's thesis.

The global village model, on the other hand, is essentially an offshoot of the process of globalization and increasing global interconnectedness in the post-Cold War and post-Soviet world. The model's origins can therefore be traced back to the disintegration of the Soviet Union and the East European countries and the increasing assertion of liberal democratic approaches by the 'hyperglobalists' in explaining the realities and conjectures of the contemporary world order. Thomas L. Friedman argued:

> The fall of the Berlin Wall in 1989 unleashed forces that ultimately liberated all the captive people of the Soviet empire. But it actually did so much more. It tipped the balance of power across the world toward those advocating democratic, consensual, free market oriented governance, and away from those advocating authoritarian rule with centrally planned economies. The Cold War had been a struggle between two economic systems – capitalism and communism – and with the fall of the wall, there was only one system left and everyone had to orient himself or herself to it one way or another. Henceforth, more and more economies would be governed from the top down, by the interests of some narrow ruling clique. Within two years, there was no Soviet empire to hide behind any more or to prop up autocratic regimes in Asia, the Middle East, Africa or Latin America. If you were not a democracy, or democratizing society, if you continued to hold fast highly regulated or centrally planned economies, you were seen as being on the wrong side of history.[102]

The global village model thus hypothesized a model of increasing global interdependence, global corporation, global regimes and the consequently increased role of non-territorial actors, multinational corporations (MNCs) and the simultaneous diminishing role of the nation-state as a central spatial actor in world order and world politics. It emphasized the increased Westernization of ideas, aspirations, values and lifestyles at a deeper global level. The assumption was that global interdependence would lead to global cooperation and, consequently, the evolution of global regimes and institutions, which would be of increased benefit to everybody – individuals and states as well as other non-state and non-territorial actors.

Richard Barnet pointed out that the nation-state was gradually being superseded by the increasingly dominant role of MNCs in world affairs.[103] Ernst Haas, also a votary of the global village model, argued that in several crucial spheres of international activity, especially with regard to global issues relating to the environment, nuclear proliferation and international civil aviation, global regimes were increasingly playing a multifaceted, proactive and dominant role.[104]

What follows from the above discussions and analysis is that, essentially, the global village model follows the 'hyperglobalist' perspective on globalization. What we can do, therefore, is to synchronize and juxtapose these two perspectives of the global village model and the globalization hypothesis into one seamless, coherent whole. We can then agree with Charlotte Bretherton that 'globalization suggests a significant intensification of global connectedness and a consciousness of that intensification with a corresponding diminution in the significance of territorial boundaries and state structures'.[105] Bretherton further identified four core and interwoven aspects of the globalization thesis, which is what the proponents of the global village model also advocated. These were 'the enabling role of technological change, the development of a global economy, political globalization and the globalization of ideas'.[106]

Jan Art Scholte regarded globalization as the proliferation of 'supraterritorial' or 'transborder relations'. What is unique and distinct about contemporary globalization is that it encompasses 'a fundamental transformation of human geography', whereby the world 'has acquired a (rapidly growing) global dimension alongside the territorial framework of old'. These are reflected in different spheres such as telecommunications and transworld finance and marketing. Therefore, summing up, Scholte observed that 'the territorial assumptions which underpin modern understandings of "international relations" have become untenable'.[107] "(B)orders are not so much crossed as transcended."[108]

In the wake of the world gradually becoming a global village, Sholte thus questioned the very notion of state sovereignty, which has guided the various notions of world order ever since the Treaty of Westphalia. To quote Scholte:

> largely owing to globalization, the Westphalian system is already past history. The state apparatus survives and, indeed, is in some

> respects larger, stronger and more intrusive in social life than ever before. However, the core Westphalian norms of sovereignty are no longer operative, nor can they be retrieved in the present day globalizing world. The concept of sovereignty continues to be important in political rhetoric, especially for people who seek to slow and reverse reductions of national self-determination in the face of globalization. However, both juridically and practically, state regulatory capacities have ceased to meet the criteria of sovereignty as it was traditionally conceived.[109]

Apart from sovereignty, new communication and information technologies have led to new and more dynamic forms of economic globalization based upon 'two principal processes – globalization of production and the globalization of finance', leading to a unified global economy. This has led to the emergence of MNCs and transnational corporations (TNCs), which are playing an increasingly dominant role in mobilizing and globalizing transnational capital. Further, globalization of ideas is occurring through new means of communication such as fax, email and mobile phones.[110]

The global village model thus relates to the liberal ideas and axioms of free market, free trade, or what the liberal international political economist, Adam Smith, referred to as the 'invisible hand of the market'. Extending Smith's argument, David Ricardo pointed out that a free market would lead to free trade and thereby to optimum economic outcomes and gain. In other words, once it adopts a free market economy, the state's purported control over its economic domain would stand weakened in a globalized world. Kenichi Ohmae, a leading globalist, pointed out:

> The nation-state has become an unnatural, even dysfunctional, unit for organizing human activity and managing economic endeavour in a borderless world. It represents no genuine, shared community of economic interests; it defines no meaningful flows of economic activity. In fact, it overlooks the true linkages and synergies that exist among often disparate populations by combining important measures of human activity at the wrong level of analysis ... . On the global economic map, the lines that now matter are those defining what may be called 'region-states'. The boundaries ... are drawn by the deft but invisible hand of the global market for goods and services. They follow, rather than precede, real flows of human activity.[111]

Charlotte Bretherton elucidated three broad issues that constituted the agenda of global politics:

- Issues that have been considered the responsibility of individual states (and jealously guarded as aspects of state sovereignty), but are increasingly seen in terms of collective responsibility, whether this be regional or universal. Here we include military security and human rights;
- Issues that are transboundary or worldwide in scope or effect, where international cooperation is widely practised and/or seen as desirable. These include international terrorism; drug related crimes; control of infectious diseases; transport and communications and transborder pollution; and
- Issues that are global in scope and require global cooperation if they are to be addressed effectively. Here we include issues associated with the global economy; development; population movements; and management of the global commons, as well as the more specific problems of stratospheric ozone depletion and climate change.[112]

Politically, the global village model promoted the values of liberal democracy, democratization and Western capitalism, which were reflected in the thinking of Western academics such as Francis Fukuyama, who propounded the 'end of history' thesis. Fukuyama contended that history had come to an end following the disintegration of the Soviet Union and the East European countries, and the consequent universal triumph of liberal democracy and human rights. Economically, the global village model posited the growing importance of the notions of liberalization, privatization and deregulation – all pointing towards the increased domination of the market forces or following the 'inscriptive' principles of a free market and free trade. However, the economic and political dimensions of globalization were inextricably intertwined. Stephanie Lawson conceptualized globalization as a 'historical process in which state or national institutions, authorities, actors and so on are increasingly bypassed in the course of interactions around the world, especially in the economic sphere'.[113]

The global village model thus underscored a world order as underpinned by the Washington Consensus of a free market, free trade economic policy. The idea of an integrated global economy was supported by certain institutions of 'global economic governance', such as the International Monetary Fund and the World Bank, which assumed that a heightened increase in economic activity would be of immense benefit to everybody.

Globalization, from the social perspective, was conceptualized as a process whereby the population of the world was increasingly bonded into a single society.[114] The same argument was put forward by David Held, who said that globalization essentially reflected a world that was 'rapidly being moulded into a shared social space by economic and technological forces and that developments in one region of the world can have profound consequences for the life chances of individuals and communities on the other side of the globe'.[115]

Endorsing the views of Francis Fukuyama and Jan Art Scholte, Joseph T. Mathews pointed out that there was a subtle 'power shift' from nation-states to a new class of non-governmental organizations (NGOs) in the contemporary world order. His assumption was that the Westphalian notion of 'state system' and 'state sovereignty' and the prevailing concepts of diplomacy and international law had been obliterated in the globalized world. He believed firmly that NGOs were able to deliver more and better welfare services and were also more active with regard to security, politico-economic and social issues. Mathews pointed out, 'Today, NGOs deliver more official development assistance than the entire United Nations system (excluding the World Bank and the International Monetary Fund).' He added, 'In many countries, they are delivering the services that faltering governments can no longer manage.'[116] It was only in authoritarian regimes and with dictatorial governments that NGOs faced a backlash; overall, the transformation from the government to the NGO and the corporate sectors seems to be the only pragmatic step in a globalized world economy.[117]

VII

The Bipolar Redux Model

This model is a refurbished image of the neo-realist theory of world order. The theoretical underpinnings of this neo-realist stability theory were laid down by John Mearsheimer, who said that the period of the Cold War reflected a period of international peace and stability. In a widely discussed and perspective article, Mearsheimer argued, "Bipolarity will disappear with the passing of the Cold War and multipolarity will emerge in the new international order."[118]

Mearsheimer argued that the defining feature of international politics in the post-Cold War period would be increasing military or security competition among the great powers, which would result in conflict and instability both at the regional and global levels, rather than ushering in peace, stability and harmony. Nuclear deterrence, as it prevailed during the Cold War period, would cease to exist because several great powers, such as Japan and Germany, as well as less powerful states would try to acquire nuclear weapons. This could possibly enhance the looming threat of a nuclear war. Mearsheimer argued:

> the prospects for major crises and war in Europe are likely to increase markedly if ... this scenario unfolds. The next decades in a Europe without the superpowers would probably not be as violent as the first forty-five years of this century, but would probably be substantially more prone to violence than the past forty-five years.[119]

However, these emerging multipolar systems would be much more unstable. Mearsheimer explained, 'The departure of the superpowers would also remove the large nuclear arsenals they now maintain in Central Europe. This would remove the pacifying effect that these weapons had on European politics.'[120] While Waltz projected the emergence of five great powers in the multipolar world – 'Japan, Germany, China, the European Union and a revived Russia',[121] Mearsheimer forecast the emergence of five major players – Germany, France, Britain, Russia and, perhaps, Italy, as well as a number of minor powers.

Harkavy, while elaborating on the evolution of the bipolar redux model, foresaw three possibilities. The first possibility was the revival of a United States-Soviet Union rivalry, while the second one visualized a United States-Japan bipolar world, as speculated upon by Huntington. Harkavy's third possible scenario was the image of a world order in which China was likely to pose a significant challenge to the supremacy of the United States, because of which a new Cold War could perhaps ensue between the United States and China. As Harkavy himself put it, 'What is more, a bipolar bloc structure might well evolve from the current or anticipated multipolar one as a China-Russia bloc faces off against a United States-European combination, or an all Asia bloc confronts a United States-European-Russian one.'[122]

Richard Bernstein and Ross H. Munro, in their book, *The Coming Conflict with China*, argued that there might be a potent threat to the United States' hegemony from China, which is trying to manoeuvre a new containment strategy.[123] But the contemporary world has further reinforced the unparalleled supremacy of the United States, so what Bernstein and Munro visualized seems to stand obliterated. The United States is now trying to push forward the Indo-US nuclear deal as a containment strategy against China. The assumption is that if India has nuclear power and enhances its energy reserves and secures some kind of energy security, the Indian military power can act as a bulwark against China. India will then act as a countervailing power to contain China. Bernstein and Munro's hypothesis, therefore, seems to have been stood on its head and, instead of China containing the United States, it is the United States, the unchallenged pre-eminent superpower, which has devised a containment strategy for China. At the moment of writing, however, the current Democrat government in the United States has reversed this trend.

The bipolar redux model seems to be of very little relevance now. Neither China nor Japan can pose a 'real' threat to the United States' unparalleled supremacy. And, even though Asia is rising, and 'Asian values' and the 'Asian tigers' are quite apparently dominant in analyzing contemporary discourses on world politics, they cannot act as any kind of countervailing and challenging power for the United States eventually. Joshua S. Goldstein rightly elucidated:

> For the present, international alignments centre on the United States; although several independence minded states such as China, Russia and France keep the United States' hegemony in check, there is little sign of a coherent or formal rival power emerging to challenge the United States. Although the United States' leadership in international security affairs fluctuated in the 1990s, the leading United States role is central to the course of world politics in the early twenty-first century.[124]

VIII

Harkavy's Typology of World Order: An Evaluation

Harkavy's seven images and models of world order often complement and supplement each other. One cannot totally accept any one model as a counterfeit to and to the detriment of another. While one can find signs of overlap between some models or images, there are also disjunctions between them. What then can be the plausible levels of analysis? Therefore, we will counter-pose all these images or models of world order against or with each other and then analyze how well they fit into the broader thematic of contemporary world order discourses. All these images of world order are neither mutually exclusive nor inclusive. This has been best exemplified by Robert E. Harkavy,[125] who pointed out how these different images or models of world order can be juxtaposed with each other in order to exhibit their commonalities or dissimilarities. While identifying their similarities, we come across the common familiar signposts between the three bloc, geo-economic model and the zones of peace and zones of turmoil model. The clash of civilizations thesis and the balance of power model posit similar overlapping tendencies. While Huntington begins his thesis with civilizational divides and civilizational clashes, he sums up by identifying civilizational alliances. On the other hand, there are models that are completely in disjunction with each other. In this regard, we can say that the primacy of the role of the nation-state varies fundamentally if we compare the global village model with the balance of power model. Similarly, again using the comparative perspective, we can argue that while the clash of civilizations thesis gives primacy to cultural division, the global village model emphasizes the role of technology and a technocratic society, which will gradually wither away these civilizational divisions. On a different plane, we can foresee that the era of balance of power politics will come to an end in the zones of peace, or wealthy, capitalist and democratic states, but the same balance of power model will continue to thrive in the zones of turmoil, or peripheral and semi-peripheral regions such as Africa and West Asia.[126]

Harkavy quoted Joseph Nye, who analyzed the distribution and the 'three layered' diffusion of power in world politics. To quote Nye:

> No single hierarchy describes adequately a world politics with multiple structures. The distribution of power in world politics has become like a layered cake. The top military layer is largely unipolar, for there is no other military power comparable to the United States. The economic middle layer is tripolar and has been for two decades. The bottom layer of transnational interdependence shows a diffusion of power.[127]

What are the implications of Harkavy's typology of world order on the present predicament of building a humane world order? How do we correlate the ontological and epistemological dimensions of the WOMP theorists' vision of world order with the contemporary positivist research agenda of world order as articulated by Harkavy? It is these two fundamental questions that form the basis of our subsequent arguments. In answering these questions, the research problematic addresses the post-positivist approaches and paradigms in understanding world order.

Within this post-positivist literature on world order, there are four different sub-schools of thought – critical theory, postmodernism, social constructivism and normative theory. We will concern ourselves with critical theory and its vision of emancipatory politics, emancipatory knowledge and an emancipatory vision of world order, which is non-hegemonic and egalitarian in character. Two prominent advocates of critical theory were Andrew Linklater and Robert Cox. World order, according to Robert Cox, 'refers to the particular configuration of forces, which successively define the problematic of war or peace for the ensemble of states'.[128] Adopting the Gramscian concept of hegemony, Cox argued that the social world was a construction and intersection of three types of forces – ideas, material capabilities and institutions. Accordingly, the three spheres of activity – social forces ('engendered by the production process'), forms of state ('derived from a study of state/society complexes') and world orders, conjoined together, defined the global historical structures of any period. These three spheres of activity were not hierarchical, but interlinked to each other and also influencing each other. The forms of state could structure and be structured by social forces and world orders. Adopting the historical materialist approach of Marx, Cox linked the political, economic and social with the domestic and the international.[129]

Social constructivists such as Alexander Wendt and Terry Nardin argued that we could acquire valid knowledge about the social world. This theory tried to bridge the gap between rationalism (essentially encompassing neo-liberal and neo-realist views as well as some variants of Marxism) and reflectivism (broadly consisting of the post-positivist approaches of postmodernism, critical theory and feminist theory), 'by adopting the ontology of the former and a very "thin" version of the epistemology of the latter'.[130]

Normative theory raises ethical and moral questions about world order. Normative theorists address fundamental questions about 'what ought to be' the nature of the social world. They raise questions such as 'What rights do individuals have?', 'What rights do communities and states have?' and 'Are individual rights prior to state rights?'[131]

The post-positivist theorists thus move away from the narrow, positivist and empirical model of world order to the larger ontological and epistemological questions. They are much more concerned with a rights based theory of justice, peace and freedom as well as critical issues of global governance, social inclusion and development, especially for the marginalized and underprivileged people and countries of the world. How do the institutions of global regimes protect both individual and group rights? How do they address the questions of violence, order, peace, equity, social and economic well-being and ecological balance? These are the perennial questions with which the WOMP theorists were concerned. These questions need to be critically addressed in our transition to a preferred and alternative world order and world futures.

Let us now quickly review Harkavy's seven-fold typology of world order. While the basic postulates of economic competition and economic rivalries among states have certainly proved to be a true axiom, many of the assumptions of the geo-economic realists have proved to be elusive. Taking a synoptic view of contemporary world politics, and especially the international political economy, we find that some of the basic presumptions of the geo-economic realists are indeed fructifying. International economic competition has increased quite rapidly. States have in reality reframed and re-orchestrated their autarchic national economies to maximize their own relative gains in conjunction with the global economy. And, the success story of the European Union and the North American Free Trade Agreement (NAFTA) countries tells us that regionalization is one of the ways to undermine globalization. Further, we can argue that the European Union is emerging as a frontrunner in the global geo-economic arena. Regional associations are growing in abundance despite the loud talk of globalization – a distinct contradiction indeed; the excuse is that these will be taken care of by the World Trade Organization rules. Moreover, the assertion of the geo-economic realists that 'great powers' will take the maximum advantage and leverage from their weaker regional partners in a regional organization seems to be a reality. This is especially so in the case of NAFTA, where the strongest ally, the United States, is trying to maximize its own relative strengths in relation to Canada and Mexico. Though some of the basic presumptions of the geo-economic realists are indeed plausible, there are many scholars who find in-built fault lines within this theory. They criticize it on several points, arguing that it has been disproved by ground realities.

Firstly, economic liberals perceive that this theory 'exaggerates the zero sum aspects of what is fundamentally a non-zero sum activity, and at worst, it encourages governments to pursue, in the name of national security, short sighted and ultimately destructive economic policies'.[132] In keeping with the view of the economic liberals, Paul Krugman found the idea of nation-states competing with each other to be an exaggerated view.[133] Taking another perception, Joseph Nye and Henry Nau pointed out that the geo-economic realists were wrong to abandon the notion of 'traditional security and alliances', which still retains its relevance in the post-Cold war period.[134]

While there is certainly the United States-led NAFTA, the Germany centred European bloc and the Japan-led Asian bloc, where does this leave countries such as Brazil, Russia, India and China (the BRIC countries)? The Cold War period saw a 'containment strategy' being pursued by both the United States and the former Soviet Union. The post-Cold War era, the Asian financial crisis of 1997 and the recent global financial crisis, which started in 2007, have proved that geo-economics is important, but that it also signals the demise and decline of the power and hegemony of the United States. The United States' hegemonic aspirations were clearly visible in its intervention in Iraq and Afghanistan in the name of upholding democracy and democratic values, but it failed to carry out the requisite rehabilitation and reconstruction programmes in both countries. The United States' intervention in these two countries met the same fate as in the Vietnam war of the 1970s.

The current emergence of countries such as Germany and France within the European Union, Russia as an energy security power and an Asia led by Japan and China clearly circumvents the growing power of the West, especially the United States and its military conglomerate, the North Atlantic Treaty Organization (NATO). It also signals and heralds the rise of the Rest vis-à-vis the West. Sanjaya Baru summarized this point quite succinctly:

> Given these trends in the past two decades, it does not require too much prescience to suggest that the recent financial crisis will have the effect of weakening of United States' power and enhancing China's. Where it will leave Russia, Japan and Western Europe is still not clear. China's massive 'bailout offer' of close to $600 billion, twice the size of India's total foreign exchange reserves, is a pointer to change under way. China's response to the trans-Atlantic financial crisis is similar to its response to the Asian crisis. It would like to be seen as being part of the 'solution' by the rest of the world, not as a part of the problem. Just as the Asian financial crisis enhanced China's profile in Asia, its response to the present crisis will enhance its global profile.[135]

Thus, the United States' hegemony seems to be in a stage of gradual decline. North Korea has openly defied it with its nuclear proliferation initiatives. Russia has emerged as an energy rich country and is trying to regain control of the Caucasian and Central Asian Republics. China has not only consolidated its own position vis-à-vis the West, but also with many Central Asian, Southeast Asian and Latin American countries. All these developments are a clear pointer to the trend towards multipolarity and a multipolar world order, rather than a United States-led unipolarity.

The clash of civilization thesis is equally worrisome. First and foremost, civilization refers to the early unwritten history of mankind before the birth of Christ and was universally accepted as a product of the land and the people inhabiting the land. There was no question of religion, as in the Indus Valley civilization and the Arabic civilization. This thesis, thus, wrongly equates and correlates the question of civilization with the question of identity, defined in terms of religion. It fails to see that an individual can have multiple identities. Pluralism and multiculturalism, the two dominant themes in contemporary liberal democracy, have been completely ignored and compensated for here. Amartya Sen argued, 'Thus, in addition to its dependence on an imaginary history of the world, the civilizational explanation of global violence is firmly moored in a particular 'solitarist' approach to human identity, which sees human beings as members of exactly one group defined by their native civilization, defined mainly in terms of religion.'[136] Sen continued:

> Trying to understand global violence through the lens of clashing civilizations does not bear much scrutiny because the reasoning on which it is based is so extraordinarily crude. And yet, it must also

> be recognized that reductionist cultivation of singular identities has indeed been responsible for a good deal of what we can call 'engineered bloodshed' across the world. However, this results from the fomenting and cultivation of targeted differences, rather than being just a spontaneous outcome from an inescapable 'clash'. We may be suddenly informed by instigators that we are not just Yugoslavs, but actually Serbs ('we absolutely don't like Albanians'), or that we are not just Rwandans or Kigalians or Africans, but specifically Hutus, who must see Tutsis as enemies.[137]

The big powers, as events show, are consciously encouraging the creation of new small states based on ethnicity and religion, which are all economically unviable. However, the big powers do not like to divide their own countries on such bases of ethnicity and religion. This is an age old strategy – seen to a considerable extent during the days of the British empire – to divide and rule, and it is now being pursued by the empire of the United States.

The clash of civilizations thesis is thus essentially based on 'politics of hatred'. It wrongly assumes that civilizational clashes are inevitable and fails to look beyond narrow, parochial and sectarian interests. Moreover, it assumes that an individual has a single civilizational identity of religion, whereas in reality, every individual has multiple and fractured identities. We need to recognize the plurality of identities to achieve peace and order as well as universal brotherhood.

The zones of peace versus zones of turmoil model is based on the hypothesis of an inherent contradiction between the two zones. It assumes that in the zones of peace, there will be democratic states that are inherently peaceful and wealthy. Pitted against these are the zones of turmoil, where there is democratic deficit and authoritarian governments. We can explain this caricature of the two zones in terms of the dualities of the North and the South, developed and underdeveloped, the United States and them. These contradictions are not easy to resolve and continue to nag at the United States' hegemony and Pax Americana. The zones of peace versus zones of turmoil hypothesis can also be explained with the help of the dependency theory, whereby the states in the zones of turmoil are economically dependent upon the states in the zones of peace. Amartya Sen observed:

> And there is indeed considerable plausibility in seeing a connection between violence and poverty. For example, many countries have

> experienced – and continue to experience – the simultaneous presence of economic destitution and political strife. From Afghanistan and Sudan to Somalia and Haiti, there are plenty of examples of the dual adversities of deprivation and violence faced by people in different parts of the world. To look at a different set of events, it would be hard to think that the outbursts of political violence in France in the Fall of 2005 had nothing to do with the economic and social deprivation of some people living in parts of the country, often living in the outskirts of Paris and other cities, who felt so badly treated and neglected. Given the coexistence of violence and poverty, it is not at all unnatural to ask whether poverty kills twice – first through economic privation and second through political carnage.[138]

How do we then map the ideas of peace, freedom, democracy and development together and provide a plausible interface between them? Should we understand these concepts only in an abstract manner or should we understand these concepts in a holistic perspective? Peace cannot be measured only by absence of war and establishment of democracy and following democratic norms, rules and institutions. Peace is related to the social opportunities of an individual and is thus related to freedom from hunger, disease and deprivation. There is a wider notion of societal and structural peace and economic development as well as structural transformation embedded in the intertwined concepts of peace and development. We take the position that the notions of peace, democracy and development should not be understood in an abstract manner; rather, a dialectical interface exists between these concepts.

An early exploration of this interface can be located in the two Brandt Commission Reports (ICDSI, 1982; ICIDI, 1983), which, according to Hettne, posed the question: 'What kind of development would facilitate the emergence of more peaceful economic, social and political structures?'[139] The Independent Commission on Disarmament and Security Issues in 1982 produced a report called 'Common Security: A Blueprint for Survival', while the Independent Commission on International Development Issues in 1983 produced a report called 'Common Crisis: North-South Cooperation for World Recovery'.[140] These two reports not only exemplified the interdependencies between the North and the South, they also provided an interface between peace and development. In answering this question, 'Hettne (1983) and Sorenson (1985) drew from the "another development" view proposed by the Dag Hammarskjold

Foundation (1975), which defined development as need oriented, endogenous, self-reliant, ecologically sound and based on structural transformation'.[141] In other words, there existed a convergence between the notions of peace, democracy and development as articulated in the dependency theory and the theories on developmental studies. Another scholar, Erich Weede, elucidated the interconnections between peace and development studies. He argued that 'the problems of economic development and prosperity, social order and liberty, and international relations and war are ... closely interdependent'.[142]

Jon Barnett articulated the theory of 'peace as freedom', which explained the dialectical interrelationship between peace and development. His theory was based on a synthesis of Johan Galtung's theory of peace as the 'absence of violence' and Amartya Sen's theory of 'development as freedom'.[143] Peace, according to Galtung, was marked 'by the absence of direct and structural violence'.[144] Structural violence, according to Galtung, "could just as well as be taken as a point of departure for development studies as for peace studies. The two are very similar and should be regarded as two sides of the same coin."[145] Galtung's theory of structural violence also echoed the basic principle of the 'human needs' provision as outlined and demanded by the Southern countries for a New International Economic Order in the mid-1970s (1973 onwards).

This North-South conflict dependency theory is also echoed and articulated in the discourses on critical security studies Critical security studies, particularly in Europe, articulates a

> debate on how the concept of security should be broadened in terms of referent objects (if the state is insufficient, is the answer the human, the global, women, society or the environment?), in terms of issue areas or sectors (should the political, environmental, religion, critical infrastructure and development be added to or replace military concerns?), and in terms of the modality of security (is it constituted through threats, dangers and exceptional measures, or everyday bureaucratic routines, or emancipation?).[146]

The Dependency School and the Frankfurt School of Critical Theory and Critical Security Studies thus 'valued emancipation, favoured structural or revolutionary change, and fundamentally challenged the legitimacy of the existing world order'.[147] The quest for a just world order thus espoused an emancipatory ontology and epistemological perspective as well as anti-imperialism and revolt against the hegemony of the United States. This can be reflected in the rise of China and Russia and the emergence of socialist regimes in Cuba, North Korea and Venezuela. Alker and Biersteker elucidated:

> Would our archaeologist be able to find intellectual order in a field which is attempting to comprehend a century characterized by as much disorder as our own? The twentieth century has been a 'century of total war' among totalizing states; it is a century which has seen the emergence of anti-capitalist, radical and often Marxist-Leninist regimes, which now govern perhaps one-third of humankind in the name of labouring classes; it is an anti-colonial century which has seen a global 'revolt against the West'.[148]

What, then, can be the bases of an alternative world order that is humane, just, non-hegemonic, promises equity and equality of opportunities in access to health and education, and is also ecologically sustainable? How can we address the question of global inequality, poverty and unemployment? How can we empower the marginalized? How can we usher in a peaceful, equitable global order? These questions inevitably led the United States to problematize the vision of an alternative global order that essentially espouses a bottom-up approach. One alternative way of solving global poverty was elucidated by Shutt:

> that the huge global problem of poverty, both absolute and relative, can be solved by seeking to maximize overall economic growth, on the questionable assumption that this will push up living standards across the board. In these circumstances, it will have to be recognized that the only alternative way of solving the problem is through redistribution of income and wealth, both within and between the nations.[149]

In other words, by shifting the emphasis from 'maximization' to 'redistribution', Shutt ensured distributive justice, both inter-state as well as intra-state. In contrast, the contemporary phase of globalization can be regarded as a form of the United States' imperialism, dominated by its hegemony. Petras regarded the contemporary phase as 'mercantilist capitalism', where the 'the imperial state (the United States) combines protectionism at home, monopolies abroad, and free trade within the empire'.[150] In a similar vein, Samir Amin believed that 'protecting against the imperialist onslaught first required a kind of delinking before we re-globalize in order to pursue certain protectionism internally and development without expansionism'.[151]

The United States' interventions in Iraq and Afghanistan were nothing short of Pax Americana. An analysis of the United States' foreign policy was well brought out by one political commentator:

if the conventional account of the Cold War were accurate, then, in the 1990s, the United States ought to have embraced demilitarization and a pacific foreign policy ... . What happened, of course, was the very opposite. Far from scaling back its military spread, the United States quickly moved to extend its presence into areas that had hitherto been out of reach. ... it signalled the turn to a new imperialism in contrast to the policy orientation that preceded it, and reminiscent of the global hegemony established by England two centuries ago.[152]

In other words, global hegemony as established by the United States had led to widespread violence, both between and across nations. It is leading to what we refer to as 'colonization of the colonized'. In other words, most of the postcolonial states have been subjected to neo-colonialism and cultural imperialism by the United States. The conflict zones of Rwanda, Somalia, Kosovo, Iraq, Afghanistan, Darfur in Sudan and Sierra Leone in Liberia show the asymmetrical nature of the contemporary world order system perpetuated by the hegemonic West, and especially the United States. The United States' domination and hegemony have once again revived the core-periphery debate. Samir Amin argued:

> Modern imperialism has nothing to offer to the large majorities of people in Asia, Africa and Latin America (75 per cent of the population of the planet). The continuation of the domination of capital over the totality of these peripheries ... requires the militarization of globalization. This rules out any genuine democratization or social progress for these peoples. The deployment of over 600 United States military bases distributed over the whole planet is intended to establish the domination of Washington over the whole world ... .[153]

Amin continued:

> The peoples of the South can meet the challenge only through preparation – including military preparation – that is adequate to the confrontation ... they have done so victoriously and formulated an appropriate military theory and a strategy, models of which have

been supplied by the Chinese People's Army and by guerrillas in Vietnam, Algeria, Cuba and the Portuguese colonies.[154]

IX

In the midst of a neo-liberal world economy, how then do we build viable alternative futures? How do we bridge the gap between the contemporary world order and proposed alternative world futures? How can we restructure the normative vision of the WOMP theorists on the basis of the four world order values of peace, economic well-being, social and political justice, and ecological balance? What are the bases of transition from the contemporary world to such a preferred world order? These are the normative ontological questions that we need to address in the search for a humane world order.

In order to map out an alternative world order, we will revert to the normative bases of the preferred world order, as articulated by the WOMP theorists. The basis of such a world order needs to be problematized on the four world order values of peace, economic well-being, social and political justice, and ecological balance. The first and foremost argument that we pose is that the state needs to be rolled back in. The state-market dichotomy should move in the direction of a strong, decentralized welfare state catering to the needs and aspirations of the vast majority of the underprivileged and deprived masses, especially in the Southern countries. The market should become secondary and be relegated to the background, so that the poor and deprived masses and the states of the South are not dependent economies. The Southern countries should ensure that they do not become appendages of the West. Keynesian welfarism needs to be revived once again in the postcolonial states of Asia, Africa and Latin America. The Southern countries should provide their citizens basic necessities such as food, housing, clothing, health care and social security as provided in the countries of the North. Minority opinion and minority rights must be respected. The state should be accommodative of the interests of new social movements, such as the women's movement, environmental movement and peace movement, as well as the 'old', class based, social movements, such as the trade union movement and the revolutionary and radical movements being waged in various Southern countries.

The discourse of globalization, which emerged in the post-Cold War period, proclaimed a unipolar world order, dominated by the hegemony of the United States and its imperialist policies. It ensured the global hegemony of the developed North over the poor and underdeveloped South. How can we, therefore, counter such hegemonic onslaughts of globalization and build a more humane, democratic and just world order? One such attempt to counter the discourse of globalization is through building up a strong civil society and new social movements, both in the North and in the South. Such movements that support an inclusive world order and build bases for the normative values articulated by the WOMP theorists need to be appropriated. These new social movements need to carve out an independent space, create the basis of a movement, and thereby lay the foundation for an alternative world order.

The movement politics as well as the politics of the new social movements received a major boost in the post-Cold War period and created the basis of an alternative discourse to counter the forces of globalism or hegemonic globalization. The movement politics thus follows a counter-hegemonic struggle. D.L. Sheth aptly summed up their basic viewpoint:

> Put differently, their aim is to create global politics of popular (civil society) movements with a view to building an alternative institutional structure of global governance, based on democratic principles of political equality, social justice, cultural diversity and non-violence, and ecological principles of sustainability and maintaining biodiversity.[155]

These new, humanist and radical micro movements need to carve out an independent social space and build the discourse of an alternative, humane and just world order. In doing so, they not only point out the new forms of exclusion being produced by globalization, but also the manner in which they are disrupting the livelihood and cultures of the marginalized communities.[156] Further, they need to have their say in the activities of state policies, especially in policy analysis. As Sheth elucidated:

> A section of social activists, and those who were relatively apolitical, but active in alternative development movements earlier, have become acutely aware of the role that the politics of discourse plays globally and nationally in influencing policy choices of governments and international organizations. Consequently, some of them are now participating actively in shaping the terms of discourse globally on such issues as biodiversity, global warming, construction of big

> dams, regulations concerning international trade and intellectual property rights, and so on. In this process, they have become active in a variety of global 'conventions', forums and campaigns opposing the policies of the global power structure as well as in building more durable transnational alliances with similar movements in other countries, both in the South and the North.[157]

We will now audit the world order values and see the extent to which they are close to the WOMP vision of achieving a humane and just preferred world order, and to what extent these values have been realized and are realizable in the near future. We will try to analyze each of these vexing questions. In answering them, we will be concerned with both what the world order 'is' and what the world order 'ought to be'. Is globalization leading to the United States' hegemony and dependencies of the South on the North? Has globalization diluted state sovereignty? Or has globalization only changed the notion of state sovereignty? Has globalization led to integration in the West and disintegration in the East? Has globalization led to a flat world?[158] Or has globalization led to a fragmented polity and deepening of poverty and economic inequalities in the contemporary world?

We begin with the basic assumption that globalization is never even and it is producing new dependencies of the South on the North. The North is reminiscent of the West. The North/West appears to have assigned to itself the role of a superpower and a 'hegemon'. G. John Ikenberry argued persuasively, "(S)weeping new ideas of circulating about the United States' grand strategy and the restructuring of today's unipolar world ... . At the extreme, these notions form a neo-imperial vision in which the United States arrogates to itself the global role of setting standards, determining threats, using force and meting out justice."[159]

On the other hand, Hardt and Negri argued, "Imperialism is over. No nation will be world leader in the way modern European nations were."[160] On the other hand, 'sovereignty has taken a new (capitalist) form, composed of a series of national and supranational organisms united under a single logic of rule'.[161] If such is the vigour of the new form of capitalism and imperialist and hegemonic practices of the West and, more appropriately, the United States, how do we construct a more peaceful and just world order?

Let the United States now evaluate how close we are to the WOMP theorists' vision of a preferred world order. What kind of transformations can we envisage for moving from the present predicament to a more just and humane world order? We need to map whether the contemporary world order is indeed peaceful or more violence prone. In doing so, we need to comprehend the concept of 'peace', not in its negative dimension of peace, but in its positive connotation. Negative peace essentially means absence of war. While it is true that no world war has taken place since 1945, conflict zones continue to exist – India-Pakistan, Israel-Palestine, Darfur-Sudan, all flashpoints of crisis. Somalia, Rwanda and Kosovo have also witnessed bitter conflicts on race, identity and civilizational issues.

The post-Soviet world saw two distinct trends – integration in the West and disintegration in the East. The United States' interventions in Iraq and Afghanistan exhibited the imperialist character of its hegemonic practices. Guantanamo Bay is a living example of how democratic civility was brushed aside brutally by the United States and the NATO forces. The United States intervened in Iraq and Afghanistan on the pretext that the countries had piled up weapons of mass destruction (WMDs). But till date, no WMD has been recovered from either country and this hypothesis has turned out to be utterly false. The United States lost both men and material in the Gulf War as well as in Iraq and Afghanistan. But it has done very little towards rehabilitation and reconstruction work in these two countries. Puppet governments and regimes have been installed there by the United States in the name of implanting democracy.

What could be the plausible alternatives to the United States' hegemony? One plausible way to circumvent the United States' imperialist policies is the rise of the non-West, or the Rest. The Rest, through various forums such as IBSA (India, Brazil, South Africa), G-77, Indian Ocean Rim and the Non-Aligned Movement, should try to promote greater South-South cooperation. The Southern countries should not accept and embrace globalization unilaterally, but develop their own indigenous models of development. The pervasive duality between us-them, inside-outside and West-Rest hampers the South both horizontally and vertically. The post-Soviet world has seen the emergence of regionalism as an alternative to globalism. Claims for self-determination as well as sovereignty and citizenship rights are proclaimed in many parts of Central Europe, Yugoslavia and the Baltic Republics, among others. Ethnic identities and loyalties have emerged stronger than ever before in most

Southern countries. These multiple identities of caste, class, gender and ethnicity as well as the overlapping identities of race and civilizational issues show that global politics is multilayered. Yale H. Ferguson and Richard W. Mansbach pointed out:

> Global politics, in our model, has always encompassed numerous, layered, overlapping and interacting politics of many types (from families to empires) that coexist, cooperate and conflict. Polities, identities and loyalties may be overwhelmed and incorporated by others, but they almost never disappear entirely; rather, they remain within the bosom of their successors in the form of what we have termed a living museum.[162]

Similarly, the rise of religious fundamentalism – Hindu fundamentalism in South Asia and Islamic fundamentalism in West Asia – triggers conflict and violence in most of these societies. Global politics has been transformed fundamentally by the events of 11 September 2001 and 7 July 2005 (the London bombings), which extrapolated terrorism to a global problem. How are the West and the Rest going to respond to these problems of religious fundamentalism and terrorism? Universal brotherhood and multiculturalism can be plausible alternatives to religious bigotry and terrorist upheavals.

Negative peace is determined by the extent to which the contemporary world is peaceful and the reason why violence is endemic today. As Ferguson and Mansbach argued:

> two key factors that determine the degree of brutality involved in global violence are (a) the degree to which the principal identities and loyalties in global politics cross-cut or reinforce each other and (b) the capacity of the territorial state to manage and channel warfare and separate legitimate from illegitimate violence. Changes in these factors, we suggest, help explain the moderation of violence following Europe's religious wars and the later increase in violence of global politics, first in relations among states in the nineteenth and twentieth centuries and then in the emerging post-international world of our present century.[163]

The above debate makes a caricature of negative peace, or how these notions of war and peace are inextricably interwoven. The dialectic of war and peace is also equally visible in the rise of the Rest and the emergence of a multipolar world, with countries such as Russia, China and Germany posing a formidable challenge to the United States' hegemony.

However, we are not concerned only with negative peace, but with a wider and more comprehensive notion of peace – positive peace. In this regard, negative peace is a prelude to positive peace. And, while emphasizing positive peace, we return to the WOMP theorists' vision of positive peace. An integral part of such a notion of positive peace has associated and interrelated values of economic well-being and social justice. Peace, then, becomes not just an abstract value – it is measured by the absence of poverty and unemployment as well as the availability of health care, safe drinking water and ecologically sustainable development.

How do we map the economic well-being of individuals as well as states in the contemporary world? Is the neo-liberal world economy promoting economic development evenly all over the world? Or is it producing inclusion in the North and exclusion in the South? We can argue that the contemporary neo-liberal world economy has led to the ascendancy of the West and is producing peripheries and semi-peripheries in the South. It is only a handful of the ruling elite and corporates that are profiting from globalization. The corporatization and marketization of the economy have hampered the nascent economies of most Southern countries. Therefore, they need to develop the notion of economic well-being, based on the notion of alternative economic development.

This notion of alternative development is very close to the premise of economic well-being articulated by the WOMP theorists. However, in formulating this notion of alternative development, we need to reinvent and restructure the state. The boundaries of the state are not transcended, as the hyper-globalists claim. But the notions of state and state sovereignty have certainly been reformulated. The state needs to be rolled back in. In order to alleviate their underdevelopment, the Southern countries need the state more than ever before. Alternative economic development is based on the premise of a strong, but decentralized, welfare state providing basic necessities to all. It is very close to the basic human needs approach articulated by the Third World countries in their struggle for a New International Economic Order. Hunger, poverty, unemployment and malnutrition – these are some of the perennial changes confronting the postcolonial states of Asia, Africa and Latin America.

We also need to learn from some of the basic postulates espoused by the neo-Marxists. Politics, economics and the cultural aspects of globalization are beneficial for the North, but proving to be disastrous for the South. The gap between the rich and the poor and the North and the South has widened as a result of globalization. As long as capitalism continues to exist in this imperialist form, further marginalization of the marginalized will continue to prevail. Therefore, we need to resist this hegemonic globalization and frame alternative economic policies. This notion of alternative economic development needs to be mapped out from the 'subaltern' and neo-Marxist perspectives.

A direct offshoot of this alternative economic policy is fulfilling the basic human needs of each and every individual. Indigenous modes of production need to be promoted. Foreign direct investment in creating basic manufacturing, namely, heavy and light engineering, needs to be encouraged. However, foreign direct investment in consumerist items needs to be reduced. The consumerist culture of the market economy needs to be altered and reworked for human benefit. The state needs to adopt pro-poor and people-centric policies. The state needs to ensure that the gap between the rich and the poor is merely semantic. The Southern countries need to adopt policies of inclusion, so that marginality of the marginalized does not continue to elude us. We need to map this notion of alternative economic policy located in radical socialist, Marxist and neo-Marxist discourses.

How has the recent economic meltdown affected the global financial architecture? The global financial crisis has affected all countries, including the dominant hegemonic superpower, the United States. Recession, unproductive employment, underemployment and unemployment, and slow economic growth are some of the hallmarks of this crisis.

What can be the other plausible alternatives to this hegemonic globalism? Richard Falk's conceptualization of globalization from below is one such attempt. Globalization from below is led by an array of transnational, new, social movements and civil society and resists the homogenizing and hegemonic tendencies of globalization from above, which are led by the transnational elites and business and corporate structures.[164] But the more viable alternative economy is promoting indigenous modes of production and resisting becoming appendages of the West. Only a state's sound economic development can ensure social and political justice for its citizens.

The 'new' social movements have a primary role to play in ensuring social justice. They can forge hands with identical revolutionary and radical movements being waged elsewhere, like the Zapatista movement in Mexico (Latin America) and the Maoist struggles in South Asia (especially in India and Nepal). These movements can not only resist hegemonic globalization and hegemonic global order, but also re-politicize development and rejuvenate the notion of participatory democracy.[165] These micro movements, through their grass roots struggles, can resist the new forms of exclusion and inequalities that globalization is producing. These new, grass roots, social movements are concerned with various issues such as peace, emancipation of women, civil liberties and ecology. They carve out independently new social and political 'space' in articulating the voices of the marginalized. In following a bottom-up approach, these new social movements can invoke the subaltern approach by focusing on peasants, women and Dalits, who essentially constitute the marginalized. These new social movements are concerned with the multiple marginal identities of caste, class, gender and ethnicity. They are concerned with livelihood and meeting the basic needs of these multiple marginalities of the people of the South. D.L. Sheth observed aptly:

> The politics of micro movements, therefore, lies not merely in fighting particular infringements of legal rights of citizens, but in creating and expanding new political and civic spaces for them by converting the survival and development needs of the poor and the deprived into struggles for their economic, political and cultural rights and these, not only of individuals qua individuals, but of groups and communities surviving on the margins of civil society. In the process, these movements' activists link rights of access to and benefits from the development process with the issues of ethnic identity and human dignity, and view the satisfaction of material needs as a pursuit not detached from the spiritual and cultural aspects of human existence. This is why several social action groups whose self-image is not of being human rights groups, almost routinely take up issues of rights and cooperate with larger human rights movements.[166]

Thus, the discourses on new social movements articulate the rights of the multiple marginalities. They also invoke the rights framework with regard to economic and developmental issues. Some of these movements are not disparate movements, but combine issues of economic development with those of gender and ecology.

While the new social movements can ensure social justice to both individuals and communities, they can also ensure political justice by building a strong civil society. Decentralization of power to the grass roots level and participatory democracy are some of the ways in which we can map political justice. The grass roots movements essentially follow a communitarian approach in advocating participatory democracy. They have not only deepened democracy at the grass roots level, but have also succeeded fairly in ensuring social and political justice. The new social movements, which promote grass roots democracy and development, are closer to the WOMP theorists' notion of ensuring social and political justice.

The new social movements, by resisting hegemonic globalism, also oppose the Washington Consensus on structural adjustment and globalization in various social and economic forums, like the World Economic Forum. They have localized global issues, and globalized local issues. At the grass roots level, these micro movements are forums of social emancipation as well as political and economic empowerment of marginalized groups. These groups seek to protect the economic rights of the subaltern classes. Thus, the movement politics of participatory democracy and democratic development ushers in humane governance at the grass roots level, national level and the global level. D.L. Sheth observed:

> The distinctive feature of movement-politics is, thus, to articulate a new discourse on democracy through a sustained political practice. This is done at three levels: (a) at the grass roots level, through building people's own power and capabilities, which inevitably involve political struggles for establishing rights as well as a degree of local autonomy for people to manage their own affairs collectively; (b) at the provincial and national levels, through launching nationwide campaigns and building alliances and coalitions for mobilizing protests on larger issues (against anti-people projects and policies) and creating organizational networks of mutual support and of solidarity among movements; and (c) at the global level, by a small section of movement-activists, who, in recent years, have begun to actively participate in several transnational alliances and movements for creating a politics of counter-hegemonic globalization. In all this, the long term goal of the movements is to bring the immediate environment (social, economic, cultural and ecological) the people live in, within their own reach and control.[167]

Movement politics has not only led to participatory democracy and democratized the notion of alternative development, it has also helped in building a large network of middle class based civil society. Taken together, the new social movements and civil society serve as forums of social, economic and political empowerment of the large number of marginalized individuals, communities and states in the South. The new social movements invoke a vocal critique of the contemporary statist notion of democracy and development. These movements, by creating a discursive space within civil society, have led to the concept of a 'creative society' and empowerment of marginalized groups. There needs to be what we refer to as a creative interplay of both the old and new social movements to lay the basis for humane governance.

Let the United States now evaluate the ecological basis of world order. We need to map how the contemporary world order can be ecologically sustainable and stable. While doing so, we need to formulate the notion of alternative economic development in an ecologically sustainable manner, so that contradictions between development, economy and ecology are resolved in laying down the basis of a humane economy as well as humane ecology. Here, again, most environmental activists have localized the global issue of ecology and environmental sustainability. These movements, as D.L. Sheth pointed out:

> have been actively associated with such counter-hegemonic global initiatives as the Convention on Biodiversity, Agenda 21, World Commission on Dams, Alliance for Comprehensive Democracy, and so on. These initiatives are not just confined to the transcendental global space. They are correctly embodied in their activities at national and local levels in the form of disseminating awareness and activating organizations at the grass roots level to identify and oppose specific policies, programmes and legislations meant to expand hegemonic global power.[168]

The ecological movements thus seek to restructure the economy in an ecologically and environmentally sustainable manner, so that sustainable development is achieved. The Chipko Movement, the Narmada Bachao Andolan, the National Alliance for People's Movements (NAPM), A Campaign for Peoples' Control over Natural Resources, There is an Alternative, The Living Democracy Movement and the Coalition for Nuclear Disarmament and Peace are some of the prominent new social movements that are concerned with the issues of peace, ecology and maintaining biodiversity, deepening democracy and women's emancipation in India.[169] The convergence and fusion of such diverse issues in the new social movements have deepened participatory democracy in various parts of the Third World. Global warming, climate change and greenhouse gas emissions are global environmental issues and have been debated at various environmental summits and conferences, such as the Earth Summit (1992), the Kyoto Protocol (1997), the Bali Summit (2007) and the Copenhagen Conference (2009). Often, there is a fusion of the women's movement with peace and ecological and developmental movements to lay the basis for a women-centric and humane economy as well as ecology. Ecological destruction caused by the creation of special economic zones (SEZs) and forcible land acquisition are being questioned seriously by diverse new social movements. These movements provide a critique of lopsided and uneven economic development between, within and across nations.

The new social movements provide a vocal critique of the Bretton Woods model of hegemonic development and the structures of dependency it created in the South. They resist the homogenization and hegemonization that is sought to be achieved by globalization through 'one worldism'. These trenchant critiques, along with the new left critique, provide the basis for alternative development. What kind of transformation can we envisage for moving from the present predicament to build a viable, humane and just world order? What are the desirable normative goals that we ought to pursue in the quest for an equitable and just world order? Is such a quest an elusive goal or can we realize it?

In answering all these questions, we can argue that we need to build on the foundational theories of WOMP in our quest for a just and equitable world order. The normative values of peace, economic well-being, social and political justice, and ecological balance, as articulated by the WOMP theorists, ought to be promoted more vigorously in laying the foundation for a humane world order. Conscious and consensual human efforts need to be channelled to transform them into universalizable values. Perhaps, a new generational change and leadership is needed to move from WOMP I to WOMP II. Most WOMP theorists have now moved into other scholarly, academic and activist pursuits. The usual binaries and dialectics between us-them, inside-outside and developed-underdeveloped need to be transcended to build a humane world order. Narratives of globalism and one worldism need to be overcome in order to remove the structural dependencies created by Pax Americana. New narratives of counter-globalism, as articulated by the WOMP theorists, need to be appropriated in laying down the foundations for an equitable and just world order, which provides the space for both individual and community identities to flourish. We need to re-envision the transition stages for moving from the present predicament of a disorderly world to a more peaceful, equitable and just world order. In doing so, we need to map the transition strategies as espoused by the WOMP theorists as well as those outlined above.

Rather than having only one globalist model of world order, we need to formulate several alternative models of world order, which are neither Pax Americana, nor hegemonic. These models, on the other hand, raise the pertinent question: What ought to be the basis of such a world order movement? The world order theorist is concerned with the realization of the desirable normative goals of peace, economic well-being, social and political justice, and ecological balance. The world order theorist is equally concerned with a viable transition strategy to move towards the preferred world. We are not concerned with only empirical observations, but in predicting the move towards a more humane world. Whether it is naïve or utopian cannot be outlined at this juncture, but certainly our vision and promise is of a normative alternative world future, which is equitable, just and humane. Humane governance and participatory democracy are the other prerequisites for a humane, benevolent and just world order.

At the same time, on a different plane, a decentralized state with varying doses of Keynesian welfarism needs to be appropriated. Southern countries need to formulate an alternative notion of world order, which is not only ecologically sustainable, but also more humane and just for all of mankind. Such a world order will lay down the basis of humane governance and, thereby, a humane world order, which is economically more just and equitable as well as peaceful in orientation. Only a humane world order will lay down the basis for emancipation of the marginalized and deprived and lay down the basis for emancipatory knowledge, society, economy and polity.

We conclude by saying that our quest for a more humane and just world order is more appropriate today than it was ever before. In this regard, WOMP and WOMP-like efforts are even more needed today in a world dominated by neo-liberals and neo-conservatives, in order to emancipate the millions of marginalized and deprived people, especially in the Southern countries. Perhaps, WOMP II will lay the foundation for a more equitable, just and humane world order.

Notes

1. Robert E. Harkavy, 'Images of the Coming International System', in *Orbis: A Journal of World Affairs* (Fall 1997), 569–90.
2. Michael Mastanduno, 'A Realist View: Three Images of the Coming International Order', in *International Order and the Future of World Politics*, T.V. Paul and John A. Hall, eds (Cambridge: Cambridge University Press, 1999), 37.
3. Ibid., 23.
4. Kenneth Waltz, quoted in Michael Mastanduno, 'A Realist View: Three Images of the Coming International Order', 23. For details, refer Kenneth Waltz, 'The Emerging Structure of International Politics', in *International Security* 18 (1993), 45–73.
5. Eric Heginbotham and Richard Samuels, quoted in Michael Mastanduno, 'A Realist View: Three Images of the Coming International Order', 23. For detailed analysis, refer Eric Heginbotham and Richard Samuels, 'Mercantile Realism and Japanese Foreign Policy', *International Security* 22 (1998), 190–4.
6. The assumption of geo-economic theorists such as Mead, Garten, Luttwak and Thurow has been summarized principally in Robert E. Harkavy, 'Images of the Coming International System', 572. For details, refer Walter Russell Mead, 'On the Road to Ruin', in *Harper's* (March 1990), 59–64; Jeffrey Garten, *A Cold Peace* (New York: Times Books, 1992); Edward Luttwak, *The Endangered American Dream* (New York: Simon and Schuster, 1993); and Lester Thurow, *Head to Head: The Coming Economic Battle among Japan, Europe and America* (New York: Morrow, 1992).
7. Robert E. Harkavy, 'Images of the Coming International System', in *Orbis: A Journal of World Affairs* (Fall 1997): 572.
8. Ibid., 573.
9. Ibid.
10. Ibid.
11. Ibid., 573–74.
12. Ibid., 574.

13. Ibid.
14. Ibid., 574.
15. Ibid.
16. Michael Mastanduno, 'A Realist View: Three Images of the Coming International Order', 24.
17. Ibid.
18. Ibid.
19. Ibid.
20. Kenneth Waltz, *Theory of International Politics* (Reading: Addison-Wesley, 1979).
21. Robert Jackson and Georg Sorenson, *Introduction to International Relations: Theories and Approaches* (New York: Oxford University Press, 2003), 51.
22. John Mearsheimer, 'Disorder Restored', in *Rethinking America's Security*, Graham Allison and Gregory F. Treverton, eds (New York: Norton, 1992), 227.
23. John Mearsheimer, 'Back to the Future: Instability in Europe after the Cold War', in *The Cold War and After: Prospects for Peace*, S. Lyn Jones, ed. (Cambridge, MA: MIT Press, 1993), 187.
24. Ibid., 142.
25. Ibid., 143.
26. Kenneth Waltz, 'The Emerging Structure of International Politics', in *International Security* 18 (1994): 45–73.
27. Christopher Layne, 'The Unipolar Illusion: Why New Great Powers Will Rise'.
28. Robert Jackson and Georg Sorenson, *Introduction to International Relations: Theories and Approaches* (New York: Oxford University Press, 2003), 91.
29. Ibid.
30. Samuel P. Huntington, 'The Clash of Civilizations', in *Foreign Affairs* (Summer 1993), 22.
31. Ibid., 23.
32. Ibid.
33. Huntington, cited in Harkavy, 'Images of the Coming International System', 579.
34. Samuel P. Huntington, *The Clash of Civilizations and the Remaking of World Order* (New Delhi: Viking Penguin Books, 1997), 20.
35. Samuel P. Huntington, 'The Clash of Civilizations', in *Foreign Affairs* (Summer 1993), 24.

36. Samuel P. Huntington, *The Clash of Civilizations and the Remaking of World Order* (New Delhi: Viking Penguin Books, 1997), 20–21.
37. Samuel P. Huntington, 'The Clash of Civilizations', in *Foreign Affairs* (Summer 1993), 25.
38. Ibid., 29.
39. Huntington, cited in Harkavy, 'Images of the Coming International System', 579.
40. Ibid., 580.
41. Samuel P. Huntington, 'The Clash of Civilizations', in *Foreign Affairs* (Summer 1993), 23.
42. Ibid., 23.
43. Stephanie Lawson, *International Relations: Short Introductions* (Cambridge: Polity Press, 2003), 68–69.
44. Huntington, cited in Harkavy, 'Images of the Coming International System', 580.
45. Michael Cox, 'International History since 1989', in *The Globalization of World Politics: An Introduction to International Relations*, John Baylis and Steve Smith, eds (New York: Oxford University Press, 2001), 116.
46. Simon Murden, 'Culture in World Affairs', in *The Globalization of World Politics: An Introduction to International Relations*, 462.
47. Ibid.
48. Samuel P. Huntington, *The Clash of Civilizations and the Remaking of World Order* (New Delhi: Viking Penguin Books, 1997), 264–65.
49. Ibid., 262.
50. Ibid., 264.
51. Samuel P. Huntington, 'The Clash of Civilizations", *Foreign Affairs* (Summer 1993), 41 and 49.
52. Samuel P. Huntington, *The Clash of Civilizations and the Remaking of World Order* (New Delhi: Viking Penguin Books, 1997), 321.
53. President Bush and Secretary of State Rice discussed the Middle East Crisis at Prairie Chapel Ranch, Crawford, Texas, on 7 August 2006; accessed at www.whitehouse.gov.
54. Charles Krauthammer, 'The Unipolar Moment', in *Foreign Affairs* 70, No. 1 (1990–91), 23–24.
55. Ibid., 29.
56. Ibid., 24.
57. Ibid., 28.
58. Ibid., 32.

59. Ibid., 24–32.
60. Samuel P. Huntington, 'The US – Decline or Renewal?', in *Foreign Affairs* (Winter 1988–89), 91.
61. Fareed Zakaria, 'The Future of American Power', in *Foreign Affairs* 87, No. 3 (May–June 2008), 27–31.
62. Modelski, quoted in Harkavy, 'Images of the Coming International System', op. cit., 1997, 579–80.
63. Ibid., 582. For details, refer George Modelski, *Long Cycles in World Politics* (Seattle, Washington: University of Washington Press, 1985).
64. Ibid., 582.
65. Cohen, Krepenvich, Perry and Owens, quoted in Harkavy, 'Images of the Coming International System', 582.
66. Richard N. Haas, 'The Age of Nonpolarity: What Will Follow US Dominance?', in *Foreign Affairs* 87, No. 3 (May–June 2008), 46.
67. Ibid., 46.
68. Ibid., 50.
69. Fareed Zakaria, 'The Future of American Power', in *Foreign Affairs* 87, No. 3 (May–June 2008), 43.
70. Richard N. Haas, 'The Age of Nonpolarity: What Will Follow US Dominance?', in *Foreign Affairs* 87, No. 3 (May–June 2008), 48–49.
71. Ibid., 52–53.
72. Bruce Hoffman, 'The Myth of Grass Roots Terrorism: Why Osama bin Laden Still Matters?', in *Foreign Affairs* 87, No. 3 (May–June 2008), 138.
73. Thomas L. Friedman, *The World is Flat: The Globalized World in the Twenty First Century* (New Delhi: Penguin Books, 2006), 265.
74. Max Singer and Aaron Wildavsky, *The Real World Order: Zones of Peace, Zones of Turmoil* (Chatham, NJ: Chatham House Publishers, 1993), 3.
75. Ibid., 3.
76. Ibid.
77. Ibid., 8–9.
78. See Norman Angell, *The Great Illusion: A Study of the Relation between Military Power to National Advantage* (London: Weidenfield and Nicholson, 1909).
79. Kant, quoted in Tim Dunne, 'Liberalism', in *The Globalization of World Politics: An Introduction to International Relations*, John Baylis and Steve Smith, eds (New York: Oxford University Press, 2001), 165–66.
80. See Robert Jackson and Georg Sorenson, *Introduction to International Relations: Theories and Approaches* (New York: Oxford University Press, 2003), 50. For more detailed reference, refer M.W. Doyle, 'Kant, Liberal

Legacies and Foreign Affairs', in *Philosophy and Public Affairs* 12, No. 4: 323–54.

81. See Bruce Russett, *Grasping the Democratic Peace: Principles for a Post-Cold War World* (Princeton, NJ: Princeton University Press, 1993).
82. Ibid., 4.
83. Max Singer and Aaron Wildavsky, *The Real World Order: Zones of Peace, Zones of Turmoil*, 36–38.
84. Ibid., 37.
85. Ibid., 42.
86. Ibid., 42–43.
87. Ibid., 14.
88. Ibid.
89. Ibid., 20–21.
90. Rummel, quoted in Singer and Wildavsky, op. cit., 22. For details, see R.J. Rummel, *Understanding Conflict and War*, Vols 1–5 (Beverly Hills, California: Sage, 1975–81) and R.J. Rummel, *The Conflict Helix: Principles and Practices of Interpersonal Social and International Conflict and Cooperation* (New Brunswick, NJ: Transaction, 1991).
91. Max Singer and Aaron Wildavsky, *The Real World Order: Zones of Peace, Zones of Turmoil*, 11.
92. Ibid., 24.
93. Robert D. Kaplan, 'The Coming Anarchy', in *Atlantic Monthly* (February 1994), 44–78.
94. Ibid., 46.
95. Robert E. Harkavy, 'Images of the Coming International System', in *Orbis: A Journal of World Affairs* (Fall 1997), 584.
96. Robert E. Harkavy, 'Images of the Coming International System', 584. For details, see Robert D. Kaplan, 'The Coming Anarchy', in *Atlantic Monthly*, 1994, 46.
97. Robert E. Harkavy, 'Images of the Coming International System', 584.
98. Max Singer and Aaron Wildavsky, *The Real World Order: Zones of Peace, Zones of Turmoil* (Chatham, NJ: Chatham House Publishers, 1993), 50.
99. Ibid., 51.
100. Ibid., 50.
101. Robert E. Harkavy, 'Images of the Coming International System', in *Orbis: A Journal of World Affairs* (Fall 1997), 584.
102. Thomas L. Friedman, *The World is Flat: The Globalized World in the Twenty First Century* (New Delhi: Penguin Books, 2006), 52.
103. Richard Barnet, *Global Dreams* (New York: Simon and Schuster, 1994).

104. Ernst Haas, 'Why Collaborate? Issue Linkages and International Regimes', in *World Politics* (April 1980).
105. Charlotte Bretherton, 'Introduction: Global Politics in the 1990s', in *Global Politics: An Introduction*, Charlotte Bretherton and Geoffrey Ponton, eds (Great Britain: Blackwell Publishers, 1996), 3.
106. Ibid.
107. Scholte, quoted in Yale H. Ferguson and Richard W. Mansbach, *Remapping Global Politics: History's Revenge and Future Shock* (Cambridge: Cambridge University Press, 2004). For details, refer Jan Art Scholte, 'Global Capitalism and the State', in *International Affairs* 73 (1997), 429–30.
108. Ibid., For details, one can refer Jan Art Scholte, "Global Capitalism and the State", *International Affairs* 73 (1997), 432.
109. Scholte, quoted in Stephanie Lawson, *International Relations: Short Introduction* (Cambridge: Polity Press, 2003/New Delhi: Atlantic Publishers and Distributors, 2004), 125. For details, refer Jan Art Scholte, 'Global Trade and Finance', in *The Globalization of World Politics: An Introduction to International Relations*, John Baylis and Steve Smith, eds (Oxford: Oxford University Press, 2001), pp. 21–22.
110. Charlotte Bretherton, 'Introduction: Global Politics in the 1990s', in *Global Politics: An Introduction*, Charlotte Bretherton and Geoffrey Ponton, eds (Great Britain: Blackwell Publishers, 1996), 4–6.
111. Ohmae, quoted in Stephanie Lawson, *International Relations: Short Introduction* (Cambridge, Polity Press, 2003/New Delhi, Atlantic Publishers and Distributors, 2004), 78. For details, refer Kenichi Ohmae, 'The Rise of the Region State', in *Foreign Affairs* 72 (1993), 78–87.
112. Charlotte Bretherton, 'Introduction: Global Politics in the 1990s', 8–9.
113. Stephanie Lawson, *International Relations: Short Introduction*, 119.
114. Martin Albrow, quoted in Richard Kilminster, 'Globalization as an Emergent Concept', in *The Limits of Globalization: Cases and Arguments*, Alan Scott, ed. (London: Routledge, 1997), 257.
115. David Held, Anthony McGrew, David Goldblatt and Jonathan Perraton, *Global Transformations: Politics, Economics and Culture* (Cambridge: Polity Press, 1999), 1.
116. See Jessica T. Mathews, 'Power Shift', in *Foreign Affairs* (January–February 1997), 53, 65, 66. Also see Laurence Jaurvik, 'NGOs: A 'New Class' in International Relations', in *Orbis: A Journal of World Affairs* 51, No. 2 (Spring 2007), 217–18.
117. Jessica T. Mathews, 'Power Shift', ibid., 53–66.

118. John Mearsheimer, 'Disorder Restored', in *Rethinking America's Security,* Graham Allison and Gregory F. Treverton, eds (New York: Norton, 1992), 227.
119. John Mearsheimer, 'Back to the Future: Instability in Europe after the Cold War', in *The Cold War and After: Prospects for Peace,* S. Lynn Jones, ed. (Cambridge, MA: MIT Press, 1993), 142.
120. Ibid., 143.
121. Kenneth Waltz, 'The Emerging Structure of International Politics', in *International Security* 18 (1993), 45–73.
122. Robert E. Harkavy, 'Images of the Coming International System', 586.
123. Richard Bernstein and Ross H. Munro, *The Coming Conflict with China* (New York: Knopf, 1997).
124. Joshua S. Goldstein, *International Relations,* 6th Edition (New Delhi: Pearson Education, 2006).
125. Robert E. Harkavy, 'Images of the Coming International System', 569–90.
126. Ibid., 586.
127. Joseph S. Nye, quoted in Robert E. Harkavy, 'Images of the Coming International System', 569–90.
128. Robert Cox, with Sinclair Timothy, *Approaches to World Order* (Cambridge: Cambridge University Press, 1996), 100.
129. Steve Smith, 'Is the Truth Out There: Eight Questions about International Order', in *International Order and the Future of World Politics,* T.V. Paul and John A. Hall, eds (Cambridge: Cambridge University Press, 1999), 102.
130. Ibid., 100.
131. Robert Jackson and Georg Sorenson, *Introduction to International Relations: Theories and Approaches* (New York: OUP, 2003).
132. Michael Mastanduno, 'A Realist View: Three Images of the Coming International Order', in *International Order and the Future of World Politics,* T.V. Paul and John A. Hall, eds (Cambridge: Cambridge University Press, 1999), 24–5.
133. Paul Krugman, 'Competitiveness: A Dangerous Obsession', in *Foreign Affairs* 70 (1994), 23–33.
134. Joseph S. Nye, 'What New World Order?', in *Foreign Affairs,* Vol. 71 (1992), 83–96.
135. Sanjaya Baru, 'Geopolitical Implications of the Current Global Financial Crisis', in *Strategic Analysis* 33, No. 2 (March 2009), 166.

136. Amartya Sen, 'Violence, Identity and Poverty', in *Journal of Peace Research* 45, No. 1 (January 2008), 6. For details, refer Amartya Sen, *Identity and Violence: The Illusion of Destiny* (London: Penguin Books, 2006).
137. Ibid., 7.
138. Ibid., 7–8.
139. Bjorne Hettne, 'Peace and Development: Contradictions and Compatibilities', in *Journal of Peace Research* 20, No. 4 (1983), 340.
140. 'Independent Commission on Disarmament and Security Issues', in *Common Security: A Blueprint for Survival* (New York: Simon and Schuster, 1982); 'Independent Commission on International Development Issues', in *Common Crisis: North–South Cooperation for World Recovery* (London: Pan, 1983).
141. Jon Barnett, 'Peace and Development: Towards a New Synthesis', in *Journal of Peace Research* 45, No. 1 (2008), 75.
142. Erich Weede, *Economic Development, Social Order and World Politics* (Boulder, Colorado: Lynne Rienner Publishers, 1996), 4.
143. Jon Barnett, 'Peace and Development: Towards a New Synthesis', 75.
144. Johan Galtung, 'Twenty-Five Years of Peace Research: Ten Challenges and Some Responses', in *Journal of Peace Research* 22, No. 2 (1985), 146.
145. Ibid., 147.
146. Lene Hansen, 'From Camps to Conversations in Critical Security Studies', in *International Studies Review* 10, Issue 3 (September 2008), 652. The book review is by Karin M. Fierke, *Critical Approaches to International Security* (Cambridge, UK: Polity Press, 2007).
147. Hayward Alker, Jr, and Thomas J. Biersteker, 'The Dialectics of World Order', in *Critical Concepts in Political Science*, Andrew Linklater, ed. (London: Routledge, 2000), 104.
148. Ibid., 101.
149. Harry Shutt, *A New Democracy* (London: Zed Books, 2001), 101.
150. James Petras, 'Introduction', in *Latin American Perspectives*, Special Issue (2004).
151. Samir Amin, 'Placing Globalization', in *Theory, Culture and Society* 14, No. 2 (1997), 123.
152. Vivek Chibber, 'American Militarism and the US Political Establishment', in *Violence Today: Actually Existing Barbarism – Socialist Register 2009*, Leo Panitch and Colin Leys, eds (New Delhi: Leftword Books, 2009).
153. Samir Amin, 'The Defense of Humanity Requires the Radicalisation of Popular Struggles', in *Violence Today: Actually Existing Barbarism – Socialist Register 2009*. Samir Amin, quoted in P.A. Sebastian, 'Reversion

to Barbarism', book review in *Economic and Political Weekly* XLIV, No. 30 (25 July 2009), 28.

154. Ibid.
155. D.L. Sheth, 'Globalisation and New Politics of Micro-Movements', in *Economic and Political Weekly* XXXIX, No. 1 (3 January 2004), 47.
156. Ibid., 47.
157. Ibid.
158. Thomas L. Friedman, *The World is Flat: The Globalized World in the Twenty First Century* (New Delhi: Penguin Books, 2006), 52.
159. G. John Ikenberry, quoted in Yale H. Ferguson and Richard W. Mansbach, *A World of Polities: Essays on Global Politics* (London: Routledge, 2008), 209. For details, refer G. John Ikenberry, 'America's Imperial Ambition', in *Foreign Affairs* 81, No. 5 (September–October 2002), 44.
160. Michael Hardt and Antonio Negri, quoted in Yale H. Ferguson and Richard W. Mansbach, *A World of Polities: Essays on Global Politics,* ibid., 208–9. For details, refer Michael Hardt and Antonio Negri, *Empire* (Cambridge, MA: Harvard University Press, 2000), xiii-xiv.
161. Ibid., xii.
162. Yale H. Ferguson and Richard W. Mansbach, *A World of Polities: Essays on Global Politics*, 61.
163. Ibid., 182.
164. See Chapter 4, Reference 41, for a detailed discussion on Falk's conceptualization of globalization from above and globalization from below.
165. D.L. Sheth, 'Globalisation and New Politics of Micro-Movements', in *Economic and Political Weekly* XXXIX, No. 1 (3 January 2004), 49.
166. Ibid., 50.
167. Ibid., 56.
168. Ibid., 50.
169. Ibid., 51.

Appendices

Interview with Rajni Kothari by Sujit Lahiry on 1 and 2 June 2002

Rajni Kothari: This is Mr Sujit Lahiry from the Panjab University Regional Centre, who is doing his PhD on 'WOMP in Retrospect: A Critical Analysis'. In between, he wants me – my name is Rajni Kothari – to give an interview to him. I was associated with WOMP (World Order Models Project) for many years and also produced a number of well known books for the future under the auspices of WOMP, alongside many of my intellectual colleagues and leading intellectuals of the time, like Falk, Mazrui, Mendlovitz, who also produced books. The credit goes to Sujit that I am here. He is going to interview me in stages. Today is the opening.

I suggested to him that I lay out my own way of methodology. He wants my views on WOMP for his doctoral work. If he has any questions, he can ask me when we conclude. I will start with a short history of (the) evolution of WOMP and, then, the theoretical approach, and then go on to the methodology, what method we adopted.

Historical Background of WOMP

WOMP was simultaneously an intellectual cum activist engagement. It was my first intellectual activist engagement. The short history of WOMP is like this:

The idea of world order had developed over time, after World War I, when the President of the United States, Woodrow Wilson, came up with the idea of one world. There were radical left wing intellectuals initially in America and later on expanded also to Europe and Japan. It had developed over the last seventy-eighty years.

So, the idea of world order was confined to the West, and within the West, especially the United States, and within the United States, especially the university system. Leading people in the peace movement were associated with WOMP. So, WOMP as an intellectual tangent had origins in the peace movement. The peace movement had its origins in the conflict between the two superpowers. The peace movement began to succeed. China did not join the peace movement directly, but there were individual intellectuals from China. So, WOMP was broadly limited to the West, and thought of as introducing into the pedagogy. The belief was that students, teachers, the academic community – all could be involved and they would bring about some changes in world order.

Generally, WOMP was an idealistic movement – it is still an idealistic movement in the West. The Pant Commission was appointed to deal with international development issues. I was at some stage associated with the Pant Commission, when I was asked by the rector of the United Nations University to visit Hiroshima and Nagasaki. In a way, all these issues are related. WOMP represents – I will not call it revolutionary, but in a radical fashion – a movement of ideas, a movement in which different streams could flow.

WOMP was not limited to the West. It established contact with the Third World countries. Saul H. Mendlovitz was the director of WOMP, teaching at Rutgers University and head of the Institute of World Order. Associated with WOMP was Professor Richard Falk, who is now a leading professor at Princeton University. When WOMP reached India, they contacted Professor Harnam Singh, who was, at that time, head of the Department of Political Science at Delhi University. There was a collaborative relationship between Delhi University and the Institute for World Order (earlier called the World Law Fund). But it didn't go too far. Basically, there took place only a series of meetings and seminars under the auspices of Delhi University because of the interest shown by some of the professors, who were specializing in international relations. However, a world order perspective could not emerge.

The next time the WOMP group visited India, in 1967, the President of the India International Centre (IIC), Dr C.D. Deshmukh, was approached by Professor Ivery Lizsum of the United States, who was a Visiting Professor at the Centre for the Study of Developing Societies (CSDS), where I used to work and am still working. Dr Deshmukh proposed my name. So, they contacted the United States and all we could do was hold some meetings and seminars at the IIC, partly due to the blessings of Dr Deshmukh, who was its president.

Dr Deshmukh also set up a leading advisory group, consisting of eminent scientists, social scientists, economists and even people in technical matters. However, at that time, I was busy with research, especially election studies, at CSDS. In 1967, we were doing a major all India level election study. So, I said that at some point of time, I would be associated with WOMP. That was how it began.

At that time, when some individuals were contacted, I had the strong support of Professor R. Bhaskaran of Madras University. I have mentioned his name in my book, *Footsteps into the Future*, as well as in *Memoirs*. Professor Bhaskaran persuaded me that I should agree to participate in WOMP. Professor Bhaskaran was the first director of WOMP India. So, with leading people like Deshmukh on the one hand and philosophers like Bhaskaran on the other hand – that was how WOMP India was born.

I was not interested in WOMP at that time for two reasons. Firstly, I was doing research in India on Indian politics. Secondly, I was going in 1968 to the Centre for Advanced Study in Behavioural Sciences. They basically invite people to sit down and write a book. So, I was at that time not willing to make a major commitment in getting associated with WOMP. It just so happened that Richard Falk, one of the leading members of WOMP USA, was a visiting professor at CSDS. He was spending a year at CSDS. He was doing a major book on environment and world order. Saul Mendlovitz visited India from time to time and extended the invitation to me to join this project.

In 1967, at a small interaction at IIC, I invited Professor Jagdish Bhagwati, a leading economist, to make a small presentation on world order from the economic point of view. He did that. At MIT, they persuaded Justice Bhagwati to join. It just so happened that Dr Pitambar Pant, who was a leading light at the Planning Commission and special assistant to Pandit Jawaharlal Nehru, also joined WOMP. So, by and large, WOMP was still then a series of meetings. Slowly, I also joined WOMP, but I was cautious about making any major commitment. That was their second visit to Delhi and that's how it moved from Delhi University to CSDS and like that and later on MIT meeting. I was on the periphery in the sense that they were contacting me, but I was not able to make major commitments. I was at Stanford University – I was doing my major book, *Politics in India*.

I formally agreed to be part of WOMP and, in the long run, director of WOMP India (the second director of WOMP India). The first director of WOMP India was Professor R. Bhaskaran, a leading political sociologist in India. I dedicated my book, *Politics in India*, to Professor Bhaskaran. So, it had Deshmukh on one side, Bhaskaran on the other and a leading group of advisory members.

It was not just that we got the WOMP project and we took it. It was not like many other projects at CSDS. From the very beginning, it was carefully thought out to take a broader look at world order, international relations and democracy, especially political democracy. It appeared to the United States that this was a liberal initiative, though radical people were there and we found it to be interesting.

As I said, I formally agreed to be a part of WOMP India. It was a general agreement. It needed a bit of funding. A small office was set up. It needed some funds, meetings had to be conducted, individuals had to be recruited and acquired. In the beginning, WOMP was located in Lokayan and CSDS was very much a part of it. That is how gradually, WOMP became a part of my intellectual interest. As I go on, I will also speak on the issues in which I was interested.

There was a WOMP India chapter and I was in charge of that section. It involved many people from the universities of India. Soon thereafter, we held a workshop under the auspices of Lokayan. It had academics and activists interested in the struggle for democracy and development. The workshop was on 'Democracy and Development', held sometime in the 1970s. It was a WOMP workshop. This is the broad history/historical background of WOMP. And gradually, WOMP appealed to me as an intellectual and to many of my intellectual colleagues. That's how, organizationally, I became a part of WOMP.

In 1975, I initiated the journal, *Alternatives* (I actually gave the name of the journal, *Alternatives*, when I was in the United States). I was the first editor of that journal. It was a collaboration between CSDS and the Institute of World Order. We had the privilege of associating with Yoshikazu Sakamoto. CSDS had now become the base. I was at its base. It contained many articles – some of them very radical, some of them very philosophical. Radical does not mean radical in the left sense of the term. Ashish Nandy wrote a number of pieces in *Alternatives*. He had gone into the roots of the culture, how to engage people not by just looking into the future, but also looking at the past. Ashish Nandy said that 2050 is going to emphasize on cultural issues, civilizational issues – all were interpreted in WOMP and *Alternatives*. So, it was multidimensional. As we grew, we had people like Ali Mazuri, who put forward the cultural perspective.

From the beginning itself, most people had written on WOMP. That was how it began. WOMP had a programme located in India. They wanted to move out of the Western auspices and visited Africa, Latin America and a number of leading professors in this part of the world. Some of the leading foundations, like the Baralochi Foundation, made the first major critic of the Club of Rome's thesis on *The Limits to Growth*. In Africa, it was basically Ali Mazrui. There were many others also at Makerere University.

WOMP was not only India, but India was important. They thought that Indian scholars would provide a different perspective. I myself had provided a critique of the dominant thinking of the West. There were different dimensions and approaches in the pursuit of WOMP. Even Saul Mendlovitz found that WOMP should have a global perspective. Mazrui emphasized culture and I emphasized decentralization, people's initiatives, Third World perspectives, all of which should be incorporated in WOMP. This is the historical background of WOMP.

Theory of WOMP

The broad theory of WOMP is the idea of world unity. How can this be in a historical situation, where there were arms build-ups everywhere, where militarization was taking place, where there were superpower rivalries of a severe kind, arms build-ups going nuclear and how to prevent that from blowing up, particularly given the experience of Hiroshima? So, to some extent, the beginnings of WOMP were located in the peace movement, as a result of the growing militarization and nuclearization of the world. So, in that way, it was an idealistic beginning.

There were perhaps differences with how to proceed with WOMP. But otherwise, I saw in it a truly liberal, radical, philosophical kind of people. I mentioned that later, people like Johan Galtung and others also joined in. Juan Somavia, who organized the Social Summit in 1995, also became part of WOMP. Many people who started with WOMP either under a UN kind of set-up, in their own embassies, in radical thinking that goes on, started with WOMP. So, it did try to mobilize leading minds from different parts of the world. To that extent, it was no longer an American project. It began with that. Even when it was an American project, it was a little idealistic. When I came, there was a theoretical development.

The idea of world unity was essentially a Western, liberal idea. It was believed that if only the world were somewhat united, there would be less friction. The world is dominated by militarization and all that. Around this time, there developed the whole federal dimension. There are a number of programmes in world federalism.

So, in the idealistic part of the West, these kinds of things were happening. There were critics of the dominant structures in the West, including the American presidency, the American political system, and so on. But at the same time, they essentially represented the left movement within the West. And it was not truly global. The effort that was made through WOMP was to make it a leading organization. I say deliberately a little more. Even today, it is not truly global in the sense that it really doesn't have deep roots in people's movements. This is what we are trying to develop at the Centre, at Lokayan, and to some extent that we participated in WOMP, that we are developing. But this was not there. So, WOMP was global in the sense of groups starting at the global level. It was not global in the sense of having any deep roots in the socio-cultural milieu of the world. That became increasingly important as groups started, articles began to be written in *Alternatives*, statements were issued, and many conferences were taking place. Gradually, it was a move towards having a social base. But by and large, it was a broad international relations and political science kind of approach, beginning with the West. So, WOMP had the idea of world unity. We also thought that socio-economic issues, like the issue of poverty, could be handled only if the world is united, only if there is no nationalism and nationalist conferences, only if there are no superpower rivalries. That was the broad thinking. WOMP was a movement for reforms in the world, which had to be thought of in macro, global terms and, through those reforms, bring about socio-economic changes and also bring about a truly federal structure of the world and, in some ways, try to have the cultural roots also.

The major contribution of Ali Mazrui in this whole thing was to emphasize the cultural roots. In participating in WOMP, each of the leading intellectuals came up with a book. The book which Ali Mazuri wrote was called *A World Federation of Cultures*. In world order, there is a world federation of cultures. The fundamental thing is culture. I will talk about my thing later. But in my *Footsteps into the Future* also, it was basically a critic of the domination by the West over the Third World and it's essentially a manifesto for how Third World regimes and Third World academics and others can reform to overcome this kind of domination. There were other works by Richard Falk, Johan Galtung, Yoshikazu Sakamoto from Japan and a number of people from Africa and Latin America – all of them had contributed to this output. So, there were a series of books which came out. Saul Mendlovitz was the person who organized all these books and gave a broad foreword and introduction.

The Westerners had a great deal of faith in the United Nations. They thought that global reforms would require the United Nations' support. Despite the fact that the United Nations was dominated by the Security Council, the Yalta Agreement got transferred to the Security Council. The Security Council is still dominated by the five big powers. Nevertheless, they had faith because they believed that the United Nations had a very large membership (116 or more) and so they had faith in the United Nations. And even today, there are advisors and so on, and an advisory panel in the United Nations. So, the United Nations on the one hand was intervening in the superpower conflict in terms of how the superpower confrontation could be reduced.

It is interesting that Saul Mendlovitz approached intellectuals, even people who belong to the overall academy, and all that, and somewhat also in terms of discussions and meetings, etc. So, there was an interest in lowering the confrontation and arms build-up between the superpowers. In some way, it was just the beginning of the global peace movement in the West. If I would have to think of it, I would think of WOMP as part of the global peace movement, as far as the West is concerned. As it moved closer to the South, many other dimensions came up – democratic development, rural development, the whole idea of culture and civilization being central to WOMP. It was not there in the original thinking. They came in eventually and gradually as members began to join. That's the broad theoretical output.

It is good to mention here right in the beginning, that almost from the beginning, there were differences – differences between the Western legal mind to join WOMP and some in the United States who differed. I, for instance, was constantly arguing for thinking of world order in federal terms, in terms in which the decentralization process is taken care of. In other words, world order is thought of as beginning from the grass roots – as it developed later on, in terms of our own thinking, the Third World thinking in India, and so on. The whole critic of parliamentary democracy that developed there, in which some in the United States played an important role, in which we emphasized on grass roots, the bottom-up process of development, rather than the top-down process of development, somehow got reflected in our participation in WOMP.

On the other hand, Saul Mendlovitz in particular and, even to some extent, Richard Falk, was thinking of world order in global terms, essentially in terms of global reforms, setting up global institutions, changing the nature of the United Nations and making it more than effective. So, the focus was global. For us, the focus was the Third World and, to some extent, also the grass roots. This internal critique was developed over time, so much so that, I, in the mid-1990s or so, began to doubt whether I should devote so much time to WOMP because it was – and still is to some extent – dominated by Western thinkers. And I gradually pulled out. I remember I had sent Ashish Nandy for one of the conferences of WOMP and, with him, I sent a draft resignation of my own participation in WOMP, which didn't mean that I was not interested in the theoretical, methodological and historical dimensions of world order. But I simply didn't want to be associated with WOMP any longer. It did not mean anything important.

Even at that time, I should mention that we had doubts about the nomenclature of the term – World Order Models Project: It was a funny name. World order was okay. But why 'models'? The United States had one model. Africa had another model. Asia had another model. So, why not think of having three or four models, or ten models, and make it a project in which these different models interact with each other? That was their justification for the World Order Models Project. And people who have not heard of it, think of it, begin to laugh. They simply say that it is radical international relations. These are some of the important things in WOMP. But by the time the critics came, WOMP had developed as an institution.

Even today, as I said, *Alternatives* is brought out by WOMP. A number of articles in *Alternatives* are provided by Richard Falk, Saul Mendlovitz and many Westerners. So, there was a kind of difference of opinion, here and there, on certain basic issues. But even then, we decided to work together in WOMP. I mentioned some discomfort with the name, but we agreed to keep it. I wrote incidentally at that time two-three interesting notes for WOMP to consider. And these are available in the Documentation Centre of the World Order Models Project. They were semi-critical and raised different dimensions – federal, intellectual, Third World issues and so on – to which we broadly agreed.

Somewhat later, while assuming the role of director of WOMP India (because, by that time, unfortunately, Professor Bhaskaran had left), I spent some time in the United States. I was at the Stanford Centre earlier and then I spent a whole year at Columbia University as a visiting professor. It was an endowed chair by one Mr Aria Walet, a fairly leading person interested in world order studies. It was called the Aria Walet Chair in World Order Studies at the University of Columbia. After every year, the chair is rotated, so that every year, there is a different person becoming the Aria Walet professor. I was the first. I inaugurated that chair. When I was doing this at Columbia, we came closer, because it was in New York. I must admit, to some extent, Saul initiated that I became the first director, the first Aria Walet visiting professor. I had no hesitation in saying that I had difficulties at that point as a result of the Emergency in India. I spent the first year of the Emergency here, in America. I had really accepted the Aria Walet chair. I think to some extent it helped me to internationally propagate against the issues. I moved around from campus to campus and the World Order Models Project was not a difficulty because it was completely with me. So, as a result of the Aria Walet chair, I was able to propagate WOMP, not directly. But Saul persuaded me to accept the co-directorship of WOMP, which I did.

As we moved on, we had intellectuals from other parts of the world. I began to play a more important role in WOMP. I ensured the participation of intellectuals from all the major regions of the world, from Eastern Europe, from Latin America, from Africa, and so on. It was the beginning of a heavyweight model in which intellectuals, universities and parties all participated.

Gradually, we were able to draw in Latin American, African and Asian scholars in it. We had a fairly large base in Tanzania, in Dar-es-Salaam, at the University of Dar-es-Salaam, fairly later in Zimbabwe. Nushan Somavarika, who is currently one of the major leaders of the government in Zimbabwe, was one of the co-directors, along with Ali Mazrui, of the African programme. These are some of the names in order. I have laid this out in greater detail in *Memoirs*, a copy of which Sujit already has, and looked into. He will definitely make use of it.

I don't know whether I have mentioned Juan Somavia. Juan Somavia was part of the early group that was developed in New York in WOMP. He later rose to become the director in charge of the social summit. They held a major social summit. Juan Somavia persuaded me that Rajni, don't give up. We need people like you. Sometimes, I thought of pulling out. But he persuaded me. He rose to become the Chilean ambassador to the United Nations. He was the head of the Social Summit Programme. I became very close to him. The Indian government didn't even allow him to see me because I was on the other side. He came to India, visited India. So, he had to make a special request to the Chilean ambassador. I met him in the Chilean ambassador's room. Those are interesting juggernauts, but nevertheless important. Juan is at present chairman and director of the International Labour Organization – he is a very leading person. I am very happy to be associated with him. I am very fond of him. It began with WOMP.

Many concepts and relationships began in the early years of WOMP. But then, not everybody stayed on. Each of them played an important role in their own countries, or in the United Nations, or in international organizations, and so on. But they all remember the WOMP relationship. Even today when we meet each other, we discuss WOMP, we discuss *Alternatives*, we discuss what's happening in the global world, particularly after the end of the Cold War. How do we respond? We are very critical of the United States, of the manner in which it is still trying to dominate. WOMP itself had been a singular critic of the American official conservative domination. So, we played a dissenting role even in the United States.

When I went to Columbia University as an Aria Walet professor, I took my whole family with me because the Emergency was going on in India. So, I had some fear that if I don't go, they would create problems for me and my family. I had taken my whole family to Columbia University during that period. My son, Miloon, stayed on after that. He joined Columbia University. I struggled against the Emergency internationally from one centre to another.

So, WOMP allowed academics and activists to play a critical role, a dynamic role, sometimes even a worthy role within their own countries and at a global level, representing that critique, so that there developed a kind of symbiosis between the struggles going on within the Third World or within the West, or even within the socialist world and the manner in which that was facilitated by our participation. In projects like WOMP, UNESCO, also UNICEF, and many other organs, we made our participation felt.

WOMP had to be seen as part of this family of institutions, global institutions, in which it was not only a world order project, but it collaborated with critiques of that. So through all these, I was able to grope with the WOMP facility, participate as co-director in WOMP itself, but at the same time, use WOMP as a base from which I could play my dissident and radical role in India. Ali Mazrui did the same thing. Ali Mazrui accepted a chair at the University of Michigan. Now he holds a chair in Birmingham (in the United States). He had been moving further with the idea of 'world culture'. So he was almost hunted out of Uganda, where he was earlier. There were some other factors, like Idi Amin and all those phenomena. He just couldn't survive. But he was there in the United Nations University essentially to promote global cultural interests. So, this is how the broad theoretical dimensions can be seen.

The African group – I have already mentioned Tanzania, Dar-es-Salaam, Juan Somavia. These persons I met were important individuals.

I have not mentioned here two other organizations – IFDA (International Foundation for Development Alternatives), of which I still happen to be the co-chairman, now I am the real chairman of IFDA. And the other organization is the Dag Hammarskjold Foundation, located in Sweden. I have mentioned in Parsi that the Dag Hammarskjold Foundation played a role in Japan getting the Right to Livelihood Award. It was an interesting combination of things in which we were involved. So, WOMP had to be seen as a multidimensional initiative with differences within, yet at some times, there were collaborations.

I think I have said enough for today. We also intervened in other debates and initiatives like *The Limits to Growth*, essentially arguing that there is reason enough in this world to halt the rate of growth. But to some extent, it was broadly conservative. There were critics of the Club of Rome's *The Limits to Growth*. Many of them participated in programmes initiated by WOMP.

Environment has been an important streak in WOMP thinking. My own interest and Richard Falk's book were the major works on environment. Later on, Vandana Shiva from India joined the effort and in fact provided and started a critique of the Western way of looking at WOMP. She was gradually accepted as a kind of participant in WOMP. In fact, she is now more involved in WOMP than I am. I have withdrawn from WOMP and am more deeply engaged in my own struggles.

I must end by saying that when I played a leading role, a critical role in WOMP, I tried to involve intellectuals from different parts of the world. I used the journal, *Alternatives*, essentially for some of my writings. There is a big critique of globalization, which I have written in *Alternatives* (in 1999) apart from three articles I have written in the *Economic and Political Weekly*, again on globalization.

So, in many ways, it was a multiple, intellectual forum, which began in WOMP along with the United Nations, in which a number of individuals and nations were involved. It required a lot of travel. I do not travel as much these days. Today, whether we are part of one organization or the other, we recognize each other, individually and otherwise. I don't travel there much these days. But I want to tell you that I always contact Saul in every way I can. Mary Kaldor was very critically important in the global peace movement. They were also from time to time invited to participate in WOMP. When we finally brought out peace as a struggle kind of thing, all of the United States participated in it. I was the director of WOMP India. Many others had set up their own institutions.

I have laid out broadly, historically and theoretically what I know about WOMP. What I have not done so far is the methodological aspect, which we can take up next time we meet.

Methodology

Why a world order kind of thing? The idea was that the world was going on in a very ignominious direction, which was started in the late 1960s and then got further. By the time the Cold War ended, new kinds of development were taking place. It took on a different shape.

The methodology was: Given the present trend, if the present trends continue, where will the world go? I was interested in 'Where should the world go?' So, if the first question is A, and the second question is B, the methodological point is how to move from A to B – from the highly conservative developments taking place, and the world is going on in that direction to a somewhat radical direction. That was called the transitional scenario. How do we make a transition from where the world is going to where the world should go? And what are the issues of transition? That is the broad methodology. If Sujit reads up things and has any questions to ask, probably some of them will be on methodology.

One other thing that I forgot to mention is that in the broad methodology, we agreed that there should be a set of values. The main purpose of WOMP was to maximize certain values, like:

- Value of peace
- Value of economic well-being
- Value of environment
- Value of social and political justice

Later on came women's role. And I brought in democratic self-reliance. These were the set of values that were sought to be maximized by this model – from where the world is moving to where the world should move.

We would like to move the world on the basis of a set of values. So it was a normative framework. It is to that extent in my own work, it made me move. I was already moving. It helped me to move away from sheer empiricism (research studies which many in my centre still continue, like election studies and all of that). So, it was a normative approach in which we follow a set of values and maximize those values. It was a shift from empirical to normative – in some ways, it has been helped by my participation in WOMP.

Q and A

Rajni Kothari: After what I have said yesterday, plus what there is in *Memoirs* and your own understanding of WOMP, if you have any questions or queries, you can ask.

Sujit Lahiry: This is the second part of our interview with Professor Rajni Kothari, who was a leading WOMP scholar and academic activist, and who was deeply engaged in WOMP for more than two decades. He was a leading light of WOMP India. He was also the director of WOMP India. I would like to express my gratitude to him that he has taken such pains at this age to find some time for me for this interview. This is very important for my doctoral work.

Based on what he said yesterday in the first sitting and my own understanding of WOMP and his recent book, *Memoirs*, in which he discusses the differences within WOMP and the idea of building WOMP, there are some small questions that I would like to put before him.

SL: Sir, you said that WOMP was a Western liberal initiative. It was global in the sense that it had leading minds from different parts of the world, such as America, Europe, Asia, Africa, Japan and Latin America. But WOMP did not have roots in a deep socio-cultural milieu (about which you talked yesterday). Do you think that WOMP succeeded in achieving the goals of a peaceful and just world that it originally intended to achieve?

RK: Yes, I think this question needs a two pronged answer. One is that WOMP had set out a set of values to be realized – peace, development, a world without superpower kind of war and all that, to the extent that WOMP was a movement for peace generally in the Western world. The reason I said it was a liberal initiative was in the sense that in WOMP, you can identify liberal, conservative as well as radical elements. By and large, I consider it the coming out of a liberal democratic space within the United States, which, later on, of course, some Europeans and Japanese joined. Some like Sakamoto from Japan joined. Sakamoto had a socialist background. But on the whole, more or less, it was a liberal initiative. Beginning with Delhi University, Professor Harnam Singh and, later on, me and my colleagues, essentially, it was a liberal democratic initiative, some of them may have in their domestic issues more radical views, but in the international arena, it was a liberal democratic initiative. That is the crux of the initiative.

They succeeded in two ways – one is for the United States itself and for the rest, the values they wanted to pursue particularly, as I mentioned yesterday, they operated through the intellectual arena – the university system, the pedagogic system, the knowledge system. They had a lot of confidence that if only the younger generation of students and the faculty would join the peace initiative and consider WOMP as part of the peace initiative, they would succeed. I think to that extent, they succeeded. My only critical reference to that phase of WOMP was that it was too much of a Western project. But, to that extent, they later on expanded. They went to Asia, visited Asia, Africa, et cetera – it certainly expanded. But for a long time, it remained fundamentally a Western liberal initiative, involving peace loving people. People wanted also a degree of justice. To that extent, as far as the domestic constituency is concerned, they seem to have made headway.

The fact that WOMP has survived for more than twenty years now, an initiative that was seen in the beginning as a romantic effort by just a few individuals who had a vision of a peaceful, single, united world and all that. But the fact that it has survived for so long and was able to bring within its fold a large number of intellectuals, peace loving people, policy makers and all that.

But I must mention that from the very beginning, even in the West, WOMP had opponents. There were people in the typical international relations field who thought of WOMP as just a romantic effort. They thought of it as a waste. There were many criticisms of WOMP, which appeared in international journals of the West, which were pursuing the typical international relations approach, international law approach.

Incidentally, I must mention that some of the key people in WOMP came out of international law. Saul Mendlovitz himself is an expert in international law. Richard Falk is a major expert in international law. As I mentioned yesterday, the first institutional initiative was taken by an organization called the World Law Fund. They wanted to create a world law, which would apply to all nations. Later on, it got converted into the Institute for World Order. From that point of view, it was influencing curricula, influencing the process of knowledge, the minds of the students. If you remember, at that time, the anti-Vietnam war protests had started. And gradually, the younger people were looking for a more idealistic, utopian kind of way out of the mess into which the state department and the government of the United States had got. Ultimately, a major citizen movement developed against the Vietnam War and, to some extent, the people in WOMP also got associated.

So, considering all these in terms of their impact within the Western parameters, it certainly shows a degree of success, despite the fact that the leading voices within international relations thought that it was a rather romantic thing. There is no question that it was to some extent romantic. If you want to create a new set of opinions, you have to start as a utopia. And that is what WOMP was to begin with, but it grew, set up institutions, and later on got associated with a journal called *Alternatives*, which I actually started and is also now brought out from CSDS here and WOMP there. To that extent, it became part of an intellectual effort within international relations, a radical thinking in international relations, of course. But people like Richard Falk are today occupying very senior and very eminent positions in the field of international relations. So, I would say that it was a partial success. It was not a complete success. It remained basically a movement on the periphery of international relations for a long time.

The fact is that WOMP has survived so far, it has an Institute for World Order and also a journal, *Alternatives*. Now the Institute has its own journal, which is different from *Alternatives*. All these show that though it was a limited success, it was a success as far as the West is concerned. The important question is whether it is also influencing other parts of the world. My answer to that would be, the fact that it involved leading individuals from Asia, Africa and Latin America and Japan – they saw the limitations of keeping it just an American venture. So, they went out. They, in fact, started with India. It began with Delhi University first, and then with me and CSDS and Lokayan. Some of the major projects, conferences that we held at that time were supported by them. They went to Makerere University – that is Ali Mazrui's university. They opposed authoritarian and military rulers like Idi Amin and others openly. So gradually, they were beginning to find acceptability within the Third World, some relatively radical elements within the Third World, not the traditional elements, not the foreign policy people, but the intellectuals, and so on. So, it was a partial success in that respect also.

I emphasize the fact, partial success, as WOMP did not bring about fundamental changes in the nature of governance. It also did not bring about fundamental changes in realizing social justice, although its aim was to create a better and just world. That is where my differences with them lay, that to create a better and just world, you have to start from the bottom. While Saul Mendlovitz and others emphasized a global institutional model and global institutional efforts under the United Nations, I emphasized a process of decentralization, federalization, et cetera. That continued to be my basic difference with them. I wrote a major booklet called 'Towards a Just World', which was also published in *Alternatives*, showing that justice demands not just dominant global thinking, but it demands also the involvement of citizens.

My whole thinking on grass roots movements and all – that also contributed to this dialogue. I don't think that the dialogue has been completely resolved. But, somehow, as I mentioned yesterday, I felt I needed to give more time to problems within India after the Emergency. And I must confess that I got full support from Saul Mendlovitz and others during the Emergency, so much so that he created a special chair for me in Columbia University called the Aria Walet Chair for World Order Studies. I would say that it remained on the whole an important effort, but did not have an effect in changing the nature of study of international relations.

SL: Considering the fact that most of the leading members of WOMP, such as Richard Falk, have gradually moved out of the WOMP movement, can WOMP succeed in today's conditions? If not, under what conditions can it succeed?

RK: No, Richard Falk has not moved out. Richard Falk continues to remain one of the leading lights of world order studies. What has happened is that international relations has moved in a way, where, for instance, after the collapse of the Soviet Union, Bush Senior talked of a new world order. The very idea of world order here meant an extremely conservative way of looking at world order. It was at this point that I moved on. Richard Falk did not give up the world order thing – he said clearly that this is not world order. It is domination by the only remaining superpower calling it the new world order, essentially taking advantage of the collapse of the Soviet Union. So now, a peculiar situation has arisen in the sense that there is a broad framework of world order studies, in which there is an official point of view, represented by the United States government, and the other in which there is an intellectual and radical point of view, represented by people like Richard Falk, Sakamoto, Ali Mazrui, et cetera.

SL: Taking into account the present fluidity of international relations, can we once again dream of a normative benevolent world order, a peaceful and just world based on the four world order values of peace, economic well-being, social and political justice, and ecological balance? Can we reinvigorate WOMP in the present international scenario?

RK: My own feeling is that the time is ripe to reassert those values, to reassert the politics of those values. Because it is the time when after the end of the Cold War, militarization is growing, authoritarian tendencies are growing, fascist tendencies are growing. Then there is the need in the academic field itself, and then, in the broad social movement, we need a WOMP kind of effort. Unfortunately, gradually, because of the differences within WOMP, and the phasing out of the key figures of WOMP, this is what is happening in all efforts – individual effort becomes more important and the collective effort that was taken on loses its clout. Today, these individuals, along with younger people added to it, motivated younger people added to it, should resume a move again to a collective effort for peace, for justice, for disarmament, for an ecologically sound world and an ethnic way of responding to it. This is my thinking, which has been laid out quite often in *Alternatives*, and also in *Economic and Political Weekly*, and so on.

If anything, this is the time WOMP, or a WOMP-like effort, is needed all the more because of the serious situation developing today, at both the domestic level and at the international level, both within the West and what we call the South.

This particular effort, WOMP, which started in the United States and then grew, on the whole, has slowed down. It is not moving. Key figures in it are seeking recognition for themselves. Ali Mazrui has his own Institute on Cultural Studies in Birmingham, a very influential person. I myself, as I said yesterday, I have sent a resignation letter to Saul Mendlovitz as I cannot travel much. It requires a lot of travel. WOMP was a big travel thing. I do not travel too much these days. Except for Westerners, who can afford it? Even if WOMP itself provided the funds, Saul Mendlovitz was a good fund raiser for WOMP, even then, it had become difficult.

What is needed, which has been my emphasis for long, is a multicultural effort. In different parts of the world, WOMP-like initiatives should be taken up for peace, for justice and for ecological balance. And as they develop in different regions of the world, they can then meet together (at international conferences, et cetera). Then they should rebuild it in a federal way. It should start from the bottom. This was what was lacking in the earlier WOMP. In fact, today, multiple regional effort, multiple cultural effort, multiple socio-economic effort, multiple political effort is needed where inequalities are growing, where injustice is growing, where violence is growing, where terrorism is growing and, in this situation, new initiative within the Third World countries, within the West, new types of communication are needed. Fortunately, there are a lot of younger people in international relations, who, without joining WOMP directly, are highly idealistic thinkers, who are writing a lot not only in *Alternatives*, but also in leading journals of international relations.

The peculiarity of the situation is that WOMP-like efforts are needed more today than when it was started. WOMP, when it was started, was a typical Western liberal initiative, starting with the thesis of one world. What is needed today is a second generation WOMP, a new WOMP, with new individuals participating and new institutional structures participating in it – organizations like CSDS, which is a leading institute in India, and is highly recognized also abroad. The fact that some of the individuals in CSDS continue to contribute to *Alternatives* and suchlike is worthwhile. But CSDS provides a major window for WOMP-like thinking. In its own way, CSDS is fighting for democracy, for justice, for better economic relations, but not within the WOMP framework. The same is the case with Africa, with Makerere University, with Uganda, with Tanzania, with Nigeria and, lately, Zimbabwe – there are a lot of problems in these countries. Nonetheless, there are a lot of individuals in these countries, like Ali Mazrui, who are there in a big way.

So, I would argue that WOMP II, not WOMP I, is needed. We have to make an effort, some of the individuals who were associated with WOMP I can play a role here – Sakamoto is a good example. I can play a role. My own thinking, my own writing, after writing about politics in India, I moved into the futuristic dimension – *Footsteps into the Future*, the five book series and one of them specially on WOMP. One of them is titled *Transformation and Survival: In Search of a Humane World Order*. There are some other individuals who are also doing that kind of thing. They are not at the moment associated in a collective way in a WOMP-like effort. What we need is both an international and global dimension and a local dimension and, of course, some form of a regional dimension to the struggle. For many struggles are going on in which young people are involved to create a better and just world. And yet, they are to an extent on the periphery.

Leading minds who were associated at one time with WOMP, or are associated with such other activities like WFSF (World Federation for the Study of Futures), need to be reworked and we have to move from WOMP I to WOMP II. Whether the leading people in WOMP I will agree to join in, whether there are vested interests, whether there are financial constraints, all of these are a matter of details, they can be gone through. We are staying in this world, for instance, where even American originated organizations are willing to support CSDS and major kinds of organizations. They should be made to support, not just research on elections and democracy, but also on creating a better world order. I think it is possible. The thinkers themselves, the writers themselves, from Ashish Nandy to D.L. Sheth, they operated at two levels – one is with respect to the human rights of local communities, the other is with respect to the global scenario. I think it is possible. It calls for a major initiative. Some of them in the United States are getting old and younger people will have to address themselves.

In my *Memoirs*, there is a section called 'Addressing the Youth', in which I have worked out that generations like ours can inspire the youth, but they also need to be inspired by the youth because the youth today is struggling in a different way. Their perspectives, their thinking, their experience have to be borne in mind by senior people, who happen to be there. Fortunately, some of the senior people still enjoy visibility with the young. Therefore, it is possible to do that. But it calls for an institutional effort, an effort to build a collective, not just a set of individuals who get senior recognition or international recognition or make inaugural speeches in the international arena. What we need is an institutional effort, an effort to build a collective effort and this is where, on the whole, there is failure. Everywhere, individuation is taking place, individuals are getting recognition, individuals are coming up all over the frame, but not institutions. We need to build a collective forum for peace, security, justice and an ecologically sound world.

SL: Thank you, sir, I don't have any more questions. I would once again like to record my thanks, my sincere gratitude, to Professor Rajni Kothari, who, at this age, has taken such pains to give me this interview. Professor Kothari is not only a great WOMP scholar and an activist, he is also deeply engaged in grass roots initiatives in India. He writes frequently. Even today, he is struggling for grass roots rights, with grass roots organizations in different parts of India and travelling all over India, struggling for human rights, social rights, political rights, economic rights. I thank him once again and express my deep gratitude to him.

RK: I must mention that the organization to which I belong and of which I am currently the chairman, CSDS, has interest in this. One of my senior colleagues, D.L. Sheth, happens to be the editor of the journal, *Alternatives*, which is brought out both in India and abroad. So, there is an institution connected with it. But this is not adequate. There are also individuals like Ashish Nandy and others who write in *Alternatives*. But we still don't have the new WOMP that I am talking about. I am hoping as a result of the new interest in grass roots politics, in the struggle for justice, struggle for a better world, to move towards that.

I am happy that I was able to give this much time to Sujit Lahiry, because he was struggling to get an audience with me, but in the beginning, I was very involved with the work at the centre. That's when we decided to make this recording at home. Then I happened to have a series of health problems. Now I am happy. He continued to persist and persevere and had the patience to wait and I was able to help in the end. It was a happy ending. I hope that his PhD, when it is published, will become a source of influence to younger scholars and younger minds.

Richard Falk's Email Communication to Sujit Lahiry on 18 June 2002

Dear Sujit Lahiry

I have received your inquiries concerning WOMP. I am living in California these days and do not have materials that might be helpful in your studies. I will try to find some items that may be of interest and send them to you from Princeton, when I return there next week.

Let me give brief answers to your very difficult questions.

Origins

WOMP originated in the late 1960s, with the first serious meeting taking place in New Delhi, hosted by Rajni Kothari. The original idea was to explore visions of a preferred world order from various perspectives that were important at that time: USA, USSR, India, Japan, China, Latin America, Africa, Europe. The idea was that such visions would reflect the diverse circumstances of culture, economic development, political ideology that existed in different parts of the world. Such diverse perspectives were best collected in a volume of essays edited by Saul Mendlovitz under the title, *Preferred Worlds for the 1990s*. Each of the main participants also agreed to work out their ideas for global reform in a separate volume, and each author was supposed to be advised by a regional group of notable individuals. The hope was to overcome the bad name of a Western oriented tradition of one world or world government proposals. There were many creative tensions in the group, reflecting world tensions as well. WOMP evolved over the years, with the benefit of meetings all over the world, and collaboration and friendship among the leading participants.

As a second stage, an effort was made to shift from diverse perspectives on world order to a consensus document. I was designated the rapporteur of such an undertaking, which produced stimulating discussion and much contention. It was finally agreed that the final product should be published under my name bearing the title, *On Humane Governance: A New Approach to Global Politics*.

As a third stage, with a greater effort to involve younger scholars, emphasis shifted to the agency role of civil society actors, new social movements, and the tensions between localism and globalism, as well as emerging issues of identity. The chief product of this period was a small volume written by R.B.J. Walker, titled *One World/Many Worlds*. There was also in this period an edited volume by Walker and Mendlovitz. I published my own book on these issues under the title, *Explorations at the Edge of Time*.

Success of WOMP

It depends on how success is measured. As a project to change the world, it failed. As a project to influence the climate of opinion and elites, it is hard to say: There were indications of influence in the early period of the Gorbachev leadership in the Soviet Union, and possibly in the approaches taken by some Latin American countries; also, the challenge in academic circles to realism was definitely helped by WOMP and its plea for a normative approach to the study and practice of international relations. It is also true that for the scholars involved, the project was a success in shaping their own evolving outlook and research agenda. It continued for more than thirty years despite the logistical problems of organizing global meetings on low budgets and raising the funds needed.

Present Opportunities for WOMP

There is a current attempt to bring WOMP back to life under the leadership of John Fousek at Rutgers University. The objective circumstances of near nuclear war in South Asia and the Global War on Terror, as well as persisting poverty and global warming, suggest the importance of alternative thinking at this time. May be, WOMP is not the right label. Probably, a new generation should rise to the challenge. We need visions of a humane future and transition strategies to bridge the gap from here to there.

I have tried as best I could in a brief space to answer your core questions. If I am able, I will send you some additional materials.

I wish you well with this research.

Sincerely,
Richard Falk

Bibliography

Primary Sources

Interview with Rajni Kothari by Sujit Lahiry on 1 and 2 June 2002.

Richard Falk's email communication to Sujit Lahiry on 18 June 2002.

Texts of WOMP Theorists

Falk, Richard, *This Endangered Planet: Prospects and Proposal for Human Survival* (New York: Vintage Books, 1971).

——. *A Study of Future Worlds* (New York: Free Press, 1975).

——. *A Global Approach to National Policy* (Cambridge: Harvard University Press, 1975).

——. *The Promise of World Order: Essays in Normative International Relations* (London: Wheatsheaf Books, 1987).

——. *On Humane Governance: Toward a New Global Politics* (London: Polity Press, 1995).

Falk, Richard and Mendlovitz, Saul H., eds, *Toward a Theory of War-Prevention: The Strategy of World Order*, Vol. I (New York: World Law Fund, 1966).

——. *The Strategy of World Order*, Vol. II: *International Law* (New York: World Law Fund, 1966).

——. *The Strategy of World Order*, Vol. III: *The United Nations* (New York: World Law Fund, 1966).

——. *The Strategy of World Order*, Vol. IV: *Disarmament and Economic Development*, New York: World Law Fund, 1966.

Falk, Richard and Kim, Samuel S., eds, *The War System: An Interdisciplinary Approach* (Boulder: Westview Press, 1980).

Falk, Richard, Kim, Samuel S. and Mendlovitz, Saul H., eds, *Toward a Just World Order*, Vol. I. *Studies on a Just World Order*, (Boulder: Westview Press, 1982).

——. *Studies on a Just World Order*, Vol. III. *The United Nations and a Just World Order* (Boulder: Westview Press, 1983).

Falk, Richard, Kratochwil, Friedrich and Mendlovitz, Saul H., eds, *International Law: A Contemporary Perspective, Studies on a Just World Order*, Vol. II. *International Law and a Just World Order* (Boulder: Westview Press, 1982).

Kim, Samuel S., *China, the United Nations and World Order* (Princeton NJ: Princeton University Press, 1977).

——. *The Quest for a Just World Order* (Boulder: Westview Press, 1984).

Kothari, Rajni, *Footsteps into the Future: Diagnosis of the Present World and a Design for an Alternative* (New York: The Free Press, 1974).

——. *State against Democracy: In Search of Humane Governance* (Delhi: Ajanta Publications, 1987).

——. *Transformation and Survival: In Search of a Humane World* Order (London: Aspects Publications, 1990).

——. *Rethinking Development: In Search of Humane Alternatives* (London: Aspects Publications, 1990).

——. *Memoirs: Uneasy is the Life of the Mind* (New Delhi: Rupa, 2002).

Mazrui, Ali A., *A World Federation of Cultures: An African Perspective* (New York: The Free Press, 1978).

Mendlovitz, Saul H., ed., *On the Creation of a Just World Order* (New York: The Free Press, 1984).

Mendlovitz, Saul H. and Walker, R.B.J., eds, *Towards a Just World Peace: Perspectives from Social Movements* (London: Butterworths, 1987).

Walker, R.B.J. and Mendlovitz, Saul H., eds, *Contending Sovereignties: Redefining Political Community* (Boulder: Lynne Rienner Publishers, 1990).

Walker, R.B.J., ed., *Culture, Ideology and World Order: Studies on a Just World Order*, No. 5 (Boulder: Westview Press, 1984).

Chapters in Edited Collections of WOMP Theorists

Falk, Richard. 'Towards a Warless World: One Legal Formula to Achieve Transition', in *The Strategy of World Order*, Vol. I: *Toward a Theory of War Prevention*, Richard Falk and Saul H. Mendlovitz, eds (New York: World Law Fund, 1966).

——. 'Historical Tendencies, Modernizing and Revolutionary Nations and the International Legal Order', in *The Strategy of World Order*, Vol. I: *Toward a Theory of War Prevention*, Richard Falk and Saul H. Mendlovitz, eds (New York: World Law Fund, 1966).

——. 'Toward a New World Order: Modest Methods and Drastic Visions', in *On the Creation of a Just World Order: Preferred Worlds for the 1990s*, Saul H. Mendlovitz, ed. (New Delhi: Orient Longman, 1975).

Falk, Richard and Kim, Samuel S. 'General Introduction', in *The War System: An Interdisciplinary Approach,* Richard Falk and Samuel S. Kim, eds (Boulder: Westview Press, 1980).

——. 'Contending Approaches to World Order', in *Peace and World Order Studies: A Curriculum Guide,* Gordon Feller, Sherle R. Schwenninger and Diane Singerman, eds (New York: Institute for World Order, 1981).

Falk, Richard, Kim, Samuel S. and Mendlovitz, Saul H. 'Introduction', in *Toward a Just World Order: Studies on a Just World Order,* Vol. 1 (Boulder: Westview Press, 1982).

——. 'Comparative Protection of Human Rights in Capitalist and Socialist Third World Countries', in *Toward a Just World Order: Studies on a Just World Order,* Vol. 1, Richard Falk, Samuel S. Kim and Saul H. Mendlovitz, eds (Boulder: Westview Press, 1982a).

——. 'On Invisible Oppression and World Order', in *Toward a Just World Order: Studies on a Just World Order,* Vol. 1, Richard Falk, Samuel S. Kim and Saul H. Mendlovitz, eds (Boulder: Westview Press, 1982b).

——. 'What New System of World Order', in *Toward a Just World Order: Studies on a Just World Order,* Vol. 1, Richard Falk, Samuel S. Kim and Saul H. Mendlovitz, eds (Boulder: Westview Press, 1982c).

——. 'Normative Initiatives and Demilitarization: A Third System Approach', in *Toward a Just World Order: Studies on a Just World Order,* Vol. 1, Richard Falk, Samuel S. Kim and Saul H. Mendlovitz, eds (Boulder: Westview Press, 1982d).

——. 'Interplay of Westphalia and Charter Conceptions of International Legal Order', in *International Law: A Contemporary Perspective: Studies on a Just World Order,* Vol. 2, Richard Falk, Friedrich Kratochwil and Saul H. Mendlovitz, eds (Boulder: Westview Press, 1982a).

——. 'A New Paradigm for International Legal Studies: Prospects and Proposals', in *International Law: A Contemporary Perspective: Studies on a Just World Order,* Vol. 2, Richard Falk, Friedrich Kratochwil and Saul H. Mendlovitz, eds (Boulder: Westview Press, 1982b).

——. 'Keeping Nuremberg Alive', in *International Law: A Contemporary Perspective: Studies on a Just World Order,* Vol. 2, Richard Falk, Friedrich Kratochwil and Saul H. Mendlovitz, eds (Boulder: Westview Press, 1982c).

——. 'Toward a Legal Regime for Nuclear Weapons', in *International Law: A Contemporary Perspective: Studies on a Just World Order,* Vol. 2, Richard Falk, Friedrich Kratochwil and Saul H. Mendlovitz, eds (Boulder: Westview Press, 1982d).

Falk, Richard. 'Evasions of Sovereignty', in *Contending Sovereignties: Redefining Political Community,* R.B.J. Walker and Saul H. Mendlovitz., eds (Boulder: Lynee Rienner Publishers Inc., 1990).

——. 'The Making of Global Citizenship', in *Global Visions: Beyond the New World Order,* Jeremy Brecher, John Brown Childs and Jill Culture, eds (Boston: South End Press, 1993).

Falk, Richard and Kim, Samuel S. 'World Order Studies and the World System', in *Contending Approaches to World Systems Analysis,* William R. Thompson, ed. (London: Sage Publications, 1993).

Kothari, Rajni. 'Toward a Just World', in *Toward a Just World Order –Studies on a Just World Order,* Vol. I, Richard Falk, Samuel S. Kim and Saul H. Mendlovitz, eds (Boulder: Westview Press, 1982).

Lasswell, Harold D. 'Foreword', in *The Strategy of World Order, Vol. I: Toward a Theory of War-Prevention,* Richard Falk and Saul H. Mendlovitz, eds (New York: World Law Fund, 1966).

Mazrui, Ali A. 'World Culture and the Search for Human Consensus', in *On the Creation of a Just World Order: Preferred Worlds for the 1990s,* Saul H. Mendlovitz, ed. (New Delhi: Orient Longman, 1975).

——. 'The Moving Cultural Frontier of World Order: From Monotheism to North–South Relations', in *Culture, Ideology and World Order: Studies on a Just World Order,* No. 5, R.B.J. Walker, ed. (Boulder: Westview Press, 1984).

Mendlovitz, Saul H. 'The Study of War Prevention: Toward a Disciplined View', in *Toward a Theory of War Prevention: The Strategy of World Order,* Vol. I, Richard Falk and Saul H. Mendlovitz, eds (New York: World Law Fund, 1966).

——. 'Introduction', in *On the Creation of a Just World Order,* Saul H. Mendlovitz, ed. (New Delhi: Orient Longman, 1975).

Mendlovitz, Saul H. and George Weiss. 'The Study of Peace and Justice: Toward a Framework for Global Discussion', in *Planning Alternative Future,* Louis Rene Beres and Harry Targ, eds (New York: Praeger, 1975).

Walker, R.B.J. and Mendlovitz, Saul H. 'Peace, Politics and Contemporary Social Movements', in *Towards a Just World Peace: Perspectives from Social Movements,* Saul H. Mendlovitz and R.B.J. Walker, eds (London: Butterworths, 1987).

Articles of WOMP Theorists in Journals

Ajami, Foujad. 'World Order: The Question of Ideology', in *Alternatives* 6 (Winter 1980–81).

Falk, Richard. 'Liberalism at the Global Level: The Last of the Independent Commissions', in *Millennium Special Issue: The Globalization of Liberalism?* 24, No. 3.

——. 'From Geopolitics to Geo-governance: WOMP and Contemporary Political Discourse', in *Alternatives* 19, No. 2 (Spring 1994).

Falk, Richard and Kim, Samuel S. 'An Approach to World Order Studies and the World System', in *WOMP Working Series, No. 22* (New York: Institute for World Order, 1982).

Kim, Samuel S. 'The United Nations, Law Making and World Order', in *Alternatives* 8 (1983).

Kothari, Rajni. 'Environment and Alternative Development', in *Alternatives* 5, No. 4 (1980).

——. 'Under Globalisation: Will Nation-State Hold?', in *Economic and Political Weekly* (1 July 1995).

——. 'Globalisation and 'New World Order': What Future for the United Nations?', in *Economic and Political Weekly* (7 October 1995).

Mazrui, Ali A. 'Global Apartheid: Structural and Overt', in *Alternatives* 19 (1994).

Secondary Sources

Non-WOMP Studies on World Order

Books

Angell, Norman. *The Great Illusion: A Study of the Relation between Military Power to National Advantage* (London: GP Putnam's Sons, 1913).

Barber, Benjamin. *Jihad vs McWorld* (New York: Times Books, 1995).

Barker, Ernest. *Principles of Social and Political Theory* (London: Oxford University Press, 1961).

Barnet, Richard and John Cavanagh. *Global Dreams* (New York: Simon and Schuster, 1994).

Baylis, John and Steve Smith, eds *The Globalization of World Politics: An Introduction to International Relations* (New York: Oxford University Press, 2001).

Beres, Louis Rene and Harry Targ, eds *Planning Alternative Future* (New York: Praeger, 1975).

Bernstein, Richard and Ross H. Munro. *The Coming Conflict with China* (New York: Knopf, 1997).

Bowler, Mike, et al., eds *From Cold War to Collapse* (Britain: Cambridge University Press, 1993).

Brandon, Henry, ed. *In Search of a New World Order: The Future of US-European Relations* (Washington DC: Brookings Institution, 1993).

Brecher, Jeremy, John Brown Childs and Jill Cutter, eds *Global Visions: Beyond the New World Order* (Boston: South End Press, 1993).

Brezinski, Zbiginiew. *Out of Control: Turmoil on the Eve of the Twenty First Century* (New York: Scribner's, 1993).

Brown, Chris. *International Relations Theory: New Normative Approaches* (Hempel Hempstead Harvester: Wheatsheaf, 1992).

——. *Understanding International Relations* (London: Macmillan, 1997).

Bull, Hedley. *The Anarchical Society: A Study of Order in World Politics* (London: Macmillan, 1977).

Burchill, Scott and Andrew Linklater, eds *Theories of International Relations* (London: Macmillan, 1996).

Burgess, Glen. *The Politics of the Ancient Constitution: An Introduction to English Political Theory, 1603–42* (London: Macmillan, 1992).

Calvocoressi, Peter. *World Order and New States: Problems of Keeping the Peace* (New York: Praeger, 1962).

Camps, Merriam. *The Management of Interdependence: A Preliminary View* (New York: Council on Foreign Relations, 1974).

Chilcote, Ronald H. *Theories of Comparative Politics: The Search for a Paradigm Reconsidered* (Boulder: Westview Press, 1984).

Chomsky, Noam. *World Orders: Old and New* (New York: Oxford, 1994).

——. *Profit over People: Neoliberalism and Global Order* (Delhi: Madhyam Books, 1999).

Clark, Grenville, and Louis B. Sohn. *World Peace through World Law, 3rd Edition* (Cambridge, Mass.: Harvard University Press, 1966).

Commoner, Barry. *The Closing Circle: Nature, Man and Technology* (New York: Alfred A. Knopf, 1971).

Council on Foreign Relations. *The New Shape of World Politics: Contending Paradigms in International Relations* (New York: Foreign Affairs, 1997).

Cox, Robert, with Timothy Sinclair, *Approaches to World Order* (Cambridge: Cambridge University Press, 1996).

Crozier, Michael, Samuel P. Huntington and Jogi Watanuki. *The Crisis of Democracy: Report on the Governability of Democracies to the Trilateral Commission* (New York: New York University Press, 1975).

Deutsch, Karl. *Political Community and the North Atlantic Area* (Princeton, NJ: Princeton University Press, 1957).

Dolman, Anthony. *Resources, Regimes and World Order* (New York: Pergamon, 1981).

Feller, Gordon, Sherle R. Schwenninger and Diane Singermann, eds *Peace and World Order Studies: A Curriculum Guide* (New York: Institute for World Order, 1981).

Ferguson, Yale H. and Richard W. Mansbach. *A World of Polities: Essays on Global Politics* (London: Routledge, 2008).

Fierke, Karin M. *Critical Approaches to International Security* (Cambridge, UK: Polity Press, 2007).

Friedman, Thomas L. *The World is Flat: The Globalized World in the Twenty-First Century* (New Delhi: Penguin Books, 2006).

Frost, Mervyn. *Towards a Normative Theory of International Relations* (London: Cambridge University Press, 1986).

Fukuyama, Francis. *The End of History and the Last Man* (New York: The Free Press, 1992).

Garten, Jeffrey. *A Cold Peace* (New York: Times Books, 1992).

Gauba, O.P. *An Introduction to Political Theory* (New Delhi: Macmillan, 1995).

Goldstein, Joshua S. *International Relations*, 6th Edition (New Delhi: Pearson Education, 2006).

Gramsci, Antonio, edited and translated by Quintin Hoare and Geoffrey Nowell Smith. *Selections from the Prison Notebooks* (New Delhi: Orient Longman, 1996).

Groom, A.J.R., and Margot Light, eds *Contemporary International Relations: A Guide to Theory* (New York: Pinter Publishers, 1994).

Gurtov, Mel. *Global Politics in the Human Interest* (Boulder: Lynne Rienner Press, 1994).

Haas, E. *The Uniting of Europe* (Stanford: California University Press, 1958).

Haas, Ernst B., Mary Pat Williams and Don Basai. *Scientists and Wold Order: The Uses of Technical Knowledge in International Organisations* (Berkeley: University of California Press, 1977).

Hardt, Michael, and Antonio Negri. *Empire* (Cambridge, MA: Harvard University Press, 2000).

Halliday, Fred. *Rethinking International Relations* (London: Macmillan Press, 1994).

Harkavy, Robert E. and Edwards Kolodziej, eds *American Security Policy and Policy Making* (Lexington, Mass.: DC Heath, 1980).

Hayek, F.A. *The Constitution of Liberty* (London: Routledge and Kegan Paul, 1960).

——. *Law, Legislation and Liberty*, Vol. 3 (London: Routledge and Kegan Paul, 1982).

Held, David, Anthony McGrew, David Goldblatt and Jonathan Perraton. *Global Transformations: Politics, Economics and Culture* (Cambridge: Polity Press, 1999).

Herz, John. *Political Realism and Political Idealism* (Chicago: Chicago University Press, 1951).

Hirisch, F., M. Doyle and Edward Morse. *Alternatives to Monetary Disorder* (New York: McGraw Hill, 1977).

Hobsbawm, Eric. *The Age of Extremes: A History of the World, 1914–91* (New York: Vintage Books, 1994).

Hoffman, Stanley, ed. *Conditions of World Order* (Boston: Houghton, 1968).

——. *Primacy of World Order* (New York: McGraw Hill, 1978).

'Independent Commission on Disarmament and Security Issues', in *Common Security: A Blueprint for Survival* (New York: Simon and Schuster, 1982).

'Independent Commission on International Development Issues', in *Common Crisis: North–South Cooperation for World Recovery* (London: Pan, 1983).

Jackson, Robert and Georg Sorensen, *Introduction to International Relations: Theories and Approaches* (New York: Oxford University Press, 2003).

Johnson, Stuart E. and Martin C. Libicki. *Dominant Battlespace Knowledge* (Washington DC: National Defence University Press, 1995).

Kaplan, Morton and Kintude Mushatoji, ed. *Japan, America and the Future World Order* (New York: Free Press, 1976).

Kaplan, Robert D. *The Ends of the Earth* (New York: Random House, 1996).

Keohane, Robert and Joseph Nye, eds *Transnational Relations and World Politics* (Cambridge, Mass.: Harvard University Press, 1971).

——. *Power and Interdependence: World Politics in Transition* (Boston: Little Brown, 1977).

Kemp, Geoffrey and Robert E. Harkavy. *Strategic Geography and the Changing Middle East* (Washington DC: Carnegie Endowment for International Peace, 1997).

Kennedy, Paul. *Preparing for the Twenty-First Century* (New York: Random House, 1993).

Keynes, J.M. *The Economic Consequences of Peace* (London: Macmillan, 1919).

Kissinger, Henry. *Diplomacy* (New York: Simon and Schuster, 1994).

Lawson, Stephanie. *International Relations: Short Introduction* (Cambridge: Polity Press, 2003).

Luttwak, Edward. *The Endangered American Dream* (New York: Simon and Schuster, 1993).

Marx, Karl and Friedrich Engels. *Manifesto of Communist Party* (Moscow: Progress Publishers, 1975).

——. *A Contribution to the Critique of Political Economy* (Moscow: Progress Publishers, 1859).

McKinley, R.D. and R. Little. *Global Problems and World Order* (London: Francis Pinter Publishers, 1986).

Modelski, George. *Transnational Corporations and World Order: Readings on International Political Economy* (San Francisco: Freeman, 1979).

——. *Long Cycles in World Politics* (Seattle, Washington: University of Washington Press, 1985).

Morgenthau, Hans J. *Politics among Nations: The Struggle for Power and Peace* (New York: Alfred A. Knopf, 1948).

Morrow, John. *History of Political Thought: A Thematic Introduction* (London: Macmillan Press, 1988).

Mukherjee, Subrata and Sushila Ramaswamy. *A History of Political Thought: Plato to Marx* (New Delhi: Prentice Hall of India, 1999).

Nozick, Robert. *Anarchy, State and Utopia* (Oxford: Basil Blackwell, 1982).

Panitch, Leo and Colin Leys, eds *Violence Today: Actually Existing Barbarism – Socialist Register 2009* (New Delhi: Leftword Books, 2009).

Pantham, Thomas. *Political Theories and Social Reconstruction: A Critical Survey of the Literature on India* (New Delhi: Sage, 1995).

Paul, T.V. and John A. Hall, eds *International Order and the Future of World Politics* (Cambridge: Cambridge University Press, 1999).

Rajan, M.S. *World Order and the UN: Essays from a Non-Aligned Perspective* (New Delhi: Har Anand Publishers, 1995).

Rosecrance, Richard. *The Rise of the Trading State* (New York: Basic Books, 1986).

Rousenau, James N., ed. *International Politics and Foreign Policy* (New York: Free Press, 1961).

Rummel, R.J. *Understanding Conflict and War*, Vols 1–5 (Beverly Hills, California, Sage, 1975–81).

——. *The Conflict Helix: Principles and Practices of Interpersonal Social and International Conflict and Cooperation* (New Brunswick, NJ: Transaction, 1991).

Russett, Bruce. *Grasping the Democratic Peace* (Princeton, NJ: Princeton University Press, 1993).

Said, Abdul A., ed. *Human Rights and World Order* (New York: Praeger, 1978).

Scott, Alan, ed. *The Limits of Globalization: Cases and Arguments* (London: Routledge, 1997).

Sen, Amartya. *Identity and Violence: The Illusion of Destiny* (London: Penguin Books, 2006).

Shams-ud-din. *Perspectives on the Emerging World Order* (New Delhi: Gyan Publishing House, 1985).

Shutt, Harry. *A New Democracy* (London: Zed Books, 2001).

Singer, Max, and Aaron Wildavsky. *The Real World Order: Zones of Peace, Zones of Turmoil* (Chatham, NJ: Chatham House Publishers, 1993).

Singh, Harnam, ed. *Studies in World Order* (Delhi: Kitab Mahal, 1972).

Sinha, Sureshwar D. *Security in the New World Order* (New Delhi: Chanakya Publications, 1993).

Smith, Steve and Ken Booth. *International Relations Theory Today* (Cambridge: Polity Press, 1995).

Sprout, Harold and Margaret Sprout. *Towards a Politics of the Planet Earth* (New York: Van Nostrand Reinhold Co., 1971).

Stallings, Barbara, ed. *Global Change, Regional Responses: The New International Context of Development* (London: Cambridge University Press, 1995).

Thompson, Kenneth W. *Politics, Realism and the Crisis of World Politics* (Princeton: Princeton University Press, 1960).

Thompson, William R., ed. *Contending Approaches to World Systems Analysis* (Beverly Hills, California: Sage Publications, 1983).

Thurow, Lester. *Head to Head: The Coming Economic Battle among Japan, Europe and America* (New York: Morrow, 1992).

Wallerstein, Immanuel. *The Modern World System*, Vols 1–3 (London: Academic Press, 1974, 1980 and 1989).

Waltz, Kenneth. *Theory of International Politics* (Reading MA: Addison Wesley, 1979).

Waslekar, Sundeep, ed. *The New World Order* (New Delhi: Konark Publishers, 1991).

Weede, Erich. *Economic Development, Social Order and World Politics* (Boulder, Colorado: Lynne Rienner Publishers, 1996).

Non-WOMP Studies on World Order: Articles in Books

Alker, Jr, Hayward, and Thomas J. Biersteker. 'The Dialectics of World Order', in *Critical Concepts in Political Science*, Andrew Linklater, ed. (London: Routledge, 2000).

Amin, Samir. 'The Defense of Humanity Requires the Radicalisation of Popular Struggles', in *Violence Today: Actually Existing Barbarism-Socialist Register 2009*, Leo Panitch and Colin Leys, eds (New Delhi: Leftword Books, 2009).

Baylis, John. 'International and Global Security in the Post-Cold War Era', in *The Globalization of World Politics: An Introduction to International Relations,* John Baylis and Steve Smith, eds (New York: Oxford University Press, 2001).

Bretherton, Charlotte. 'Introduction: Global Politics in the 1990s', in *Global Politics: An Introduction,* Charlotte Bretherton and Geoffrey Ponton, eds (Great Britain: Blackwell Publishers, 1996).

Brown, Chris. 'Human Rights', in *The Globalization of World Politics: An Introduction to International Relations,* John Baylis and Steve Smith, eds (New York: Oxford University Press, 2001).

Carruthers, Susan L. 'International History 1900–45', in *The Globalization of World Politics: An Introduction to International Relations,* John Baylis and Steve Smith, eds (New York: Oxford University Press, 2001).

Chibber, Vivek. 'American Militarism and the US Political Establishment', in *Violence Today: Actually Existing Barbarism-Socialist Register 2009,* Leo Panitch and Colin Leys, eds (New Delhi: Leftword Books, 2009).

Clark, Ian. 'Globalization and the Post-Cold War Order', in *The Globalization of World Politics: An Introduction to International Relations,* John Baylis and Steve Smith, eds (New York: Oxford University Press, 2001).

Cox, Michael. 'International History since 1989', in *The Globalization of World Politics: An Introduction to International Relations,* John Baylis and Steve Smith, eds (New York: Oxford University Press, 2001).

Dunne, Tim 'Liberalism', in *The Globalization of World Politics: An Introduction to International Relations,* John Baylis and Steve Smith, eds (New York: Oxford University Press, 2001).

Dunne, Tim, and Brian Schmidt. 'Realism', in *The Globalization of World Politics: An Introduction to International Relations,* John Baylis and Steve Smith, eds (New York: Oxford University Press, 2001).

Hobden, Stephen and Richard Wyn Jones. 'Marxist Theories of International Relations', in *The Globaliastion of World Politics: An Introduction to International Relations,* John Baylis and Steve Smith, eds (New York: Oxford University Press, 2001).

Jackson, Robert H. 'The Evolution of International Society', in *The Globalization of World Politics: An Introduction to International Relations,* John Baylis and Steve Smith, eds (New York: Oxford University Press, 2001).

Kilminster, Richard. 'Globalization as an Emergent Concept', in *The Limits of Globalization: Cases and Arguments,* Alan Scott, ed. (London: Routledge, 1997).

Lamy, Steven L. 'Contemporary Mainstream Approaches: Neo-Realism and Neo-Liberalism', in *The Globalisation of World Politics: An Introduction to*

International Relations, John Baylis and Steve Smith, eds (New York: Oxford University Press, 2001).

Mastanduno, Michael. 'A Realist View: Three Images of the Coming International Order', in *International Order and the Future of World Politics*, T.V. Paul and John A. Hall, eds (Cambridge: Cambridge University Press, 1999), 24–5.

Mearsheimer, John. 'Disorder Restored' in *Rethinking America's Security*, Graham Allison and Gregory F. Treverton, eds (New York: Norton, 1992).

——. 'Back to the Future: Instability in Europe after the Cold War', in *The Cold War and After: Prospects for Peace*, S. Lynn Jones, ed. (Cambridge, MA: MIT Press, 1993).

Modelski, George. 'The Theory of Long Cycles and US Strategic Policy', in *American Security Policy and Policy Making*, Robert E. Hakavy and Edward Kolodziej, eds (Lexington, Mass.: DC Heath, 1980).

Owens, William. 'Introduction', in *Dominant Battlespace Knowledge*, Stuart E. Johnson and Martin C. Libicki, eds (Washington, DC: National Defense University Press, 1995).

Parsons, Talcott. 'Order and Community in the International Social System', in *International Politics and Foreign Policy*, James N. Rousenau, ed. (New York: Free Press, 1961).

Scott, Len. 'International History 1945–90', in *The Globalization of World Politics: An Introduction to International Relations*, John Baylis and Steve Smith, eds (New York: Oxford University Press, 2001).

Sen, Amartya. 'Assessing Human Development', in *UNDP Human Development Report* (New York: Oxford University Press, 1999).

Smith, Steve. 'Is the Truth Out There: Eight Questions about International Order', in *International Order and the Future of World Politics*, T.V. Paul and John A. Hall, eds (Cambridge: Cambridge University Press, 1999).

Smith, Steve. 'Reflectivist and Constructivist Approaches to International Theory', in *The Globalization of World Politics: An Introduction to International Relations*, John Baylis and Steve Smith, eds (New York: Oxford University Press, 2001).

Ullman. 'Foreword: The 1980s Project', in *Alternatives to Monetary Disorder*, F. Hirisch, M. Doyle and Edward L Morse, eds (New York: McGraw Hill, 1977).

Woods, Ngaire. 'International Political Economy in an Age of Globalization', in *The Globalization of World Politics: An Introduction to International Relations*, John Baylis and Steve Smith, eds (New York: Oxford University Press, 2001).

Non-WOMP Studies on World Order: Articles in Journals

Ajami, Foujad. 'The Summoning', in *Foreign Affairs* (September–October 1993)

Barnett, Jon. 'Peace and Development: Towards a New Synthesis', in *Journal of Peace Research,* 45, No. 1 (2008), 75.

Baru, Sanjaya. 'Geopolitical Implications of the Current Global Financial Crisis', in *Strategic Analysis,* 33, No. 2 (March 2009),166.

Bell, Daniel. 'The Future of World Disorder', in *Foreign Policy,* 27 (Summer 1977).

Bergsten, C. Fred. 'Globalizing Free Trade', in *Foreign Affairs,* (May–June 1996).

Brezinski, Zbigniew. 'Recognizing the Crisis', in *Foreign Policy,* 17 (Winter 1974–75).

Carpenter, Ted Galen. 'The New World Disorder', in *Foreign Policy* (Fall 1991).

Cohen, Eliot. 'A Revolution in Warfare', in *Foreign Affairs* (March–April 1996).

'Columbus and the New World Order', in *Monthly Review,* 44, No. 3 (July–August 1992).

David, Steven R. 'Explaining the Third World Alignment', in *World Politics* (January 1991).

Doyle, M.W. 'Kant, Liberal Legacies and Foreign Affairs', in *Philosophy and Public Affairs,* 12, No. 4, 323–54.

Farer, Tom J. 'The United States and the Third World: A Basis for Accommodation', in *Foreign Affairs,* 54 (October 1975).

Fukuyama, Francis. 'The End of History', in *The National Interest,* 16 (1989).

Galtung, Johan. 'Twenty-Five Years of Peace Research: Ten Challenges and Some Responses', in *Journal of Peace Research,* 22, No. 2, (1985).

Haas, Ernst. 'Why Collaborate? Issue Linkages and International Regimes', in *World Politics,* (April 1980).

Haas, Richard N. 'The Age of Nonpolarity: What Will Follow US Dominance?', in *Foreign Affairs,* 87, No. 3 (May–June 2008), 48–9.

Hardin, Garrett. 'The Tragedy of the Commons', in *Science,* 162 (December 1968).

Harkavy, Robert E. 'Images of the Coming International System', in *Orbis: A Journal of World Affairs* (Fall 1997), 569–90.

Hansen, Lene. 'From Camps to Conversations in Critical Security Studies', in *International Studies Review,* 10, Issue 3 (September 2008), 652.

Hettne, Bjorn. 'Peace and Development: Contradictions and Compatibilities', in *Journal of Peace Research* 20, No. 4 (1983), 340.

Hoffman, Bruce. 'The Myth of Grass-Roots Terrorism: Why Osama bin Laden Still Matters?', in *Foreign Affairs*, 87, No. 3 (May–June 2008).

Huntington, Samuel P. 'The US – Decline or Renewal?', in *Foreign Affairs* (Winter 1988–89), 91

——. 'The Clash of Civilizations', in *Foreign Affairs*, 72, No. 3 (1993).

Ikenberry, G. John. 'America's Imperial Ambition', in *Foreign Affairs*, 81, No. 5 (September–October 2002), 44.

Jaurvik, Laurence. 'NGOs: A 'New Class' in International Relations', in *Orbis: A Journal of World Affairs* 51, No. 2 (Spring 2007), 217–8.

Kaplan, Robert D. 'The Coming Anarchy', in *The Atlantic Monthly* (1994).

Kissinger, Henry. 'How to Achieve the New World Order', in *Time* (14 March 1996).

Krauthammer, Charles. 'The Poverty of Realism', in *New Republic*, 17 (February 1986).

——. 'The Unipolar Moment', in *Foreign Affairs* 70, No. 1 (1990–91), 23–4.

Krepenvich, Andrew. 'From Cavalry to Computers', in *The National Interest* (Fall 1994).

Krugman, Paul. 'Competitiveness: A Dangerous Obsession', in *Foreign Affairs* 70 (1994), 23–33.

Lahiry, Sujit, et al., 'The Emerging World Order and India', Paper presented at Academic Staff College, Jawaharlal Nehru University, New Delhi, on 5 May 2000.

Lampton, David. 'China: The Coming Power', in *Foreign Affairs* (Winter 1992–93).

Lilley, James R. 'Nationalism Bites Back', in *The New York Times*, 24 October 1996.

Mathews, Jessica T. 'Power Shift', in *Foreign Affairs* (January–February 1997).

Mead, Walter Russell. 'On the Road to Ruin', in *Harper's* (March 1990).

Mearsheimer, John. 'Back to the Future: Instability in Europe after the Cold War', in *International Security*, 15 (Summer 1990).

Nye, Joseph. 'What New World Order?', in *Foreign Affairs* (Spring 1992).

Ohmae, Kenichi. 'The Rise of the Region State', in *Foreign Affairs*, 72 (1993), 78–87.

Perry, William J. 'Desert Storm and Deterrence', in *Foreign Affairs* (Fall 1991).

Petras, James. 'Introduction', in *Latin American Perspectives* (Special Issue 2004).

Rosecrance, Richard. 'Long Cycle Theory and International Relations', in *International Organization* (Spring 1997).

——. 'A New Concert of Powers', in *Foreign Affairs* (Spring 1992).

Sen, Amartya. 'Violence, Identity and Poverty', in *Journal of Peace Research* 45, No. 1 (January 2008).

Sheth, D.L. 'Globalisation and New Politics of Micro-Movements', in *Economic and Political Weekly* XXXIX, No.1 (3 January 2004).

Swazo, Norman K. 'The 'Ontological' Meaning of the World Order Movement', in *Alternatives* X, 1984.

Tonelson, Alan. 'Beyond Left and Right', in *The National Interest* (Winter 1993–94).

Wallerstein, Immanuel. 'Friends and Foes', in *Foreign Policy*, No. 40 (Fall 1980).

Waltz, Kenneth. 'The Emerging Structure of International Politics', in *International Security* 18, 45–73.

Weigel, George. 'On the Road to Isolationism', in *Commentary* (January 1992).

Zakaria, Fareed. 'Realism and Domestic Politics: A Review Essay', in *International Security*, 17 (1992).

——. 'The Future of American Power', in *Foreign Affairs*, 87, No. 3 (May–June 2008), 43.

Index